IMAGES
of America

Mexicans in San José

On the Cover: Taken in 1949, this image shows Mexican women taking an afternoon break on the lawn outside of the Tri-Valley Cannery located on Tenth and Taylor Streets in San José. From left to right are Rachel ?, Edelmira ?, Idolina Garcia, Maria Guerrero Alvarado, and Alicia Saenz. (Courtesy of Maria Guerrero Alvarado.)

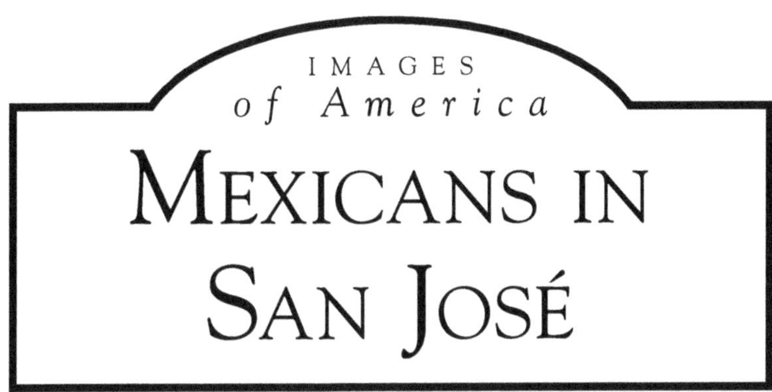

Nannette Regua and Arturo Villarreal
Foreword by Stephen Pitti

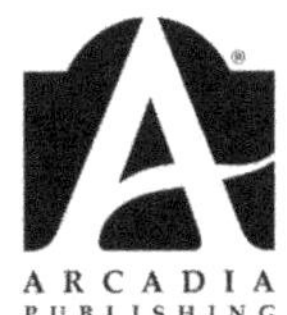

Foreword by Stephen Pitti
ISBN 978-0-7385-6930-7

Published by Arcadia Publishing
Charleston, South Carolina

Library of Congress Control Number: 2008940093

For all general information contact Arcadia Publishing at:
Telephone 843-853-2070
Fax 843-853-0044
E-mail sales@arcadiapublishing.com
For customer service and orders:
Toll-Free 1-888-313-2665

Visit us on the Internet at www.arcadiapublishing.com

We dedicate this book to the first indigenous inhabitants, the Ohlones, and to the Mexicans and Mexican Americans who made and continue to make history happen in San José.

Contents

Foreword

This book tells many stories. It must be because Mexican and Mexican American people in San José, California, have accumulated countless experiences, many good times, more than their share of struggles, and therefore have abundant stories to tell. If a single picture is in fact worth a thousand words, then the dozens of images collected in this volume for the first time should go a long way toward starting new conversations about our past. Too often in recent years, books, museum exhibits, and media that have intended to describe the history of the San Francisco Bay Area have ignored the people featured in *Mexicans in San José*. This would seem a startling omission, since Spanish-speaking settlers, missionaries, and military personnel were so critical in the 18th and 19th centuries to the making of Missions San José and Santa Clara, of San José pueblo, and of much more. It would seem startling, too, in light of the number of local Mexican residents by the 21st century, a time when so many have come to play important roles in the city's schools, churches, organizations, and neighborhoods.

This volume makes clear that the San José area has an important Mexican history and that people of Mexican descent can rightly claim to have shaped many of the region's most important historical developments. The authors of *Mexicans in San José* have brilliantly assembled a visual record of this place and of people who in fact have mattered to the city. The images in the following pages call for a rethinking of San José's fascinating past. These images show that the history of Mexicans in San José was one defined by working people, by families and individuals who contributed their labor in many types of jobs. But it is clear that local Mexicans have done far more than collect paychecks. As the following pages suggest, tens of thousands of Mexican children have passed through city schools and churches. Residents have established clubs and held parties to stay in touch with kin from the same town, state, or region—for instance, Eagle Pass, Texas, or Jalisco, Mexico. Local families have held memorable gatherings in city parks, they have competed on area baseball diamonds, and they have spent their money in downtown businesses. Some have led national organizations working to end racial and economic discrimination in the United States. The history of Mexicans in San José is, therefore, a history of families, of leisure and good times, and of efforts to achieve civil rights.

This book reminds us to celebrate these truths, to recognize the long-standing presence of Mexicans in San José, and to preserve our photographs and memories of people whose histories have too often been forgotten in Santa Clara County.

—Stephen J. Pitti
Professor of History and American Studies
Yale University

Acknowledgments

We would like to thank all of the individuals, organizations, and institutions that helped make this book possible. Many thanks to archivists Jeff Paul, Kathryn Blackmer Reyes, Stacy Mueller, and Ralph Pearce, San José Public Library and San José State University Library; Jim Reed, History San José; Cristina Jimenez, University California, San Diego; librarian staff, Library and Technology Center, Evergreen Valley College; the Bancroft Library, University California, Berkeley; Polly Armstrong, Special Collections, Stanford University; Santa Clara University; Vanessa Flores, City of San José; Lisa Christiansen, California History Center; Marcela Davison Aviles, Mexican Heritage Plaza; New Almadén Quicksilver Mines Archives; Mary Andrade, *La Oferta* newspaper; and Bill Highlander, *Evergreen Times*.

We are very grateful to the community members who welcomed us into their homes and places of business to share their photographs, including Elizabeth Alvarez; Adriana Garcia Cabrera; Arturo "Huitzilin" Mata; Ernesto "Tlahuitollini" Collin; Abraham Menor; Gina and Felipe Portales; Felix Garcia; Johnny Guitar; Roberto Duran; Felipe Rodriguez; Victor Garza; Greg Bernal-Mendoza Smestad; Paul Ortiz; Adrian Vargas; Ernie de la Torre; Saul Valenzuela; Manuel and Vickie Romero; Moses and Connie Carrasco; Ralph and Connie Chavira; Art Peredia; Carmen Solórzano; Dr. Susan Cashion; Chris Arriola; Richard Regua; our students Mabeel Garcia, Esmeralda Anaya, and Skye Jacquez; and to all others who contributed images. Anne Castaneda and Art Partida at Evergreen Valley College provided copying assistance. Reporters Damian Trujillo from KNTV Channel 11 and Ramón Adame from KDTV Channel 14 kindly raised awareness of the book in their televised segments. We acknowledge our college president David Wain Coon for his support and promotion of this endeavor. Thank you to Arcadia Publishing and to acquisitions editor Kelly Reed for all of the positive support and expertise that she provided. Regrettably, we could not include all images that were kindly shared with us because of space constraints for the book.

Introduction

Located 45 minutes south of San Francisco, San José is a rich cultural epicenter of which Mexicans are historical and contemporary contributors and builders. Founded by José Joaquin Moraga on November 29, 1777, El Pueblo de San José de Guadalupe became the first Spanish civilian settlement in California, then called Alta California. San José emerged as a rancho farming community, growing food for the military forces in San Francisco and Monterey. Mexico won its independence from Spain in 1821, and in 1845, Capt. Andres Castillero was sent by the Mexican army on a scouting mission to Northern California. On his expedition, he arrived in San José and encountered a thriving Ohlone Indian population who told him of a red rock they used for paint. The red rock was cinnabar, which is a high-grade mercury ore.

This amazing discovery later put San José on the map as it became one of the highest producing mercury mines in the world in the 19th century. After the Mexican-American War of 1846–1848, the mercury mines were called the New Almadén quicksilver mines. By the mid-1800s, owners of the mines hired Mexicans for low-wage mine work. Mexican mine workers and their families lived in a segregated community called Spanishtown. In addition to laboring, Mexican miners participated in several other activities in the New Almadén mining community. For instance, they joined the musical band Mountain Echo and baseball teams named New Almadén Quicksilver Miners and the Cinnabars. They formed *Juntas Patrioticas*, patriotic committees. Yet Mexican miners faced unequal wages, segregation, inadequate schooling for their children, expensive company housing, lack of water and sanitation services, and exorbitant prices for food and goods sold at the company store they were forced to patronize.

By the 1900s, after the mine production decreased, the Mexican population moved out of Spanishtown. A new industry was gaining momentum in San José—agriculture. San José soon became known as "The Valley of Heart's Delight" for its rich agricultural products of apricots, prunes, and peaches. Agricultural production in San José became "factories in the field" for countless Mexican laborers. Mexicans established in San José competed for jobs with Italians, Portuguese, and recent Mexican immigrants who fled a war-ravaged Mexico to find employment in San José.

Mexicans in San José labored every day to feed the nation and put food on American tables by working in the fields and the canning, drying, and packing industries. Canning and drying of fruits and vegetables became lucrative businesses in San José. By World War II, San José, with 18 canneries and 13 packinghouses, became the world's largest canning and dried-fruit packing center. By the 1950s, Mexicans began to fill positions in canneries and packinghouses that Italians and Portuguese left behind for better employment. Faced with housing and other forms of discrimination, Mexicans found East San José to be a safe haven to live, work, and raise their families. However, East San José was short on city services, such as paved streets, paved sidewalks, protection from annual flooding, and adequate housing. So Mexicans united to form mutual aid societies to address shared needs.

For many Mexican families, culture and spirituality are closely entwined. With a majority of Catholic followers, the Mexican community in San José attended several Catholic churches, such as St. Joseph's Cathedral (Basilica after 1997), Most Holy Trinity, and Our Lady of Guadalupe. Churches offered places for worship, a sense of community, cultural reinforcement, job assistance, food for the poor, counseling for the youth, assistance for senior citizens, and buses for transportation to work in the fields in nearby Salinas, Monterey, or Watsonville.

Mexicans who worked in the fields and canneries became active in labor unions, such as the National Farm Labor Union under the leadership of Mexican community activist, educator, and labor organizer Dr. Ernesto Galarza. In a prominent East San José district, known as Mayfair, the Community Service Organization was active and recruited *Sal Si Puedes* resident and organizer Cesar Chavez to get involved in the 1950s. Chavez later became a labor organizer and the cofounder of the National Farm Workers Association, a precursor to the United Farm Workers union.

During the mid-1960s, Mexicans throughout the Southwestern states fought for social justice and equality. The Chicano movement was launched during this time. Many Mexicans in San José began to identify themselves as Chicanos and expressed their commitment to cultural pride and ethnic identity. La Confederacion de La Raza Unida emerged as a powerful voice for Mexicans in San José.

San José is often overlooked for its significant contributions to the Chicano movement in spite of having the first Mexican American Graduate Studies program and Chicano Commencement at San José State University and the first Chicano student walkout at Roosevelt Junior High School. Sofía Mendoza and Ernestina Garcia played key roles in the Chicano movement.

The Mexican community of San José has also produced a wealthy share of musicians, artists, and writers. Several poets and writers, such as Roberto Duran, are published and respected in their fields. Musical groups of San José have produced albums. As an example, Los Tigres del Norte is known internationally and is the recipient of many Grammy Awards. Luis Valdez is recognized nationally and internationally for his productions in theater with Teatro Campesino and feature films like *La Bamba* and *Zoot Suit*. In 1999, the Mexican community of San José celebrated the grand opening of its world-class cultural center, the Mexican Heritage Plaza, which showcases local, national, and international acts of Mexican and American theater, music, poetry, dance, and art.

This book is an introductory documentation of Mexican cultural history in San José from 1777 to 1999 through photographs. It is a stepping stone for future scholars and writers to complete further research and publications about the rich history of Mexican people. We will use Mexican, Mexican American, and Chicano interchangeably.

One

The Early Years

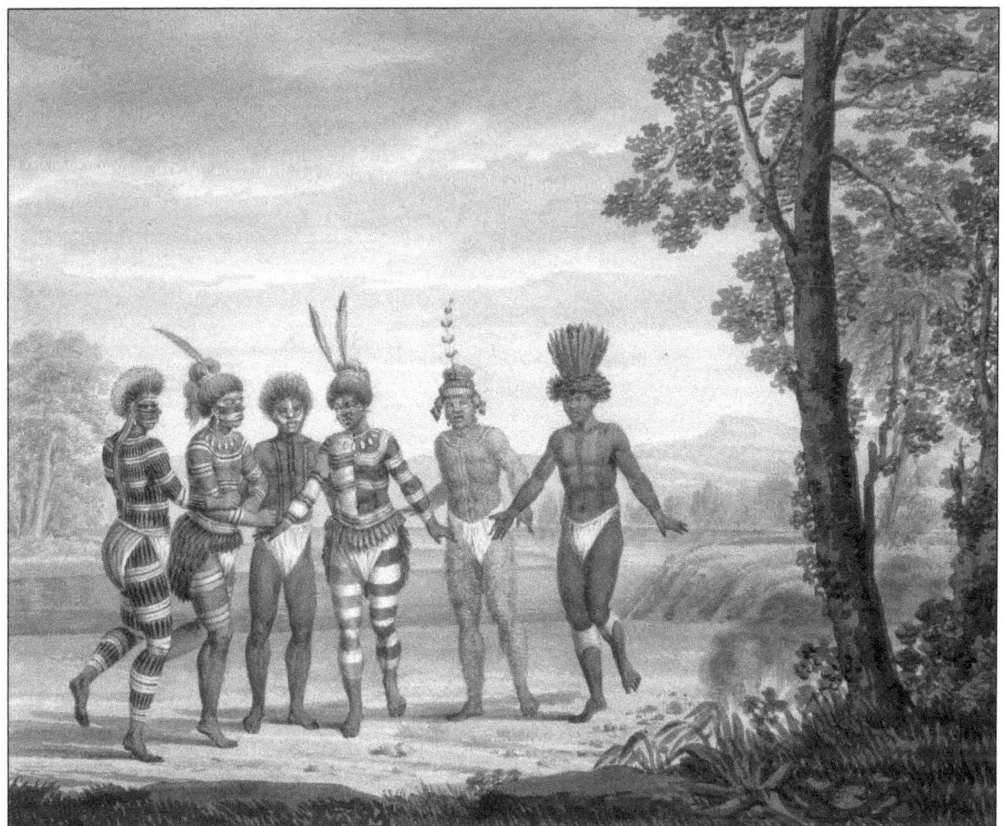

By 1777, there were between 10,000 and 20,000 Ohlone inhabitants living throughout the San Francisco Bay Area, with approximately 50 nations or tribes. Each tribe held its own territory and numbered between 50 and 500 people, with an average of 200. This sketch is an 1806 representation of Ohlone dancers at Mission San José. (Courtesy of the Bancroft Library, University of California, Berkeley.)

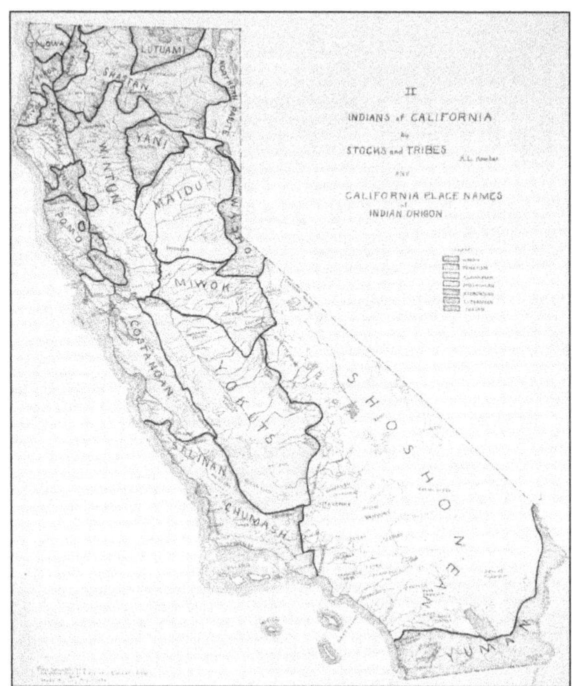

In this 1926 map, A. L. Kroeber lists the Ohlones as Costanoans, an anglicized version of the Spanish word *costenos*, which refers to the people of the coast. Many descendants embrace Ohlone or Ohlone Muwekma as alternative names. The linguistic term for Ohlones from the San José area is Tamien. (Courtesy of the Bancroft Library, University of California, Berkeley.)

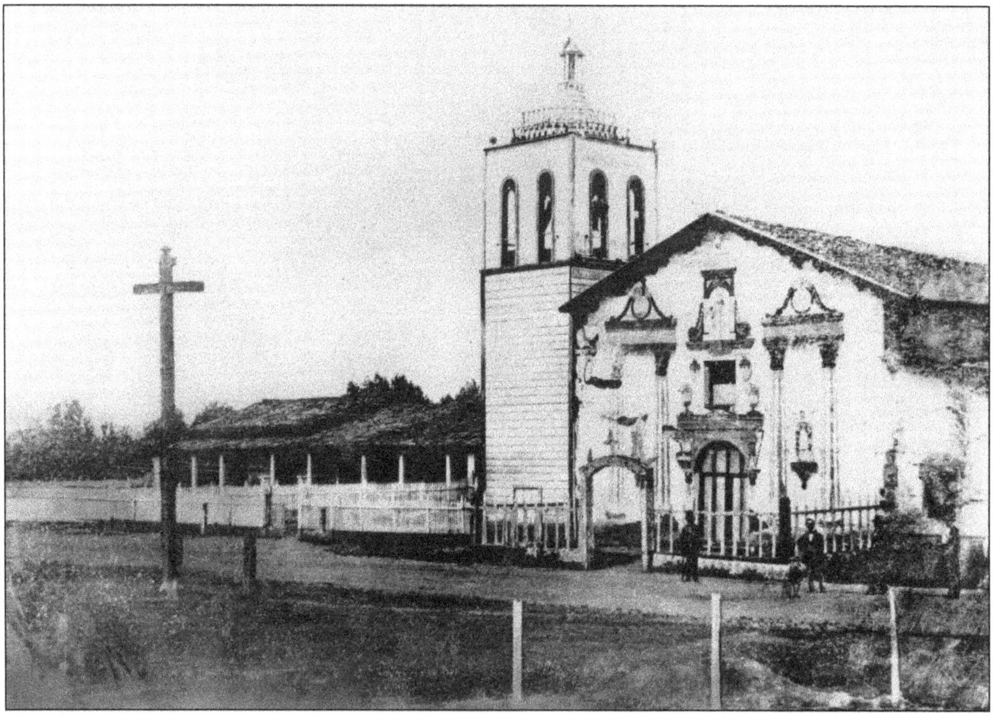

Mission Santa Clara de Asisi was founded on January 12, 1777, by Fr. Junipero Serra. It was the eighth in the 21 missions built in California. Named for St. Claire of Assisi, the mission was a self-sustaining village of growing agriculture, tending livestock, and Christianizing Ohlone Indians. This image from 1854 is the oldest known photograph of the mission. (Courtesy of University Archives, Santa Clara University.)

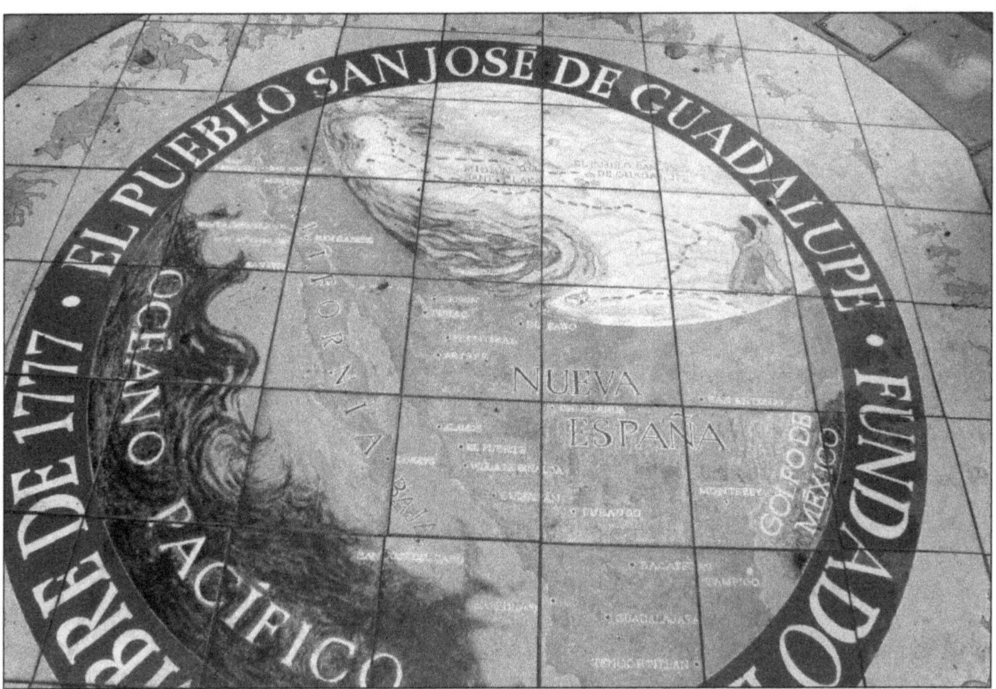

Juan Bautista de Anza led an expedition of settlers into California between 1775 and 1776. Two hundred settlers (called *pobladores*) of various castes, including mestizos (Indian and Spanish), mulattos (African and Spanish), and Indians, established a permanent Spanish colony called El Pueblo de San José de Guadalupe. Spanish colonizing required a combination of three elements: missions (religious), presidios (military), and pueblos (civilian settlements). This photograph was taken at the Parque de los Fundadores in San José. (Both photographs by and courtesy of Ernie de la Torre.)

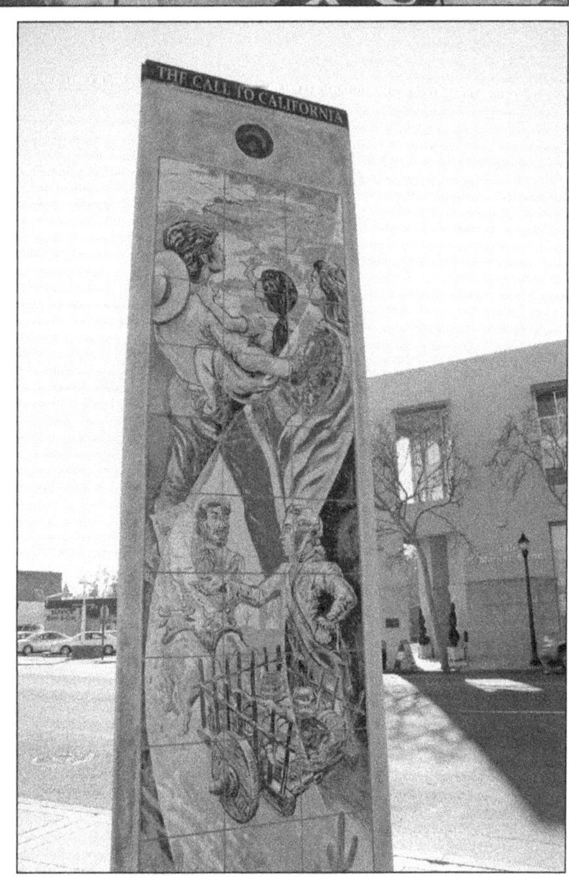

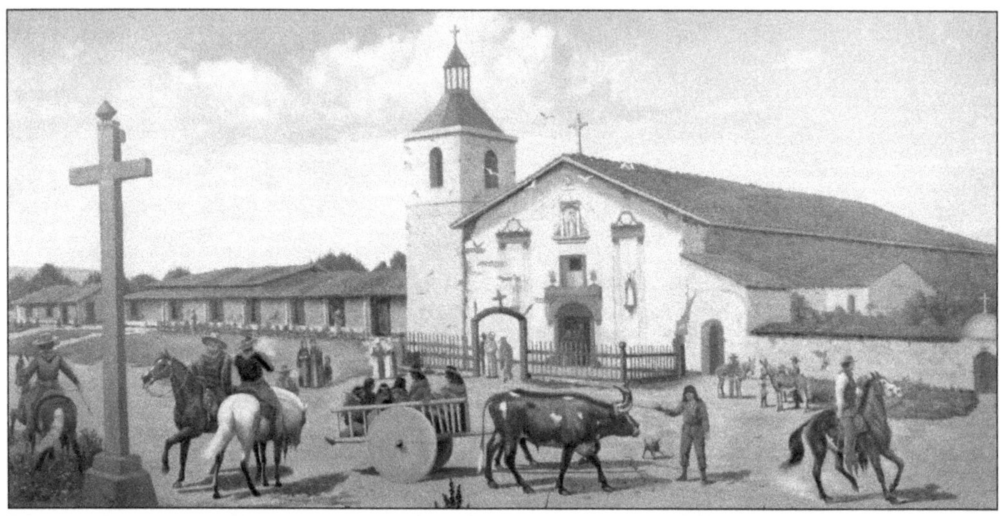

This 1849 painting of Mission Santa Clara de Asisi depicts an idyllic relationship between the Spanish priests, pobladores, and Indians. In reality, countless Indians were captured, forced to help build the missions, and expected to convert to Christianity. Culture shock, mistreatment, and diseases brought immediate and deadly impact for many Indians. (Courtesy of University Archives, Santa Clara University.)

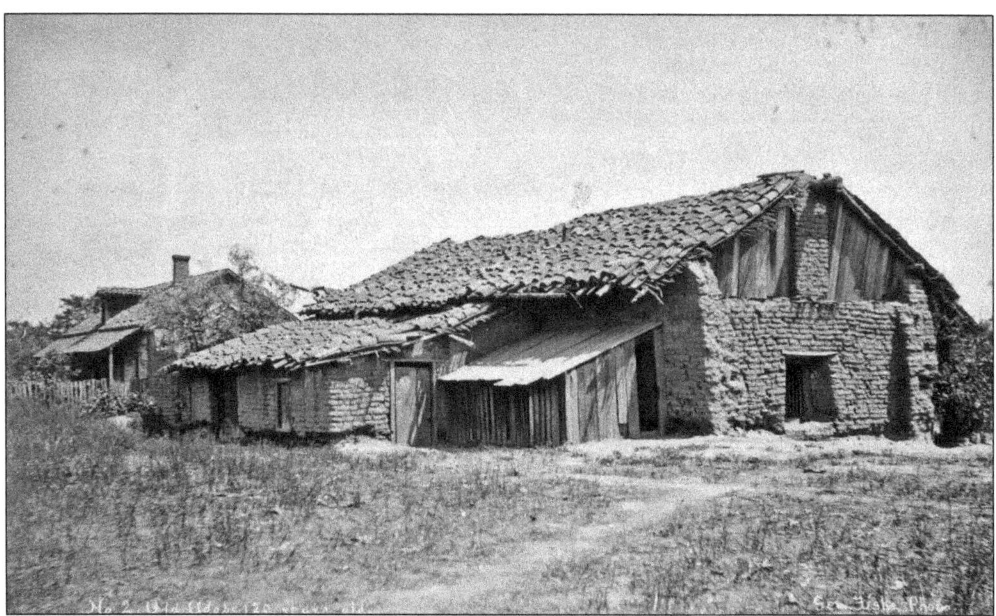

Two old adobes located near the Mission Santa Clara are depicted in this 1910 image. The adobes served as housing for Ohlone and other Indians. With lack of support and funding after Mexico won its independence from Spain in 1821, the missions in California closed their doors. By 1834, the mission Indians were scattered throughout California, looking for employment and permanent residence. Many Indians found employment as vaqueros, or cowboys, and domestic servants in multiethnic ranches. Some Indians intermarried with Mexicans and acquired Spanish surnames. (Courtesy of San José Public Library, California Room.)

This photograph taken in 1860 is of Ynigo Lopez, who was a Mission Santa Clara Indian. In 1844, Lopez, a talented musician and singer, was one of the few Ohlone Indians to be granted a land title. (Courtesy of University Archives, Santa Clara University.)

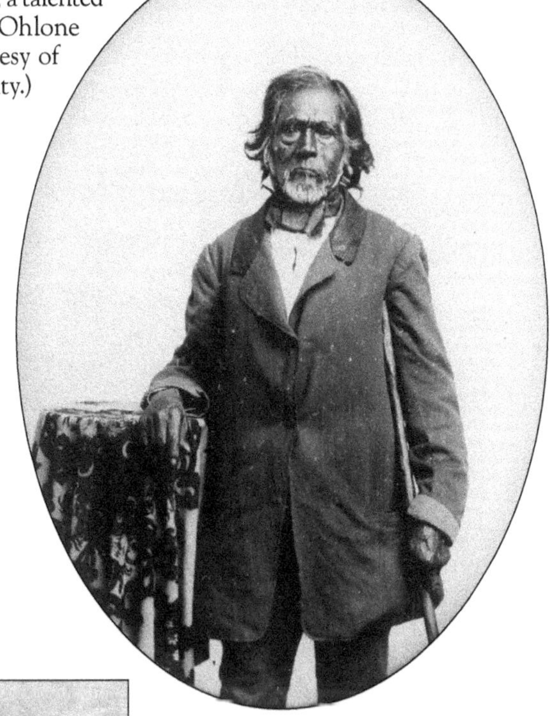

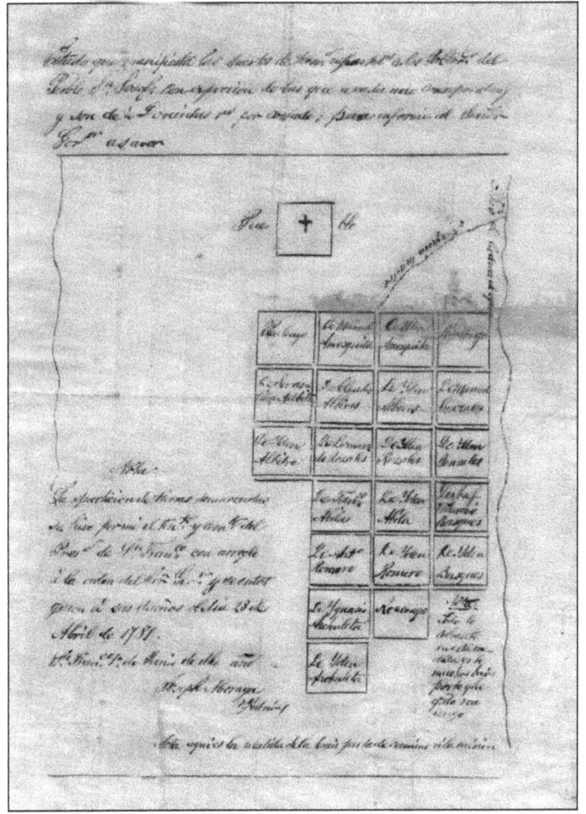

A *diseño*, or sketch, dated 1781, shows the allotment of lands to the early settlers. José Joaquin Moraga drew the diseño map on April 23, 1781. The cross is the present-day site of St. Joseph's Cathedral. (Courtesy of History San José.)

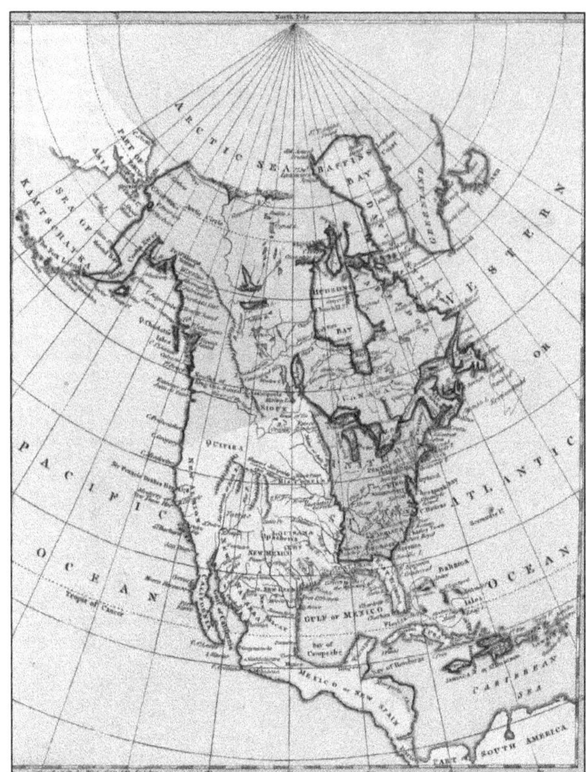

These were the lands that were part of Nueva España, which Mexico was known as until its liberation from Spain in 1821. This 1797 map highlights the vast amount of Nueva España lands in contrast to the U.S. lands. (Courtesy of the Bancroft Library, University of California, Berkeley.)

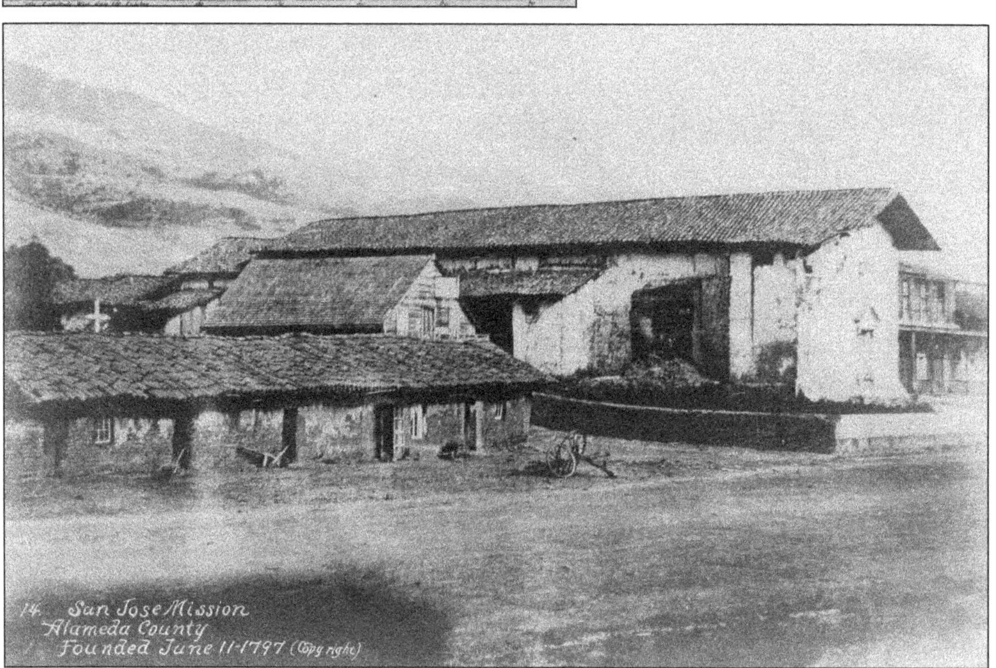

Mission San José, the 14th California mission, was founded on June 11, 1797. The original name was El Mission del Gloriosismo Patriarca Señor San José. The founding priest was Fermin Lausen. This photograph was taken prior to a 7.0-magnitude earthquake in 1868 that caused tremendous destruction to the mission and its buildings. (Courtesy of History San José.)

An economy centered on the hide and tallow trade developed in the farms and ranches in San José. By 1819, there were 45 ranches in San José. By the close of the Spanish period in 1821, the population was at 240. This illustration depicts vaqueros, or cowboys, lassoing a cow. (Photograph by and courtesy of Ernie de la Torre.)

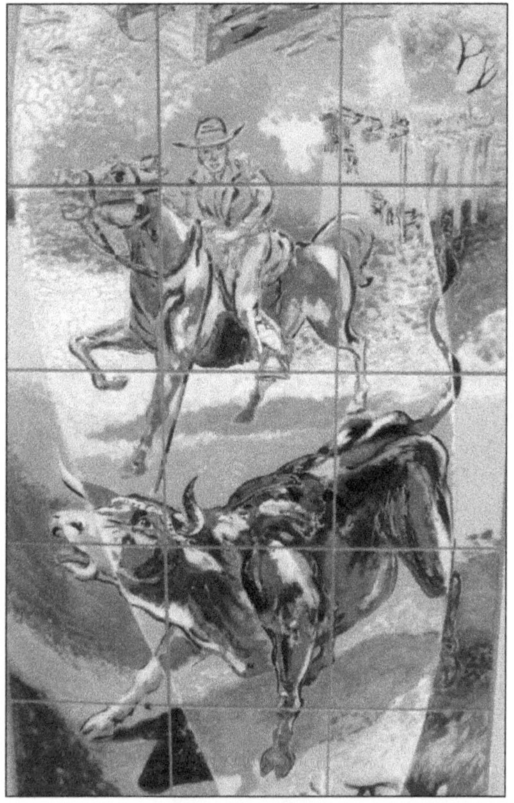

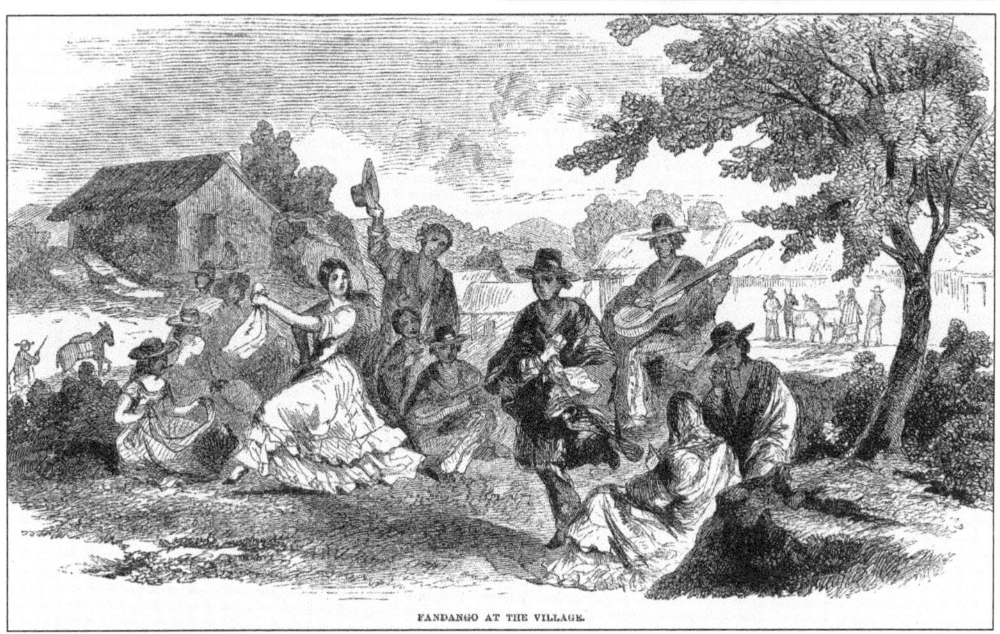

Fandangos, or dances, were held on the ranches. The music consisted of a violin, guitar, and two or three singers. The dances were called *sones* and included songs like "La Bamba" and "El Fandango." Other amusements at the ranches included horse racing, bullfights, cockfights, and bear and bull fights. (Courtesy of Cornell University Library, Making of America Digital Collection.)

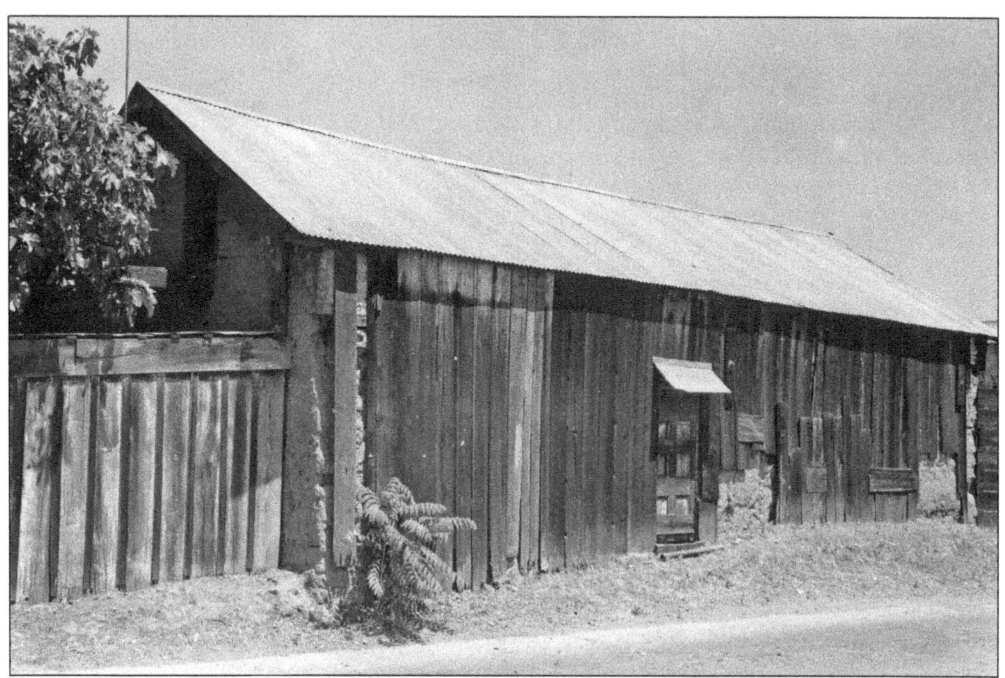

The Peralta Adobe House was built in 1797 by Manuel Gonzalez, an Apache Indian. He was the first resident and second mayor of San José. The second occupant was Luis Maria Peralta. He held the highest office in the community as commissioner. Gonzalez and Peralta were part of the De Anza expedition. The image above is a 1947 photograph of the Peralta Adobe house when it was used as a warehouse. Peralta's home is now the oldest surviving structure in San José and the only remaining adobe. (Above courtesy of San José Public Library, California Room; below photograph by and courtesy of Ernie de la Torre.)

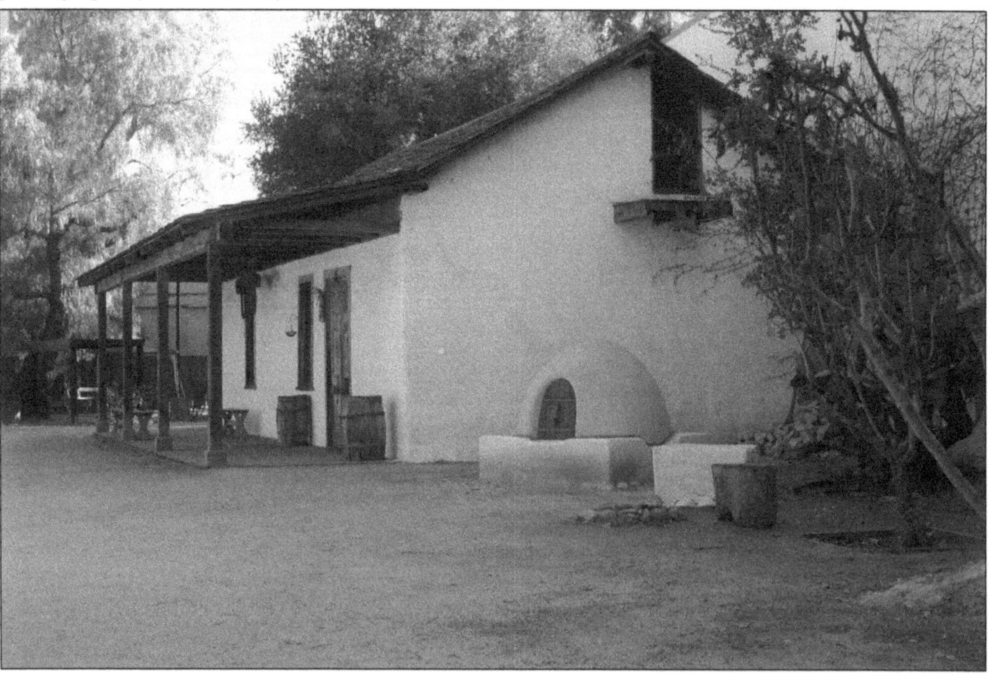

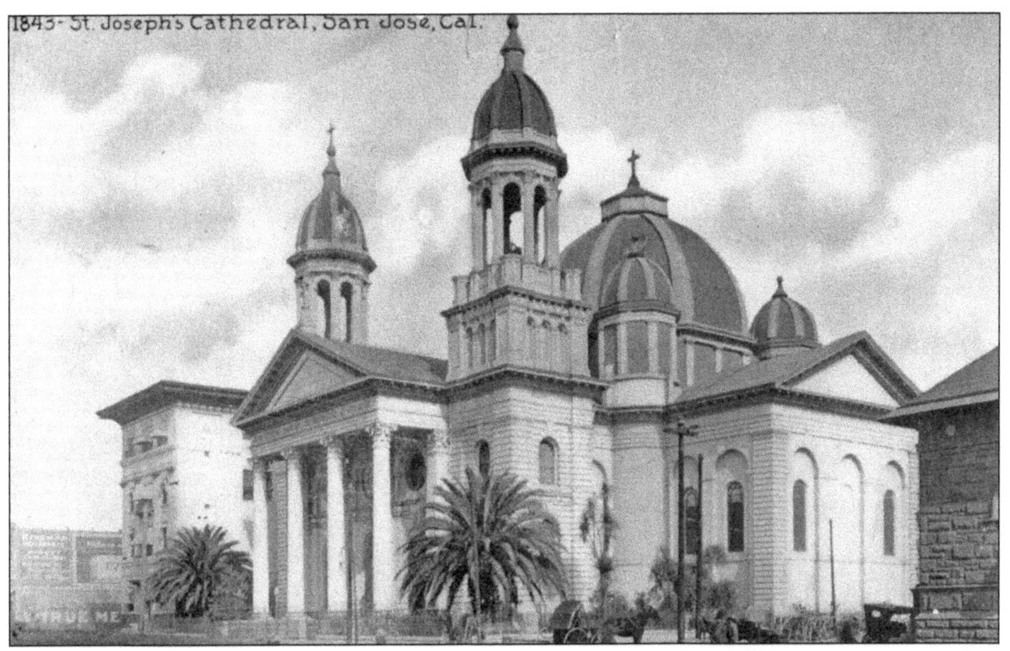

The "little adobe church" of 1803 was originally considered a dependency of the Mission Santa Clara de Asisi. This 1843 image is of St. Joseph's Cathedral, the fifth to occupy the site on the corner of Market and San Fernando Streets. (Courtesy of the San José Public Library, California Room.)

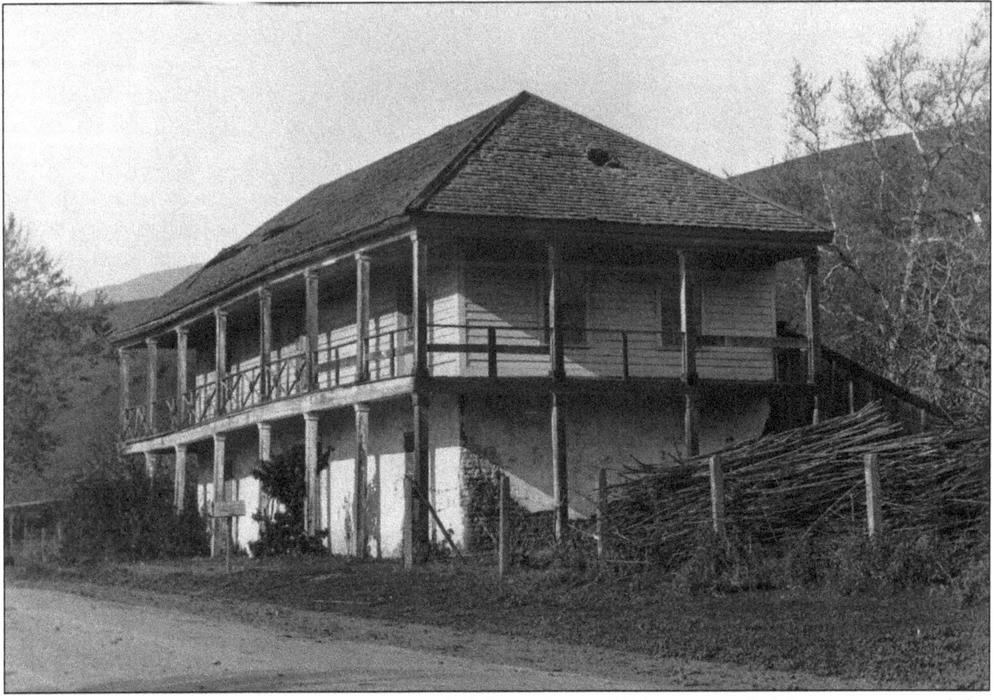

Ygnacio Alviso was a child when he traveled from Central Mexico to California as part of the Juan Bautista de Anza expedition. In 1836, he was granted an area of land called Rincon de los Esteros, which later became the city of Alviso. His adobe was built in 1837. (Courtesy of History San José.)

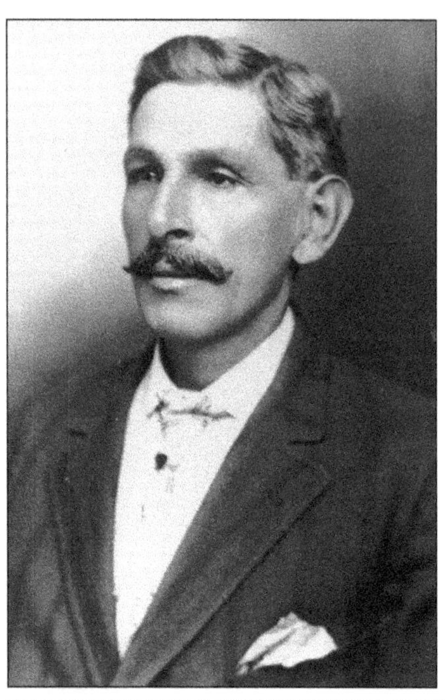

Pictured is Dionisio Bernal y Sibrian. He was the great-grandson of José Apolonario Bernal of the Juan Bautista de Anza expedition. In the 1900s, he married Henrietta Escobar, a miner's daughter from the New Almadén quicksilver mines. Some members of his family were the owners of Rancho Santa Teresa in South San José. (Courtesy of Greg Bernal-Mendoza Smestad.)

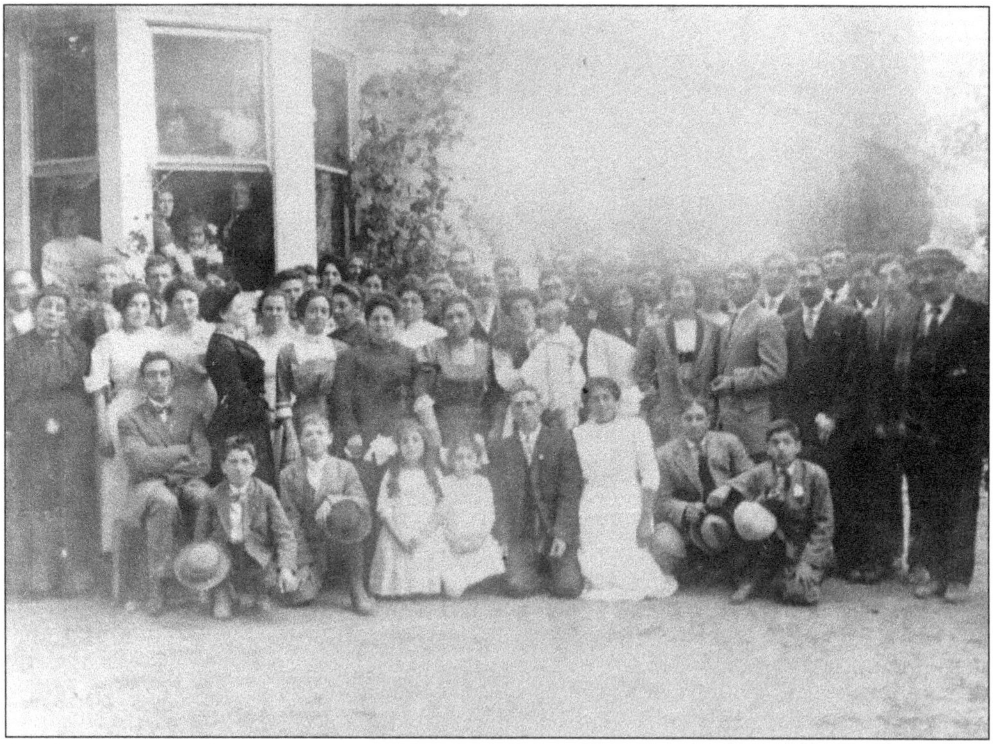

California governor José Figueroa granted the Rancho Yerba Buena y Socayre to Antonio Chabolla in 1833. Around 1845, an adobe residence was built in the East San José foothills. Antonio was the son of Marcos Chabolla and Teresa Bernal. Marcos was born in Spain and served as alcalde, or mayor, from 1796 to 1797. This early-1900 photograph shows at least three generations of the Chabolla family. (Courtesy of the Heritage Room, Evergreen Valley College.)

On September 16, 1821, Mexico secured her independence from Spain. Between 1834 and 1839, Mexico began to secularize, or end the religious ownership of the missions and lands to civil use, because of the high costs of maintenance. Between 1834 and 1842, throughout California, more than 300 ranches were carved out of mission-held lands and were granted to Mexican citizens. Some of the mission holdings were distributed to heads of Indian families. (Courtesy of History San José.)

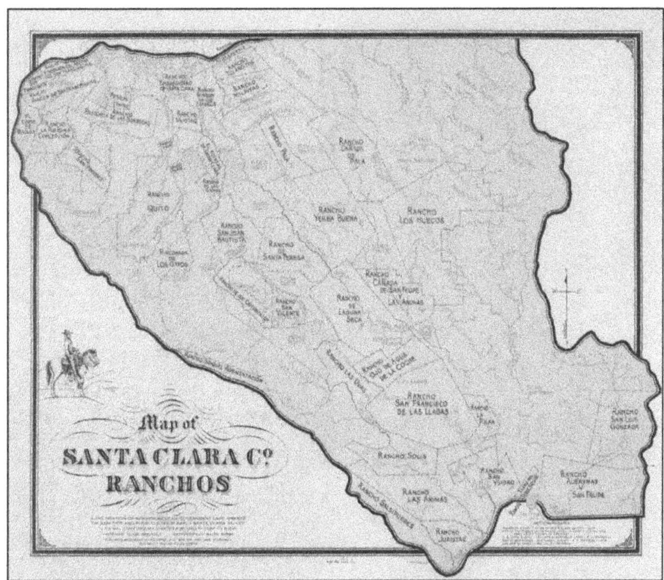

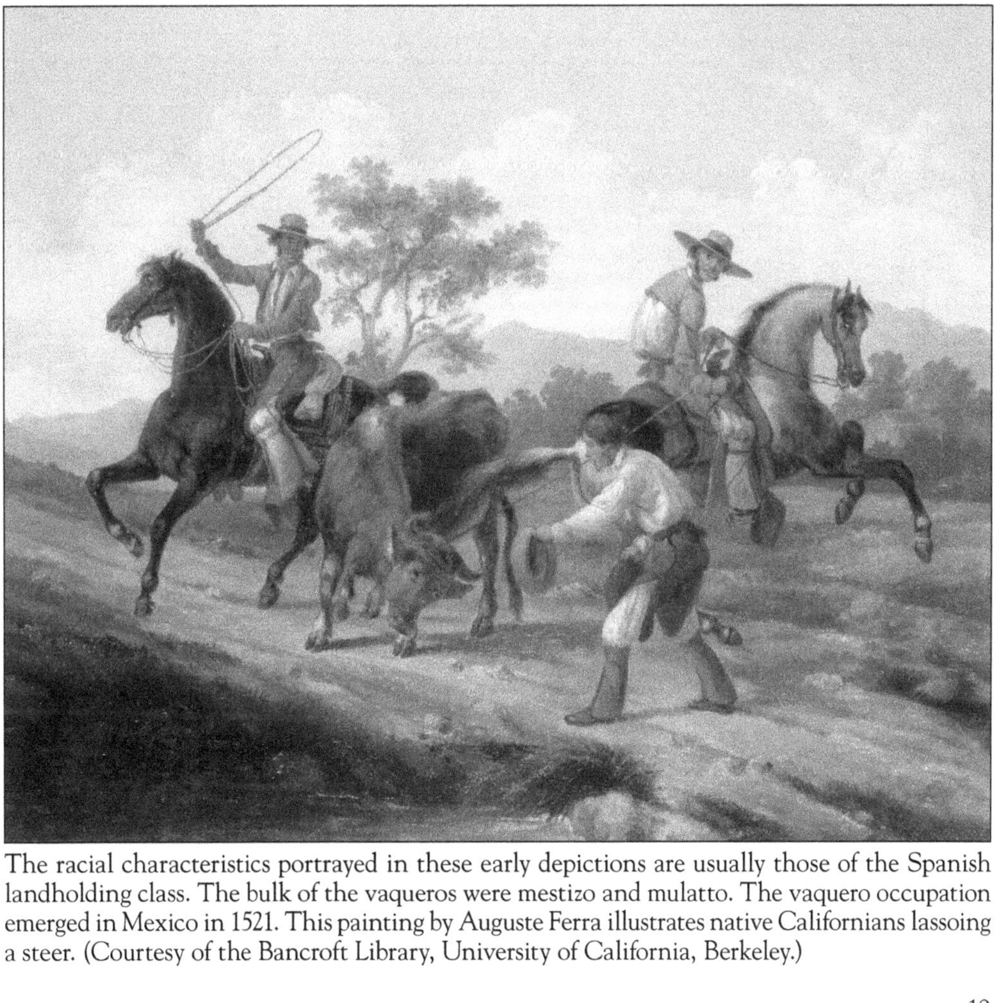

The racial characteristics portrayed in these early depictions are usually those of the Spanish landholding class. The bulk of the vaqueros were mestizo and mulatto. The vaquero occupation emerged in Mexico in 1521. This painting by Auguste Ferra illustrates native Californians lassoing a steer. (Courtesy of the Bancroft Library, University of California, Berkeley.)

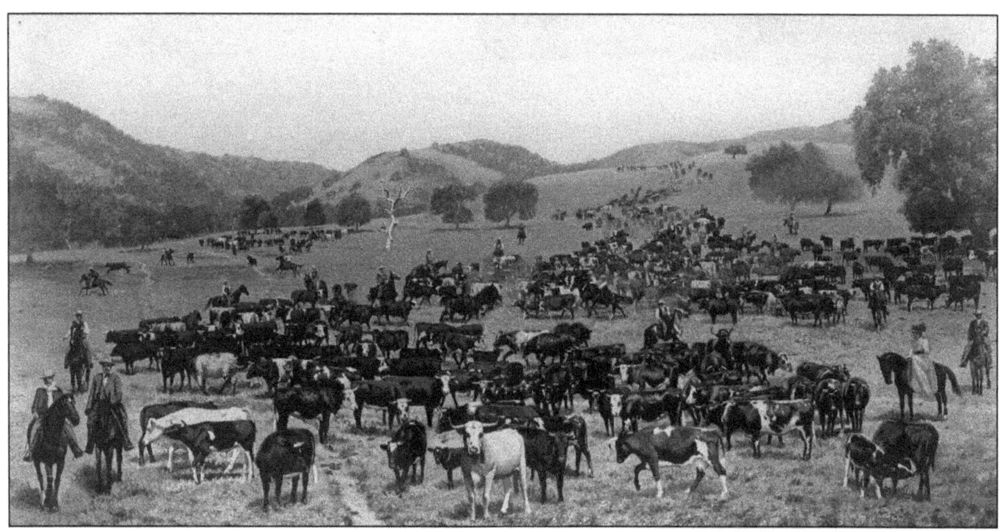

During the Mexican period from 1822 to 1846, there was significant economic growth and diversification in San José. During this time, grain was sold to the Russians at Fort Ross in Northern California, grape and wine production increased, and land was granted to Mexican Californians for raising cattle and other livestock. (Courtesy of History San José.)

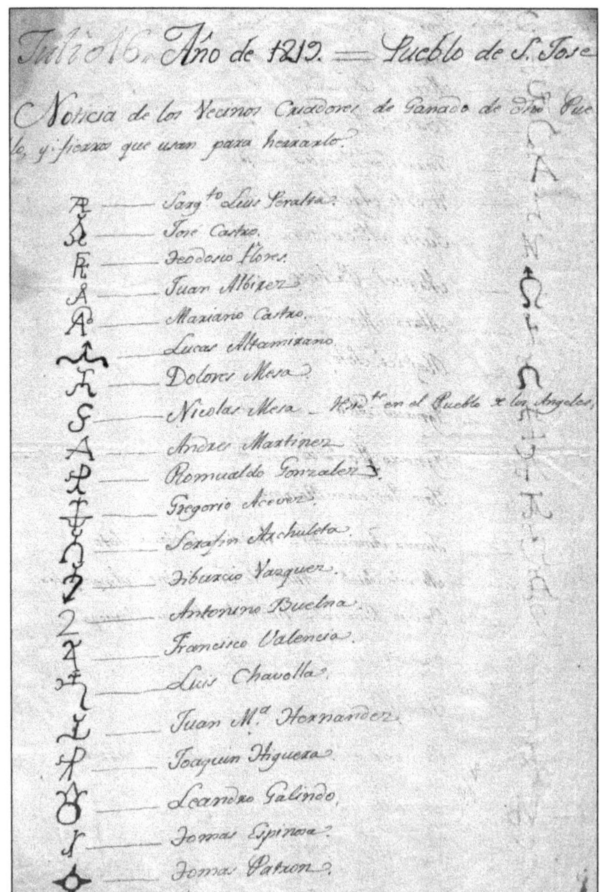

Julio 16. Año de 1812. — Pueblo de S. José

Noticia de los Vecinos Criadores de Ganado de dho Pueblo, y fierros que usan para herrarlo.

[illegible] — Sarg.to Luis Peralta.
[illegible] — José Castro.
[illegible] — Teodoro Flores.
[illegible] — Juan Alvirez.
[illegible] — Mariano Castro.
[illegible] — Lucas Altamirano.
[illegible] — Dolores Mesa.
[illegible] — Nicolas Mesa — Vecino en el Pueblo de los Angeles.
[illegible] — Andres Martinez.
[illegible] — Romualdo Gonzalez.
[illegible] — Gregorio Acevez.
[illegible] — Serafin Archuleta.
[illegible] — Ygnacio Vazquez.
[illegible] — Antonino Buelna.
[illegible] — Francisco Valencia.
[illegible] — Luis Chavolla.
[illegible] — Juan Ma. Hernandez.
[illegible] — Joaquin Higuera.
[illegible] — Leandro Galindo.
[illegible] — Tomas Espinosa.
[illegible] — Tomas Patron.

This document, dated July 16, 1812, displays cattle brands prepared by Comisionado Sgt. Luis Maria Peralta. A yearly roundup was usually held in mid-March, at which time the cattle were sorted and branded. The cattle were driven into corrals, lassoed, and tied while the branding iron was applied. (Courtesy of the William McPherson Collection, Special Collections, Libraries of the Claremont Colleges, Claremont, California.)

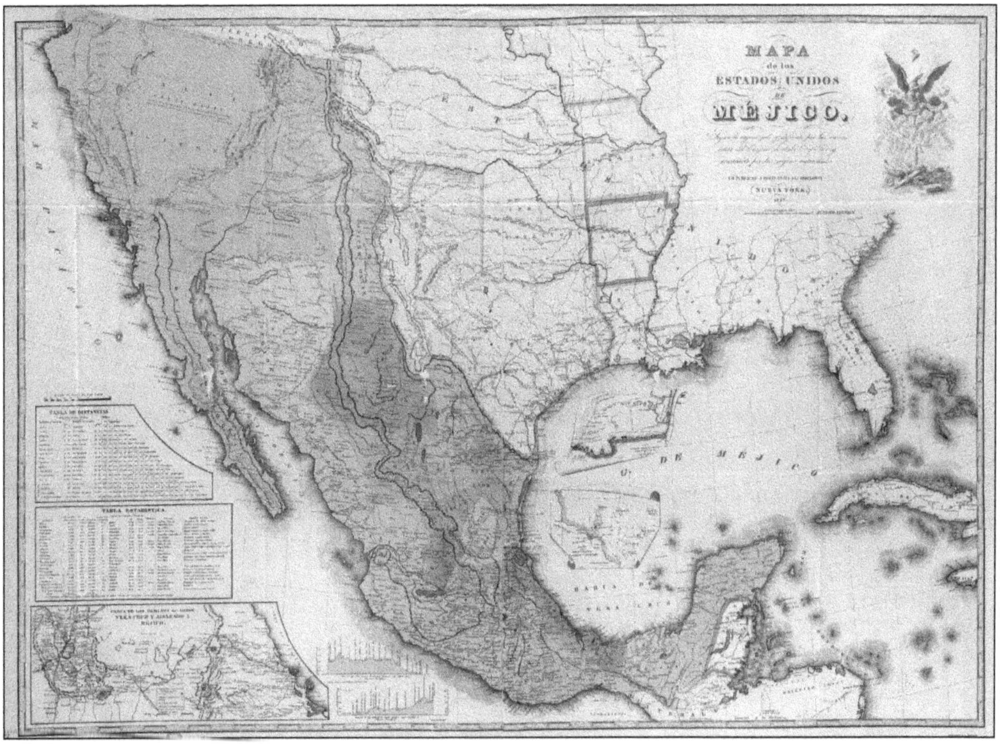

At the end of the Mexican-American War, the Treaty of Guadalupe Hidalgo was signed in 1848 between the United States and Mexico. Its terms included the United States's purchase of over one-third of Mexico's territory. The treaty guaranteed Mexicans their full U.S. citizenship rights and respect for their land, language, and religion. This 1847 map shows the Mexican territory, which includes the present-day southwest United States. (Courtesy of the Department of Special Collections, University of California, Los Angeles.)

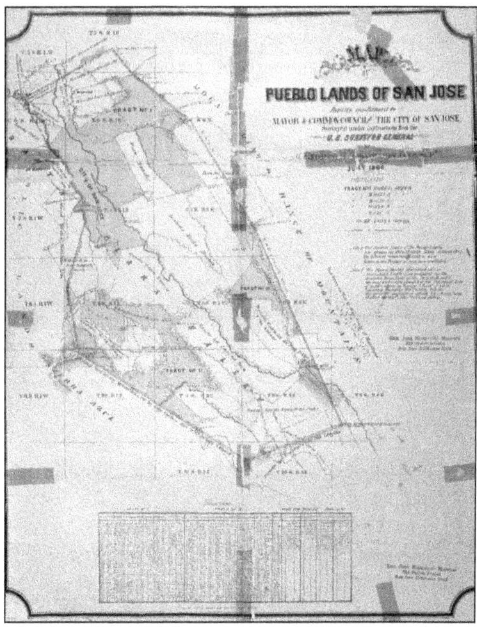

This 1866 map of the pueblo lands of San José shows significant loss of land ownership for Mexicans as a result of the Mexican-American War. One prominent Mexican family that lost their land was the Berryessa family. Nicolas Antonio Berryessa came with the Juan Bautista de Anza expedition. His ancestors were the original grantees of Rancho Milpitas and Rancho Las Putas, which includes Lake Berryessa. (Courtesy of History San José.)

Tiburcio Vasquez was the grandson of one of the original settlers and mayors of San José. Vasquez was born in Monterey, California, on August 11, 1825. He was educated and fluent in Spanish and English. After the Mexican-American War, he witnessed Mexicans' loss of land and their descent into second-class status. Rebelling against those in power, he became a social outlaw. To many Mexicans, he is viewed as a cultural hero. (Courtesy of History San José.)

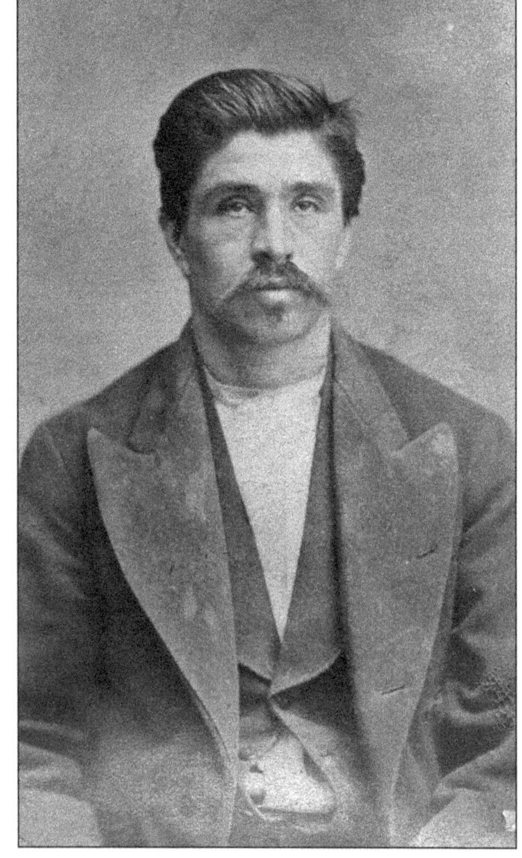

Abdon Leiva, a Chilean miner, rode with Tiburcio Vasquez in the 1870s. They were involved in the Los Piños Tragedy, in which Vasquez and his band killed several men. Leiva later ended his support of Vasquez and provided evidence against him in a trial. Vasquez was convicted of murder in the Santa Clara County court, hanged at St. James Park on March 19, 1875, and buried at Mission Cemetery in Santa Clara. Because he was considered an outlaw, his headstone was placed at an angle. (Courtesy of History San José.)

Two

The New Almadén Quicksilver Mines and Spanishtown

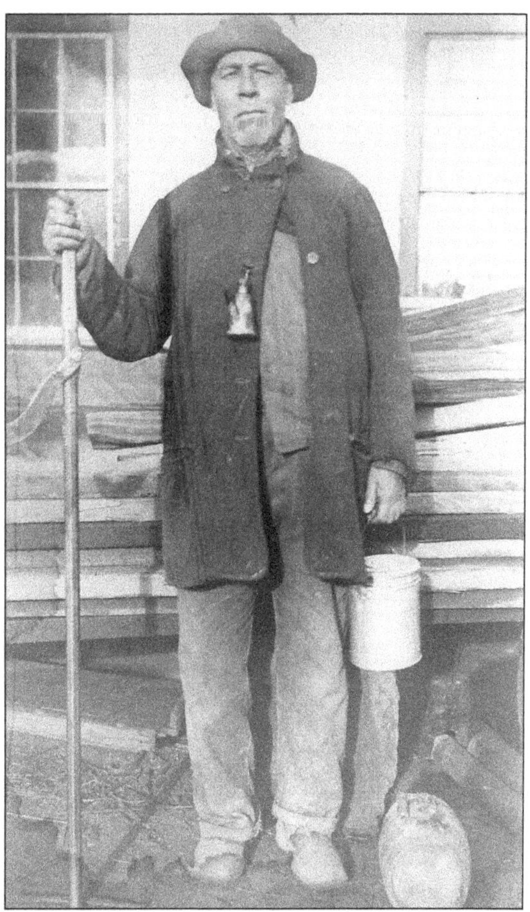

In 1845, Capt. Andres Castillero discovered a cinnabar deposit in the Capitancillos hills 12 miles south of downtown San José. The mine established at Castillero's discovery site changed ownership several times over the next 50 years. In this 1890s image, Patricio Avila stands with his mining equipment—a drill, a lamp, and lunch and water buckets. Absent in this photograph is a hard hat or other protection for his head. In 1851, all but two of the approximately 700 employees were either Mexican or Chilean. A majority of the Mexican workforce were from Sonora, Mexico. For miners, the average life expectancy was 45 years. (Photograph by Laurence Bulmore, courtesy of History San José.)

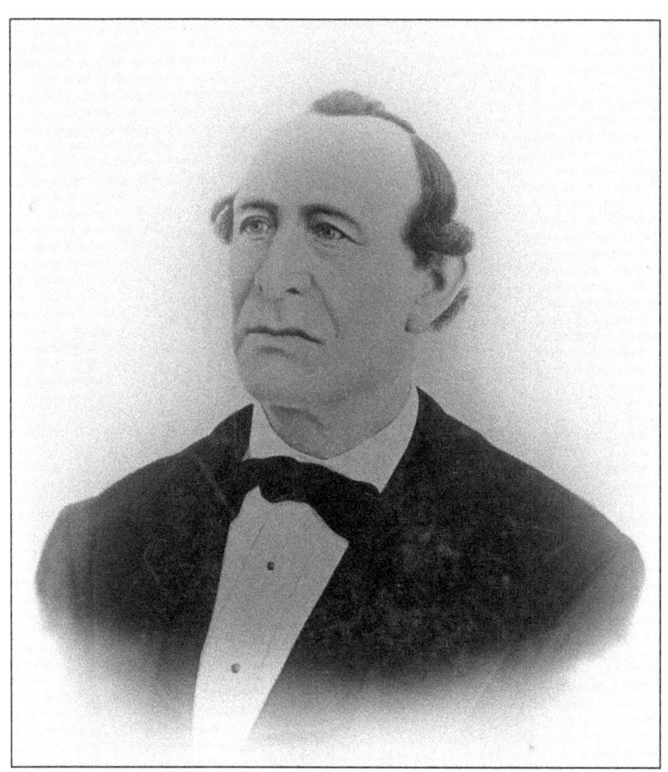

Secundino Robles learned from an Ohlone Indian the location of a cave with red rock the Ohlones used for decorative paint. He investigated the Capitancillo hills, called New Almadén, with an Ohlone guide, hoping to find gold or silver. But he failed to understand that the red rock was cinnabar, a high grade of mercury. In 1824, he told Antonio Sunol and Luis Chabolla about his discovery. Sunol and Chabolla also investigated the hills for gold or silver, but abandoned their venture after finding cinnabar instead. (Courtesy of the Society of California Pioneers.)

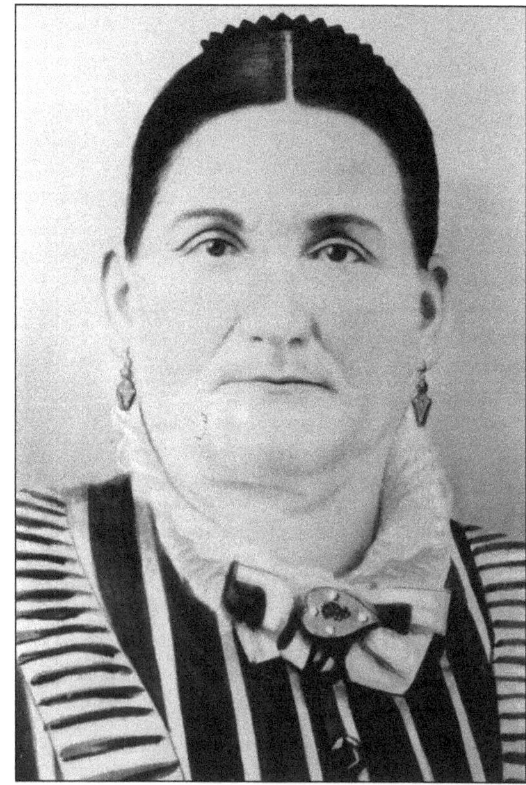

Antonia Garcia Robles was the wife of the New Almadén mine cinnabar investigator, Secundio Robles. She gave birth to 29 children, 12 boys and 17 girls. (Courtesy of the California History Center.)

Capt. Andres Castillero was on a scouting mission and encountered cinnabar on Justo Larios's land grant Rancho de los Capitancillos, which was near José Berryessa's land grant as the map illustrates. In 1845, Castillero filed a mine claim in San José and traveled to Mexico City for its financial support, but the Mexican government was preoccupied with a war against the United States and could not lend their support. (Courtesy of the New Almadén Quicksilver Mining Museum.)

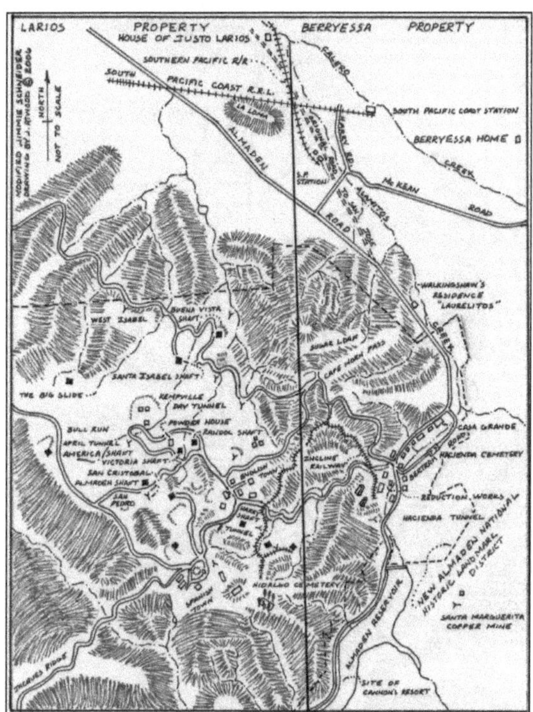

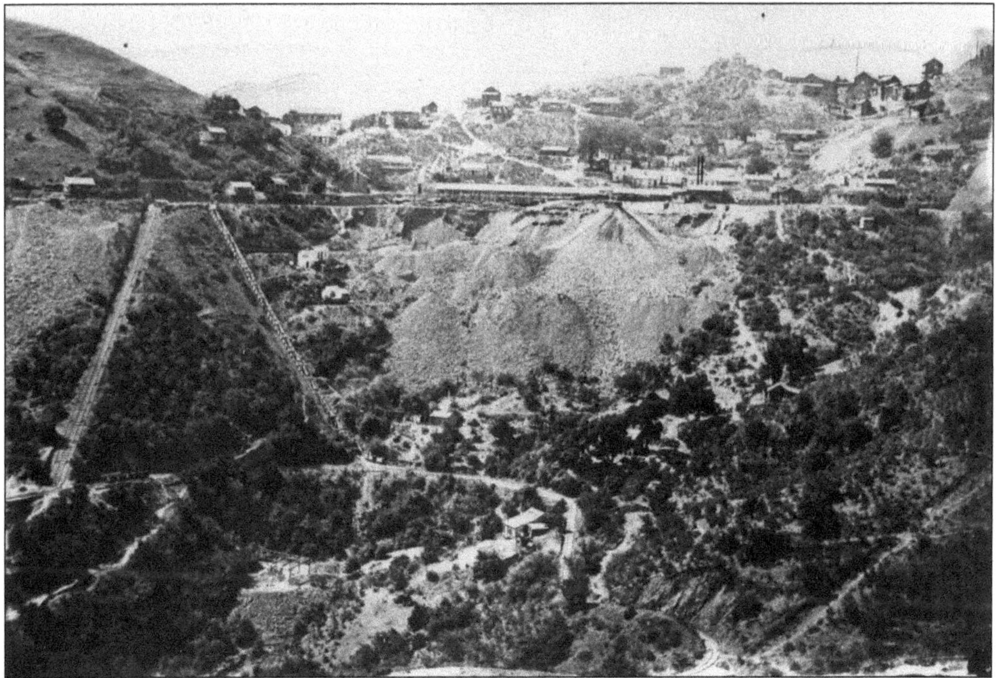

This aerial photograph displays the operations of the mine and routes. Down the steep hill on the left is a railroad line that moved the mercury ore in a small car from the mine to nearby railroad cars for shipment. On the right is a ladder for miners to walk up and down the hill. (Courtesy of the Department of Special Collections and University Archives, Stanford University Libraries, New Almadén Mine collection [M270].)

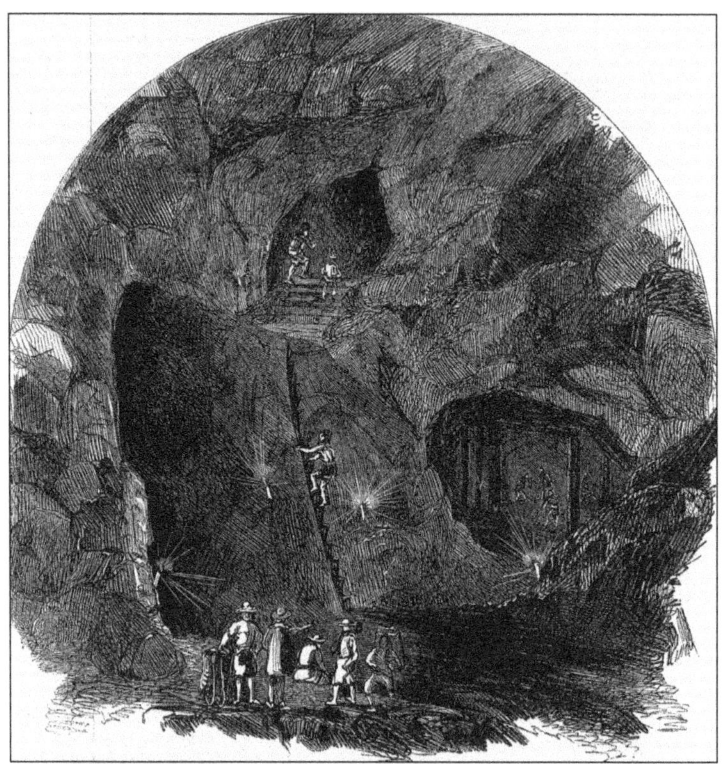

Mine owners took pride in noting that Mexican miners were "more adventurous" than Cornishmen, who were known to be excellent miners. This illustration from *Harpers New Monthly Magazine* shows Mexican miners climbing up steep shafts. (Courtesy of Cornell University Library, Making of America Digital Collection.)

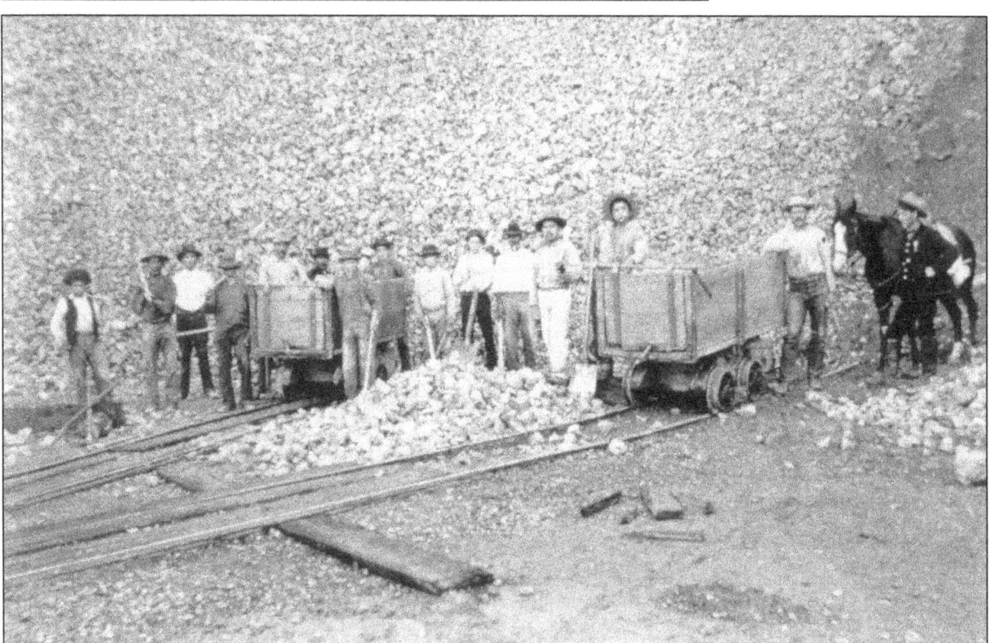

From 1865 to 1868, there were at least four strikes by miners fighting to increase wages, to improve dangerous working conditions, to end the financial exploitation by the company store, and to address other labor grievances. Several leaders of the strikes were Mexican, and for some, the consequences for their activism included loss of mine employment, removal from their homes, and damage to their reputation. (Courtesy of the California History Center.)

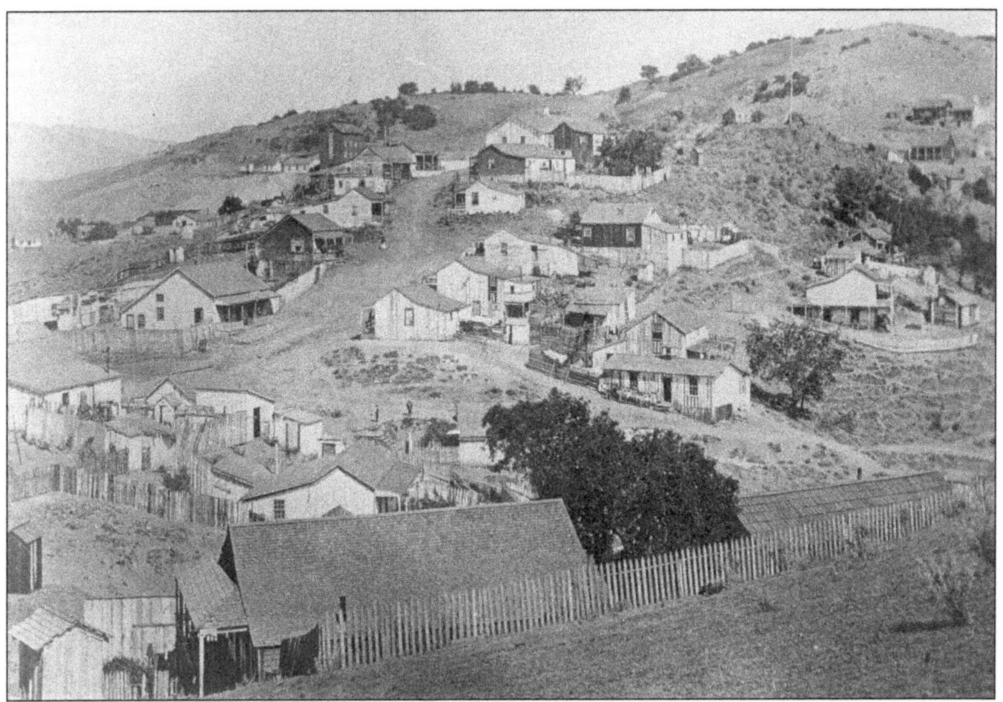

Mexican miners and their families lived near the mines in a segregated area called Spanishtown. Some of the homes were built by the mine company and others by the Spanishtown residents. Outhouses were built behind the homes. (Courtesy of the Department of Special Collections and University Archives, Stanford University Libraries, New Almadén Mine collection [M270].)

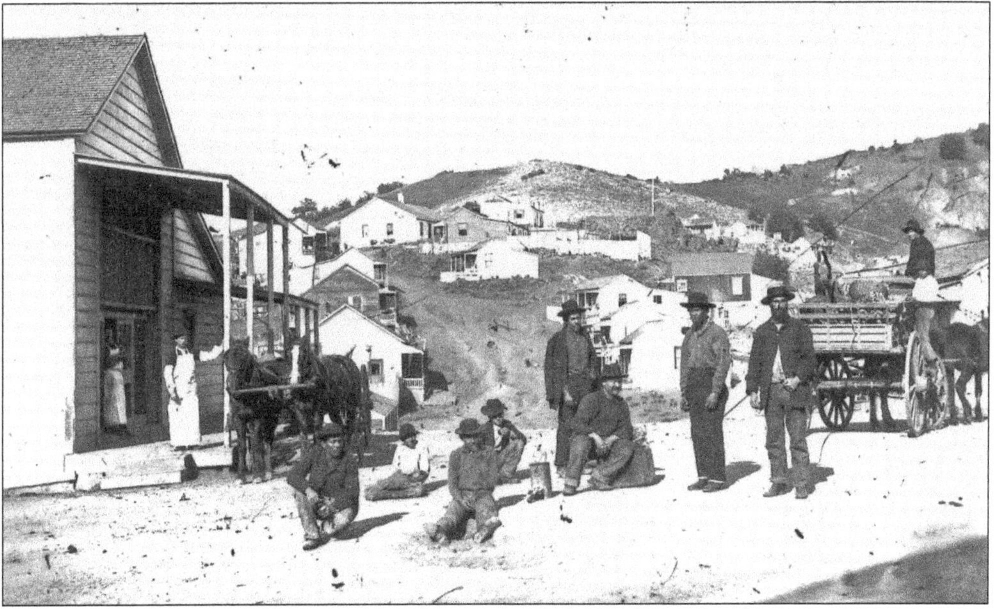

Miners stand in front of the butcher shop in Spanishtown in the 1880s. From left to right are Matt De Leon (butcher), Dave Neddy (butcher), and spectators (standing) Walker Brown, Patricio Andrada(e), Nicholas ?, and Francisco Palayo. (Courtesy of the Department of Special Collections and University Archives, Stanford University Libraries, New Almadén Mine collection [M270].)

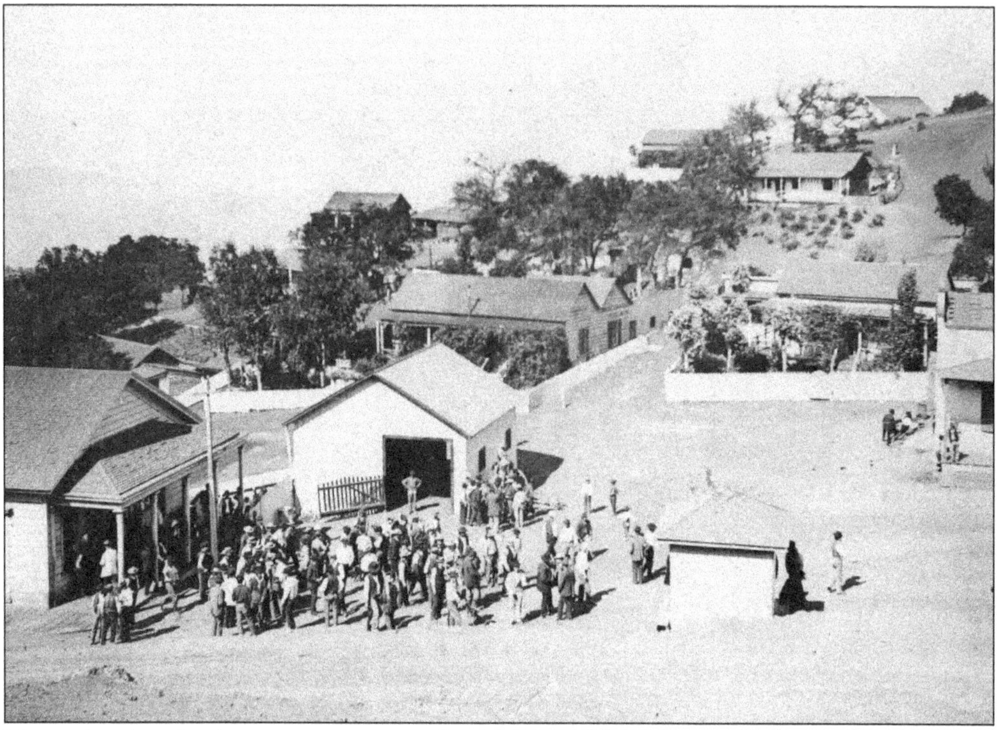

Miners lined up for their earnings on the last Sunday of the month, called the "dia de raya" or payday. In the late 1880s, their earnings were paid in silver dollars or cardboard boletos. Boletos could be redeemed for credit at the company store, yet purchasing food items at the company store proved to have its challenges, as perishable food was often rotten and overpriced. (Courtesy of the New Almadén Mining Quicksilver Mining Museum.)

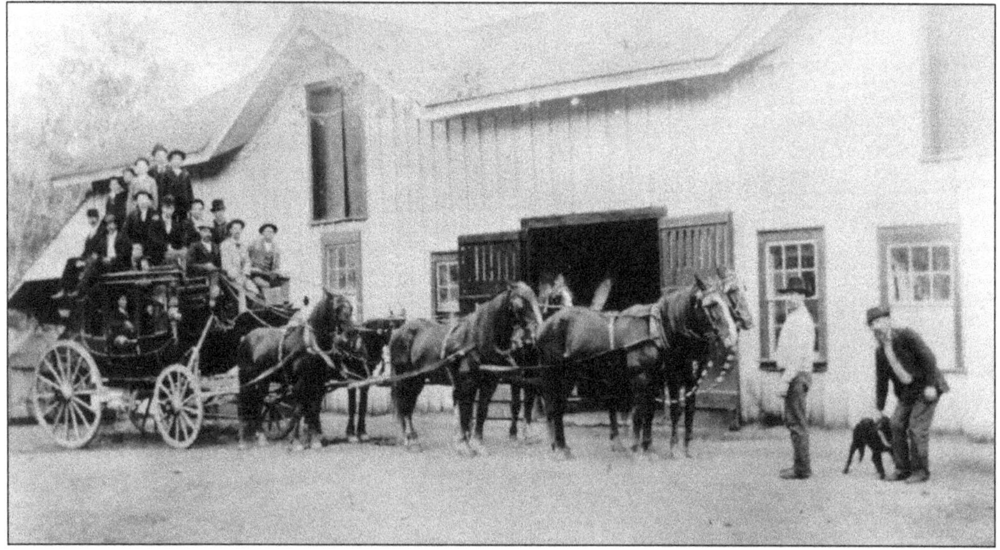

Pancho Alcaraz, a Concord stagecoach driver, drove daily from New Almadén to San José in 1896. The stagecoach could safely carry 18 passengers, nine inside the coach and nine on the top, yet this photograph shows the coach exceeding capacity. (Photograph by Laurence Bulmore, courtesy of the California History Center.)

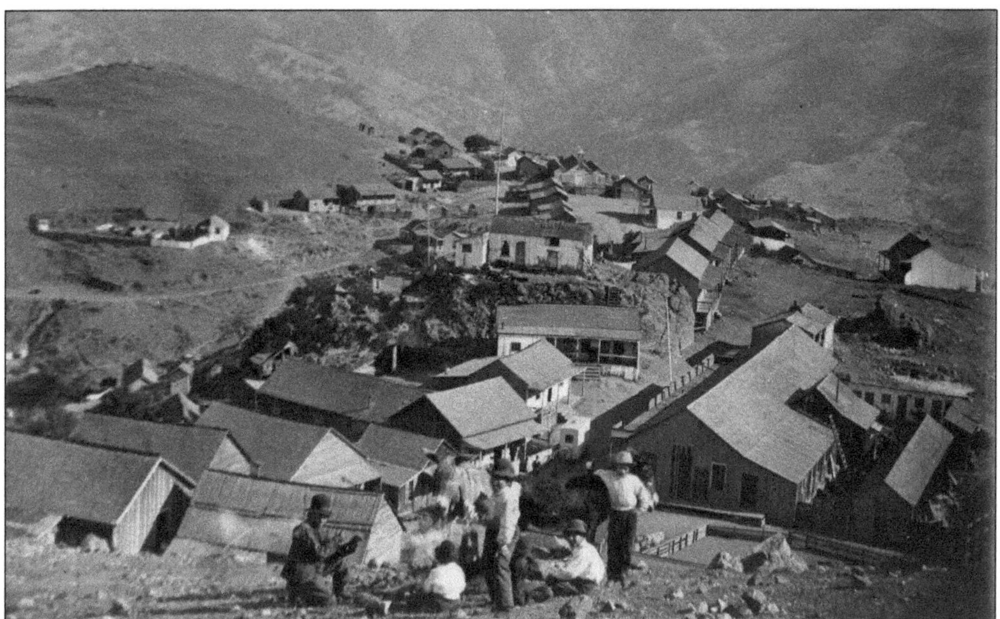

Living in Spanishtown proved to be deadly to countless Mexican children. They were exposed daily to life-threatening illnesses and toxic gases from the mines. As one doctor noted in 1891, there was a disproportionate number of deaths of children in Spanishtown under the age of 13. (Courtesy of the Department of Special Collections and University Archives, Stanford University Libraries, New Almadén Mine collection [M270].)

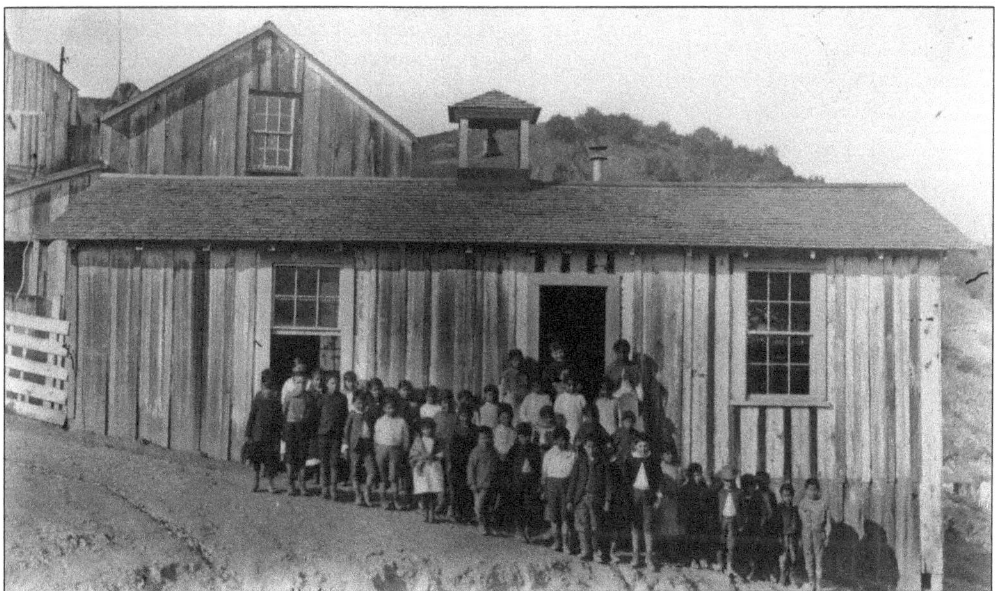

Mexican schoolchildren residing in Spanishtown had to traverse long distances in dangerous conditions to attend school in a nearby mining community called Englishtown. In response to concerned parents of Mexican schoolchildren, a single one-room school was erected by the mine company next to St. Anthony's Catholic Church in Spanishtown. This was one of the first segregated schools for Mexicans in the nation. (Courtesy of the Department of Special Collections and University Archives, Stanford University Libraries, New Almadén Mine collection [M270].)

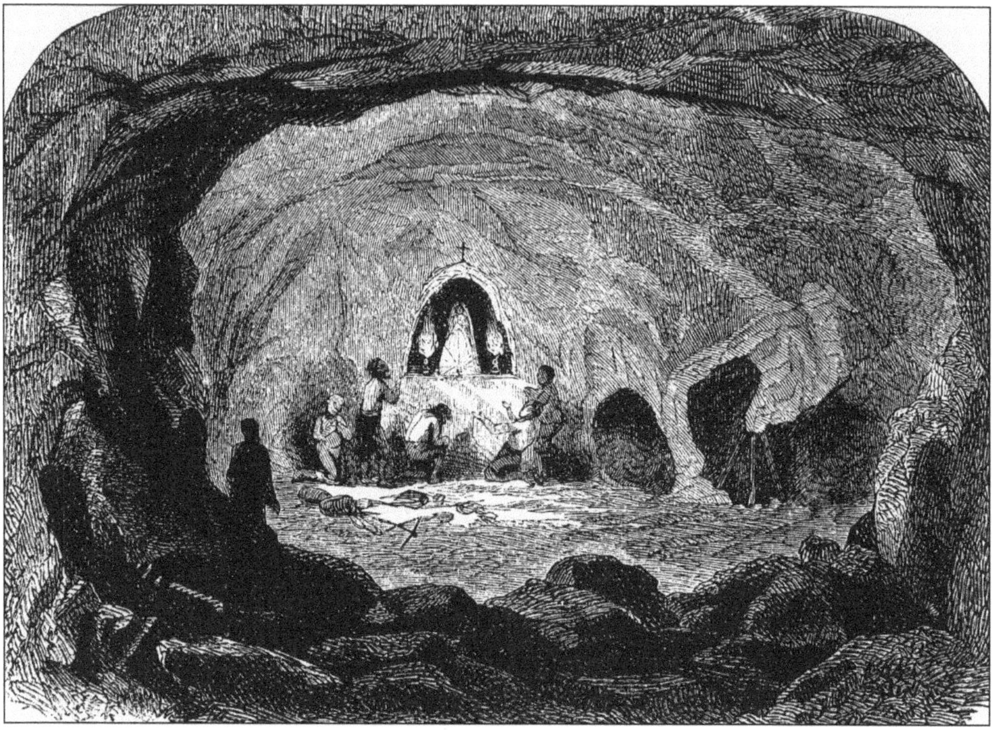

Due to their dangerous working conditions, Mexican miners erected Catholic altars dedicated to the revered La Virgen de Guadalupe. Candles were constantly kept burning at the altars to protect the workers from cave-ins or explosions called fire-damps. (Courtesy of Cornell University Library, Making of America Digital Collection.)

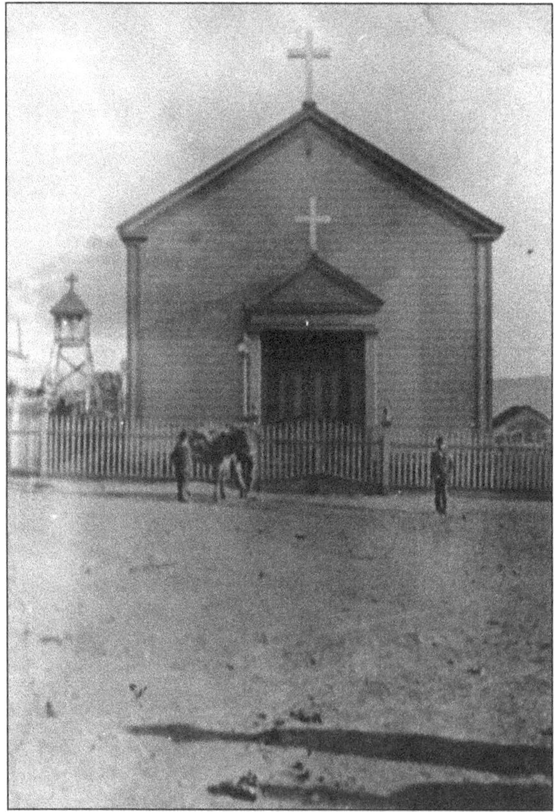

St. Anthony's Church was a magnificent sight in the New Almadén mines community. The church stood at the top of a hill near the Mexican School, overlooking Deep Gulch. (Courtesy of the Department of Special Collections and University Archives, Stanford University Libraries, New Almadén Mine collection [M270].)

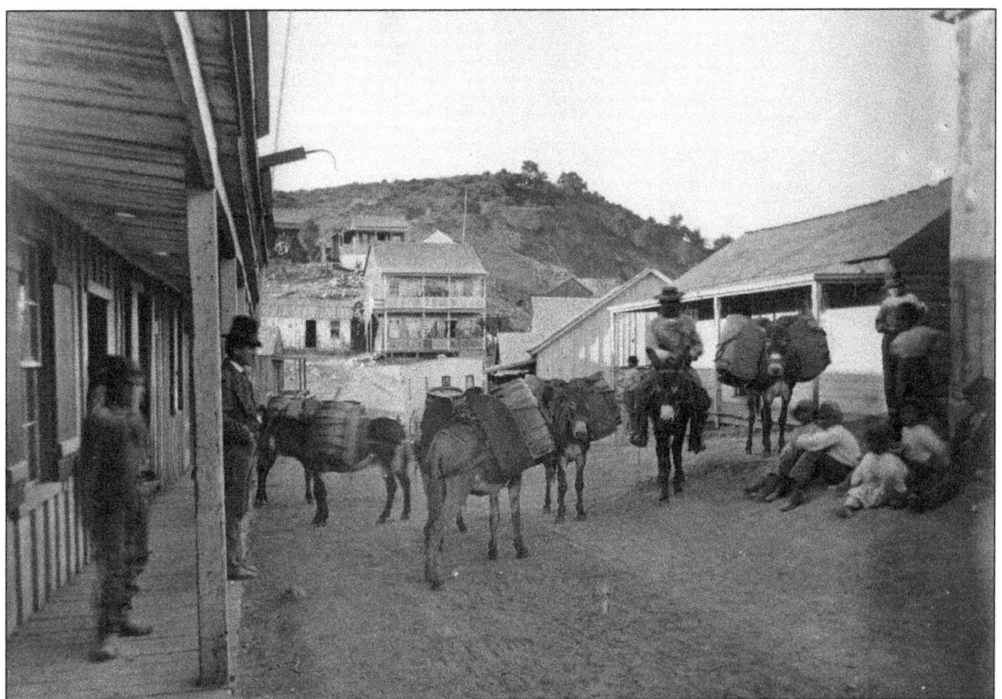

Available water was a mile away from Spanishtown inhabitants. Mine owners resorted to using burros to haul in barrels of water. Eventually, water pipes were installed in Spanishtown by the mine company in 1881. (Courtesy of the Department of Special Collections and University Archives, Stanford University Libraries, New Almadén Mine collection [M270].)

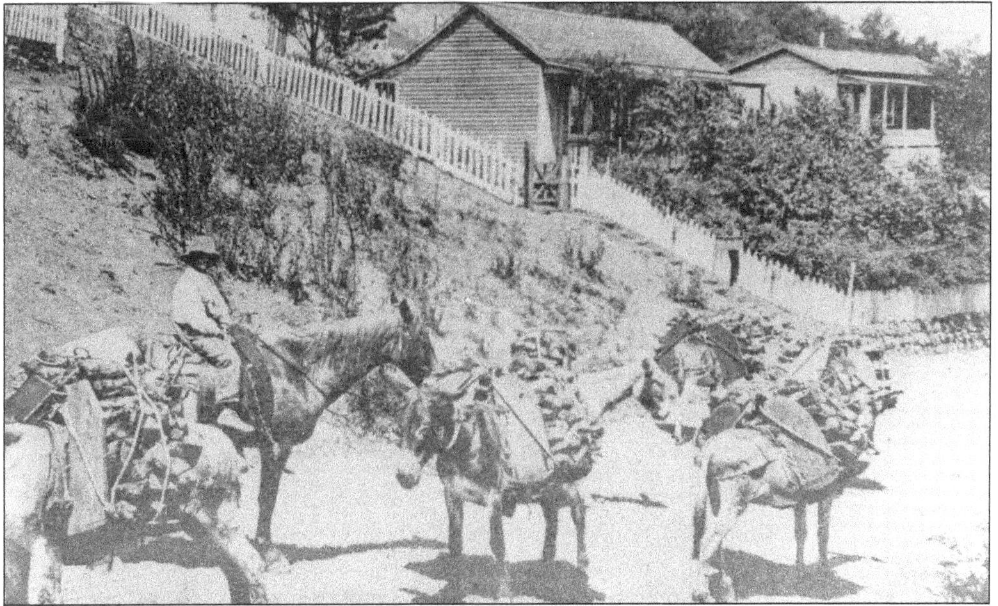

Remotely located in steep terrain, residents of Spanishtown were dependent on mine owners to provide provisions for them. A young Mexican guide in the fall of the late 1880s leads burros to deliver stove wood to the Spanishtown residents. The burros' wood packs weighed approximately 300 pounds. (Courtesy of the California History Center.)

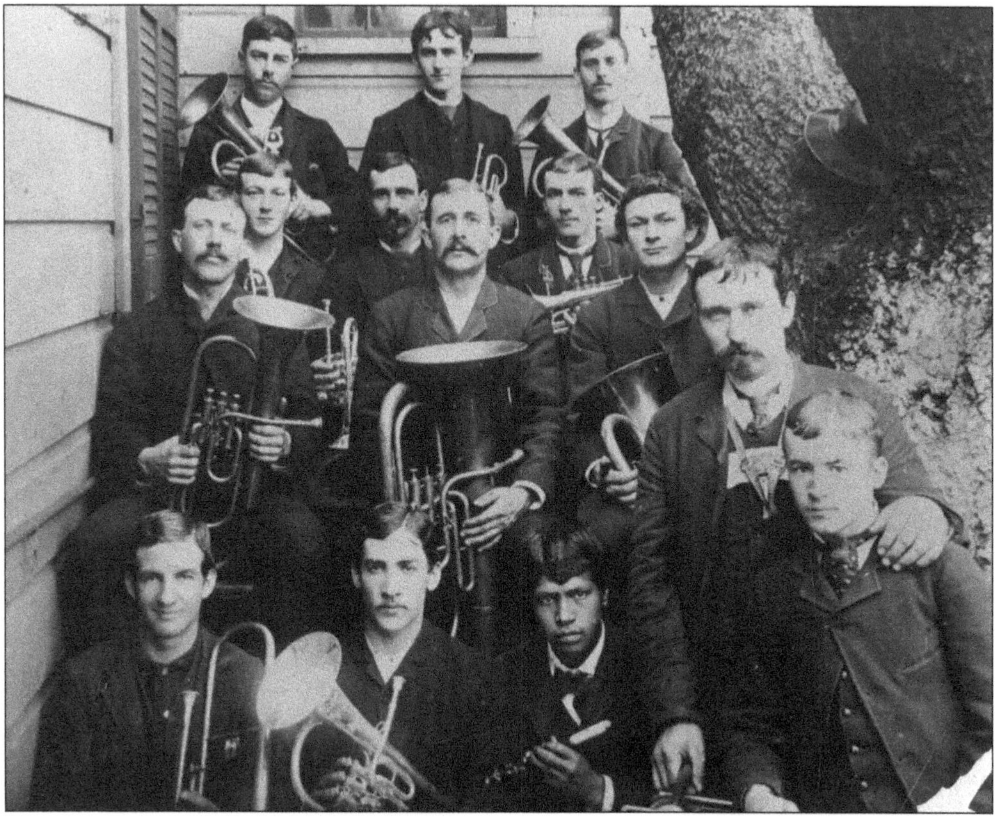

Named Mountain Echo, the musical band had members from both Englishtown and Spanishtown. Posing with their instruments are, from left to right, (first row) William Bunney, John Robbins, Amado Gonzales (flute), William Luxom, and Dick Jacka (with Luxom's arm over his shoulder); (second row) Thomas Williams, Dick Colins, and Joe Pearce; (third row) James Williams, bandmaster Joseph Bishop, and William Jacka; (fourth row) Thomas Matthews, Nicholas Grey, and John Williams. (Courtesy of the Department of Special Collections and University Archives, Stanford University Libraries, New Almadén Mine collection [M270].)

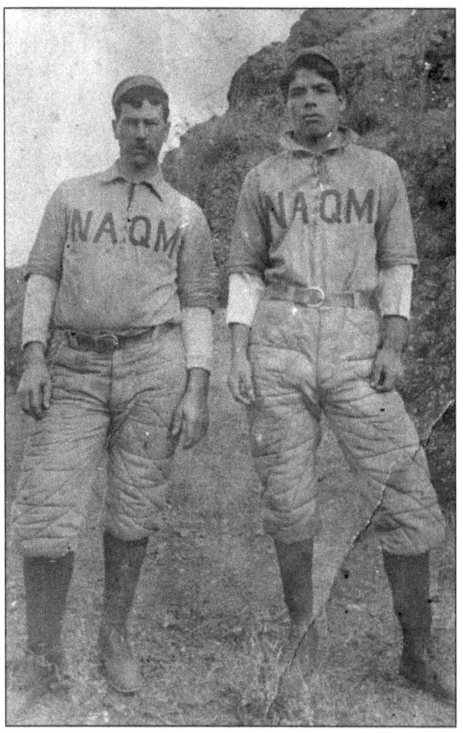

Baseball players Joe Victor (left) and Evaristo San Ibanes are teammates for the New Almadén Quicksilver Miners (NAQM) team in 1894. Baseball games were extremely competitive between townships and no doubt exciting for the spectators. (Courtesy of the California History Center.)

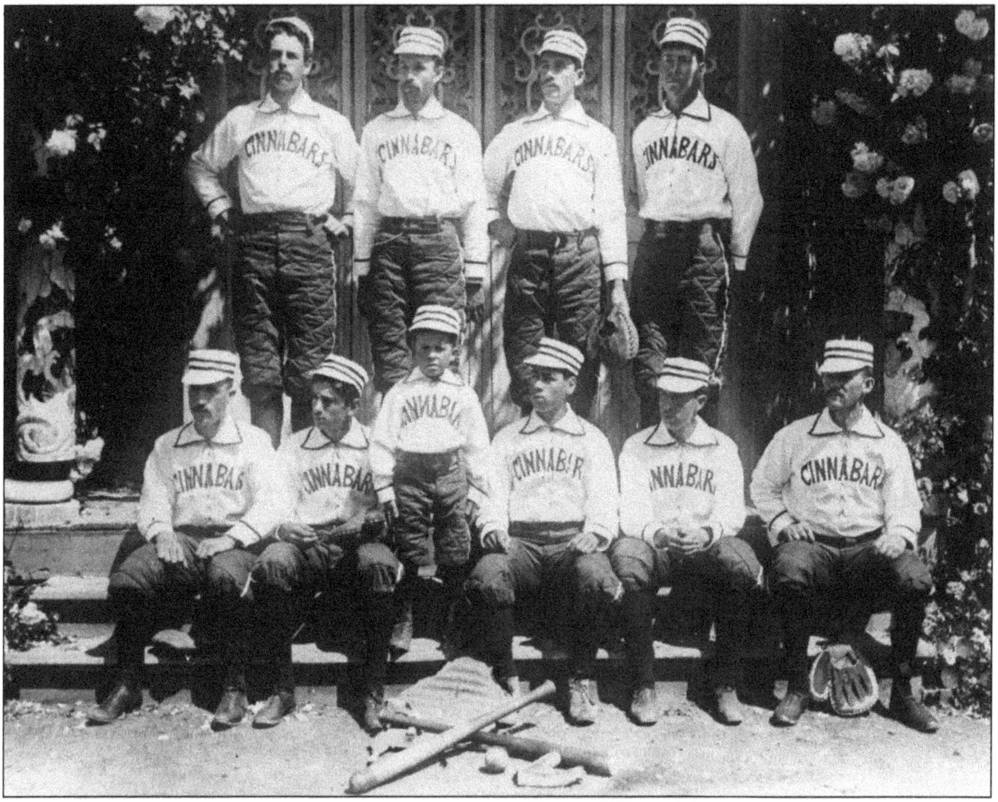

The Cinnabar baseball team members pose proudly in their home game uniforms in 1897. From left to right are (seated) Frank McComas, Alma Bulmore, Johnny Selaya (mascot), Al Acevida, Tom Ynostrosa, and Bud McCracken; (standing) Dave Bulmore, Jim Fiedler, George Bulmore, and Joe Moore. (Photograph by Robert Bulmore, courtesy of the California History Center.)

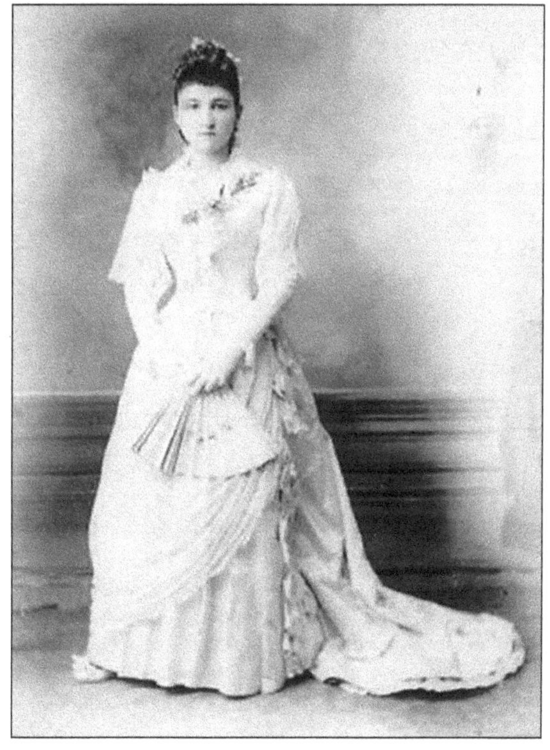

Henrietta Escobar y Caseres stands in her wedding gown at the New Almadén mines. She was born at the mines in 1873. Her waist was smaller than 18 inches when she was 18 years old. (Courtesy of Greg Bernal-Mendoza Smestad.)

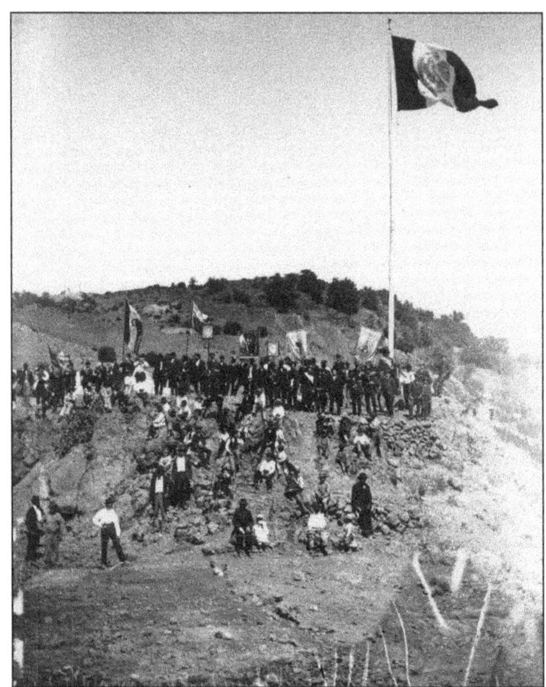

In this photograph, Mexicans united to maintain their ties and cultural identity with their home country in the late 19th century. Spanishtown residents celebrated the annual festivities of Cinco de Mayo. (Courtesy of the Department of Special Collections and University Archives, Stanford University Libraries, New Almadén Mine collection [M270].)

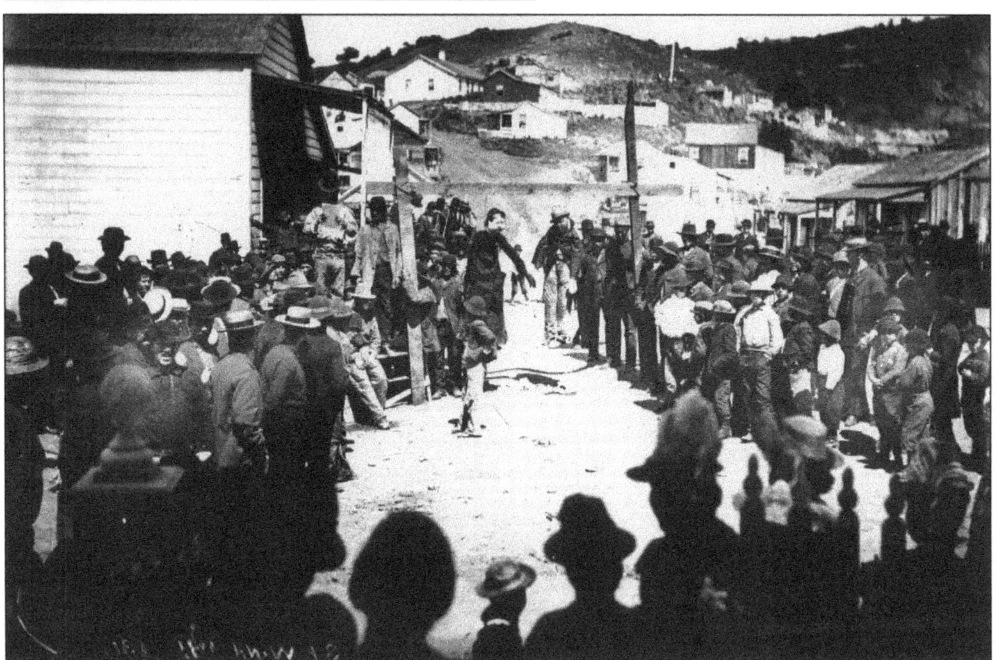

In the late 1800s, the hanging and burning of an effigy of Judas Iscariot was part of the annual Catholic Good Friday celebration in Spanishtown. Named the Colgante de Judas, the celebration began with the parade of a mannequin of Judas and ended with the hanging of the mannequin. Inside the mannequin were firecrackers and a kitten. The event climaxed when the firecrackers were lit. The frightened kitten frantically escaped from the mannequin, symbolizing the release of Judas. (Courtesy of the Department of Special Collections and University Archives, Stanford University Libraries, New Almadén Mine collection [M270].)

Three

Cannery and Agriculture Work

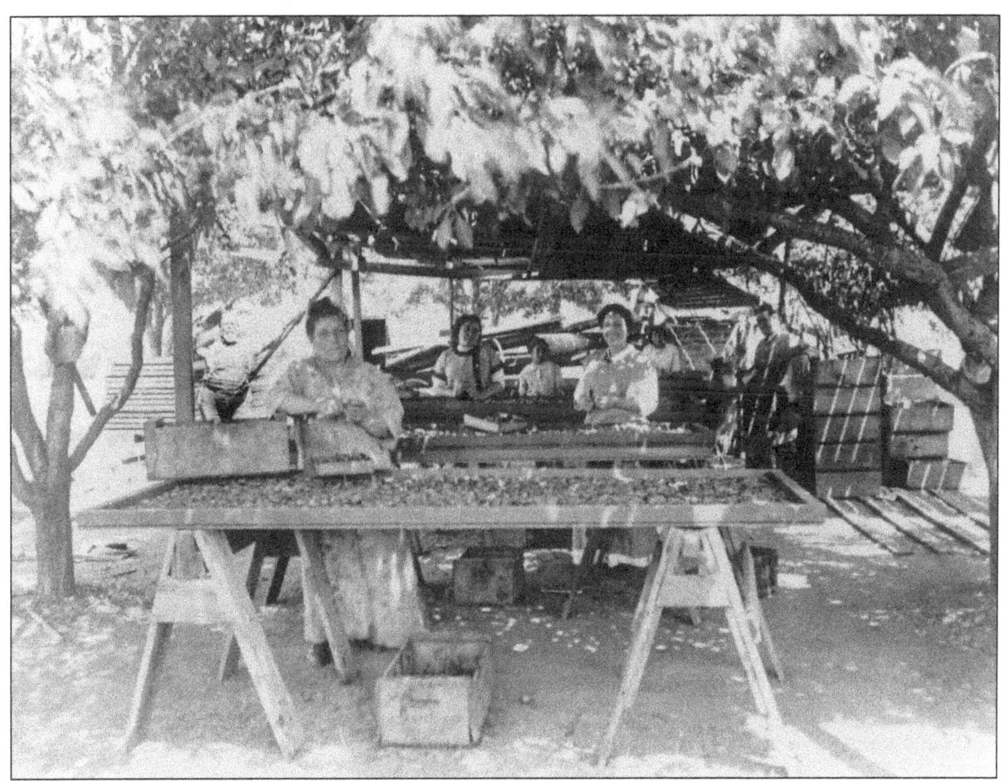

At the Chabolla ranch in the Evergreen area of San José, women slice open apricots to place on drying trays in 1914. Ramon Chabolla (right) and an unidentified gentleman observe in the background. The Chabolla family was originally granted the land by the Mexican government, its ownership ratified by the U.S. government in 1859. The land grant of approximately 24,342 acres was used originally for cattle grazing and later for agricultural harvesting. (Courtesy of Evergreen Valley College, Heritage Room.)

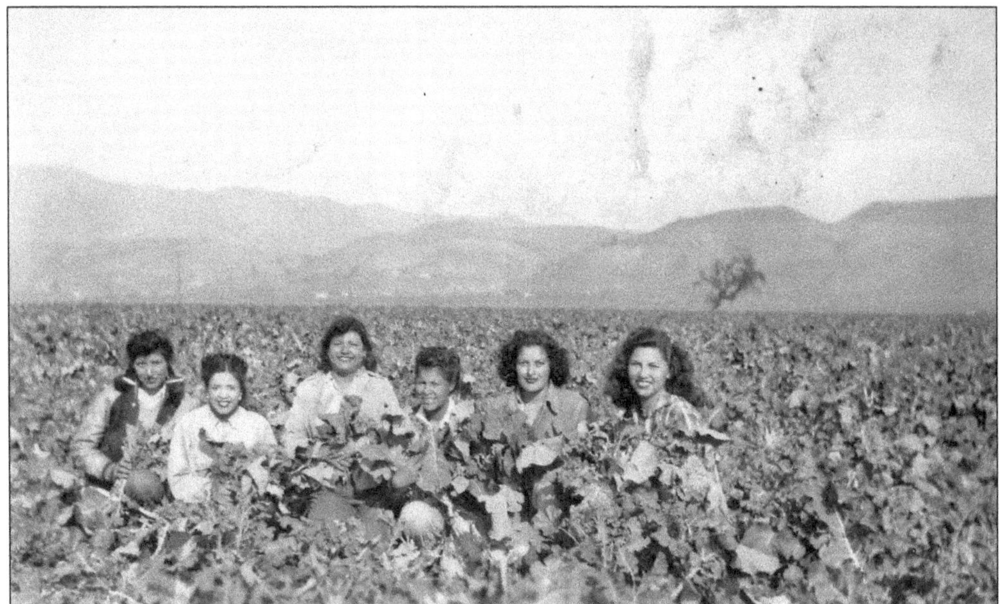

San José was a pivotal location for the production of many crops. Its varied agricultural production contributed to the label "The Valley of Heart's Delight" given to Santa Clara Valley in the 20th century. San José provided fresh, dried, and canned fruits and vegetables, domestically and internationally. In the 1950s, these six women are posing in one of many agricultural fields. (Courtesy of the Felix Garcia family.)

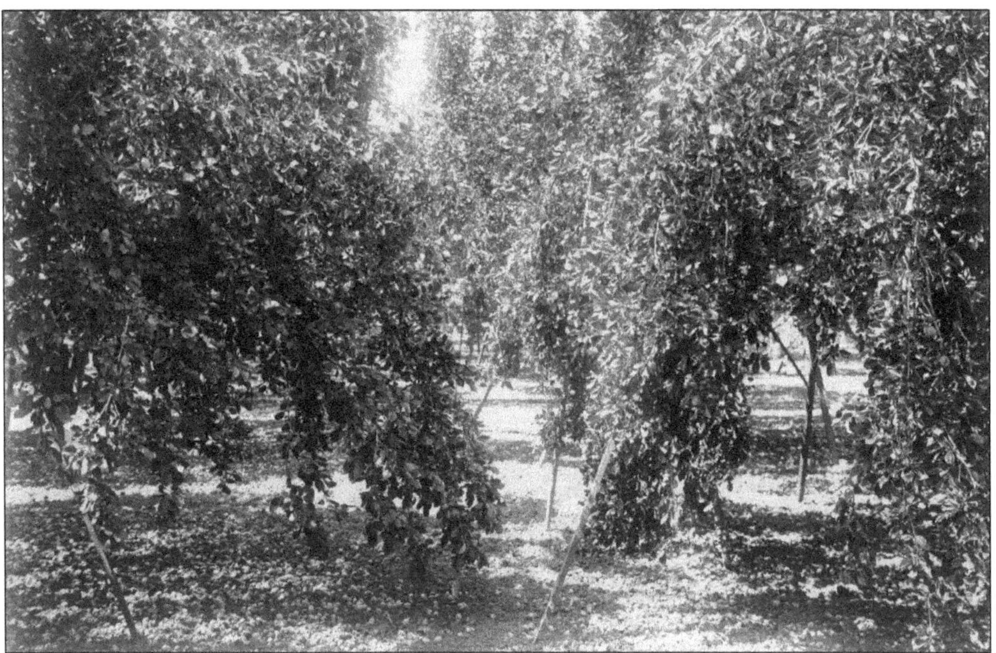

In the 19th century, San José farmers planted grains such as wheat, barley, oats, nuts, and flour. By the mid-19th century, farmers began planting fruit orchards, vegetables, and vineyards. This image illustrates the abundance of fruit as wooden stakes hold up branches heavy with prunes at harvest time. (Courtesy of San José Public Library, California Room, Clyde Arbuckle Collection.)

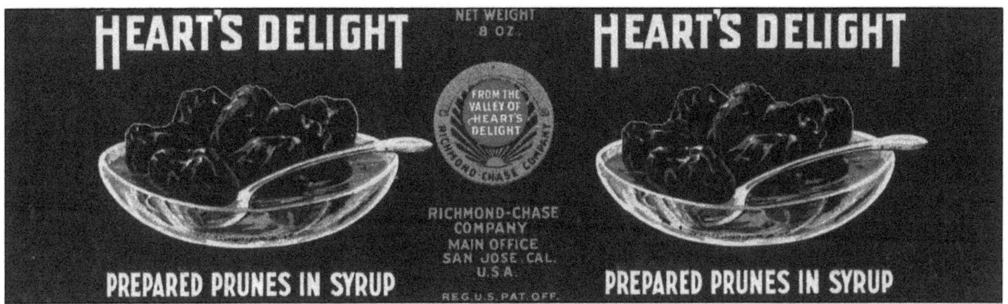

From the 1870s, agricultural production growth in California increased 25 percent per year. By 1919, California produced 57 percent of the oranges, 70 percent of the prunes and plums, over 80 percent of the grapes and figs, and virtually all of the apricots, almonds, walnuts, olives, and lemons grown in the United States. This label from Richmond-Chase Company was fixed on metal cans containing prunes with syrup. (Courtesy of History San José.)

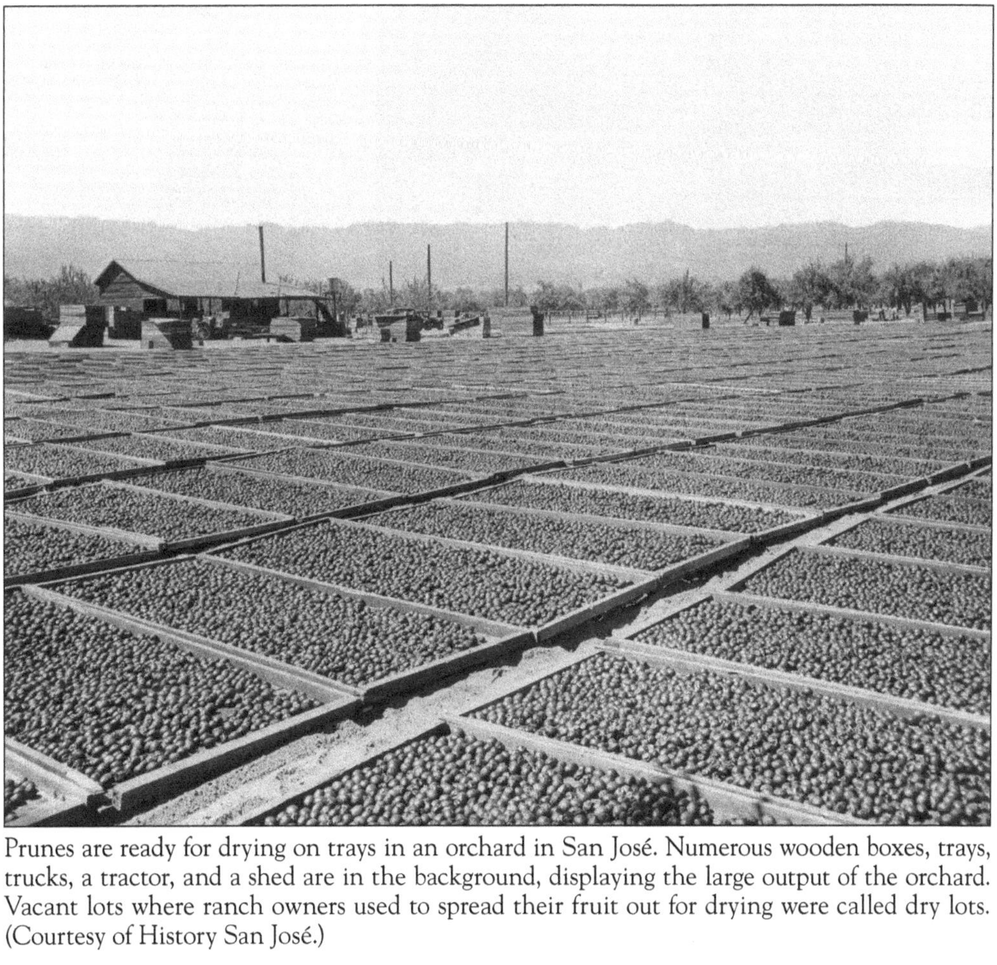

Prunes are ready for drying on trays in an orchard in San José. Numerous wooden boxes, trays, trucks, a tractor, and a shed are in the background, displaying the large output of the orchard. Vacant lots where ranch owners used to spread their fruit out for drying were called dry lots. (Courtesy of History San José.)

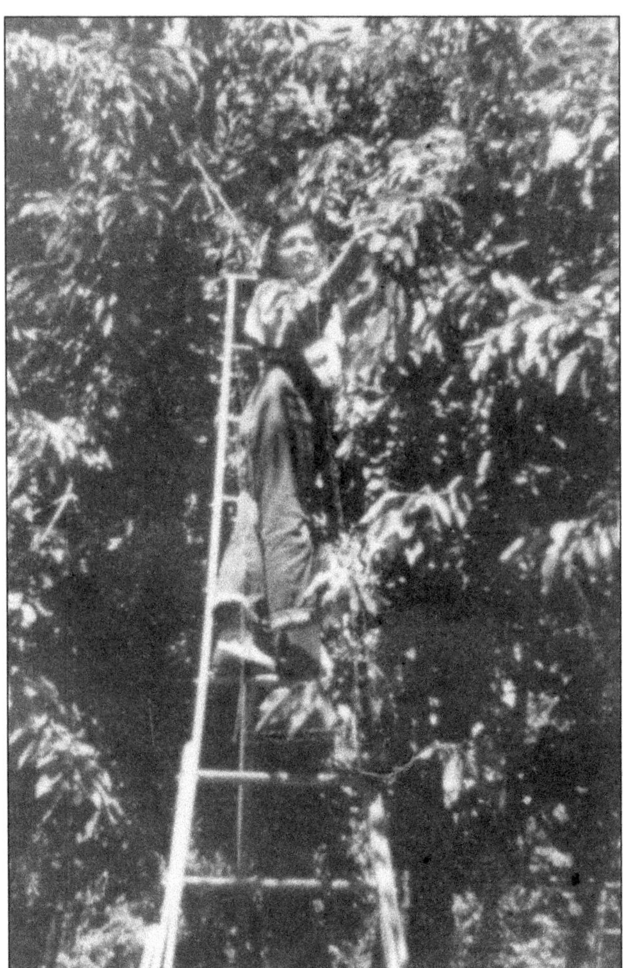

Maria Guerrero Alvarado poses on a narrow ladder while picking bing cherries in one of San José's orchards in 1955. It was rare for women to climb and pick on ladders, which were usually 12 feet tall. (Courtesy of Maria Guerrero Alvarado.)

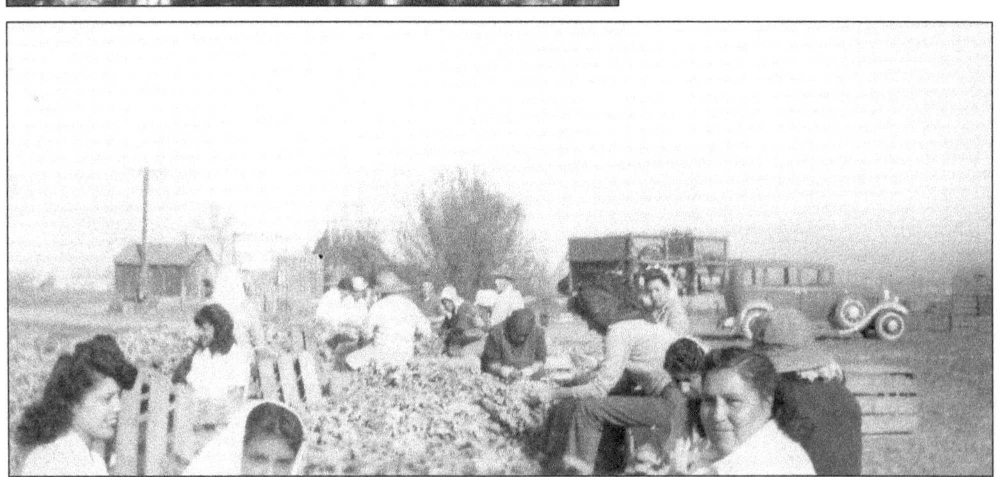

In this photograph, women pack boxes of agricultural items. Some women look at the photographer while others concentrate on their work. Women wore a variety of hair items, including pioneer-style bonnets, to protect themselves from sun exposure, insects, and fuzz from the crops. (Courtesy of the Felix Garcia family.)

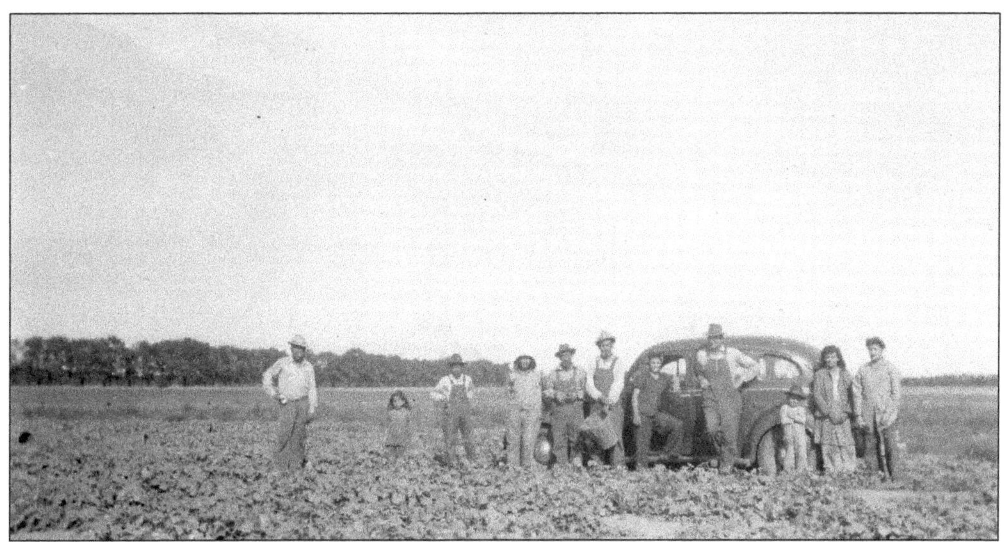

Family members pose next to their car in the agricultural fields. Most often, field workers were not paid a fixed salary but were paid according to the amount of produce picked. Generally, all members of the family, including children, labored in the fields, combining their income for the survival of the family. (Courtesy of the Felix Garcia family.)

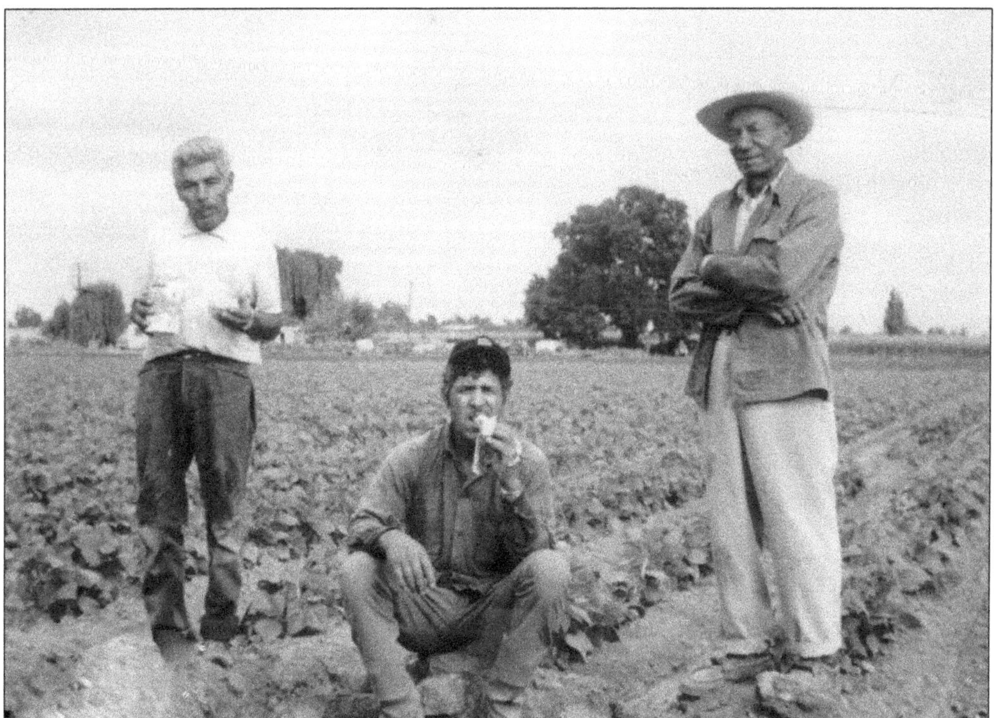

Jesus Anaya (center) and coworkers have a snack in the fields. Anaya, originally from Mexico, walked from Los Angeles to San José to find employment. Other Mexican males were part of the United States and Mexico's Bracero Program of 1942, leaving their rural communities and heading north to the United States as guest workers in the agricultural fields and railroad industry. (Courtesy of Esmeralda Anaya.)

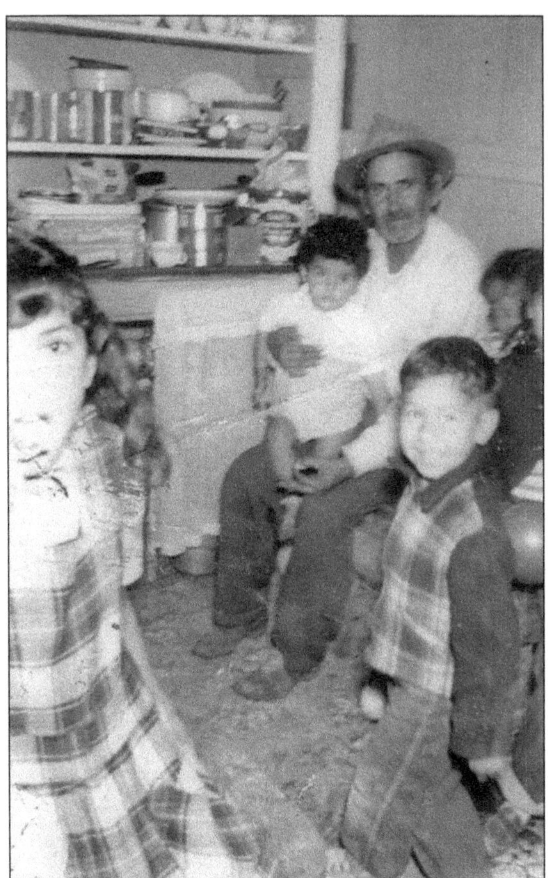

A farm worker's family lives in a home provided by the landowner in the 1950s. Children play around their father, José Garcia. A carpet covers the dirt floor of the home. Pots and pans in the cabinet illustrate the tight living quarters of the Garcia family. (Courtesy of the Felix Garcia family.)

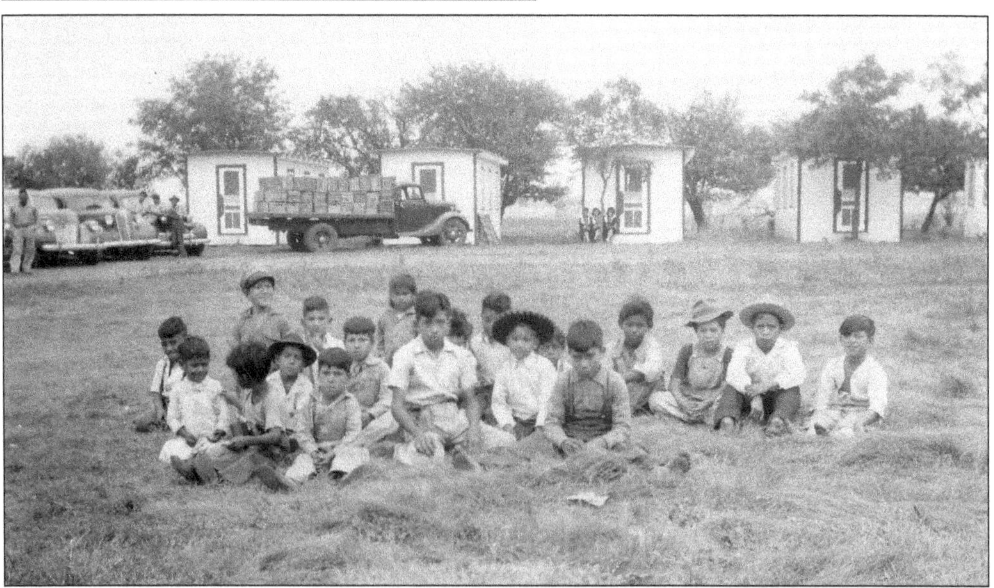

Children pose in front of a row of farm workers' homes as their parents look on. The children appear tired, possibly from helping their parents labor in the fields that day. (Courtesy of the Felix Garcia family.)

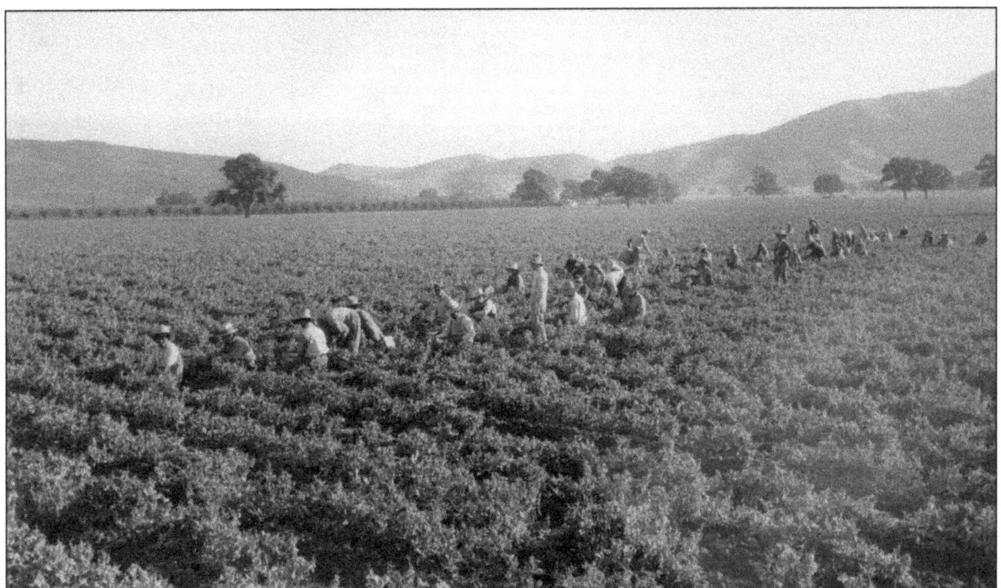

Filipino and Mexican male field workers pick peas in a field in San José. Many Filipinos met single Mexican women working in the fields. They fell in love, married, and started families. However, they faced anti-miscegenation laws in which California did not legally recognize interracial unions. (Courtesy of San José Public Library, California Room, Clyde Arbuckle Collection.)

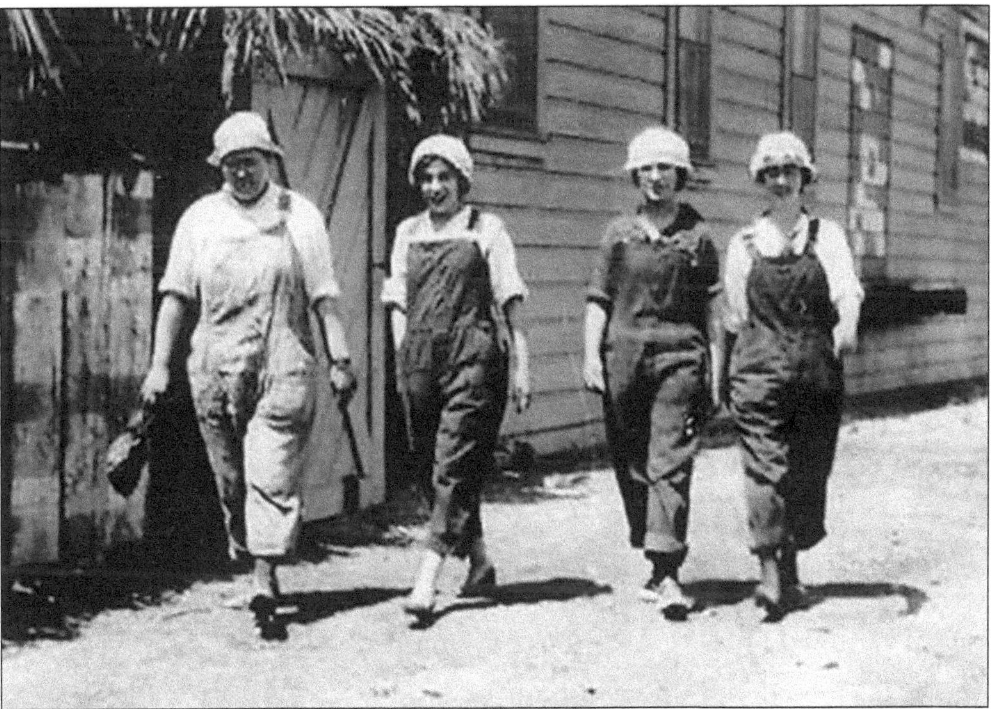

Velma Bernal (second from the left) walks with friends to the American Can Company in 1918. She lied about her age so she could be permitted to work there and earn enough money to help support her family. She lived on Gregory Street with her family. (Courtesy of Greg Bernal-Mendoza Smestad.)

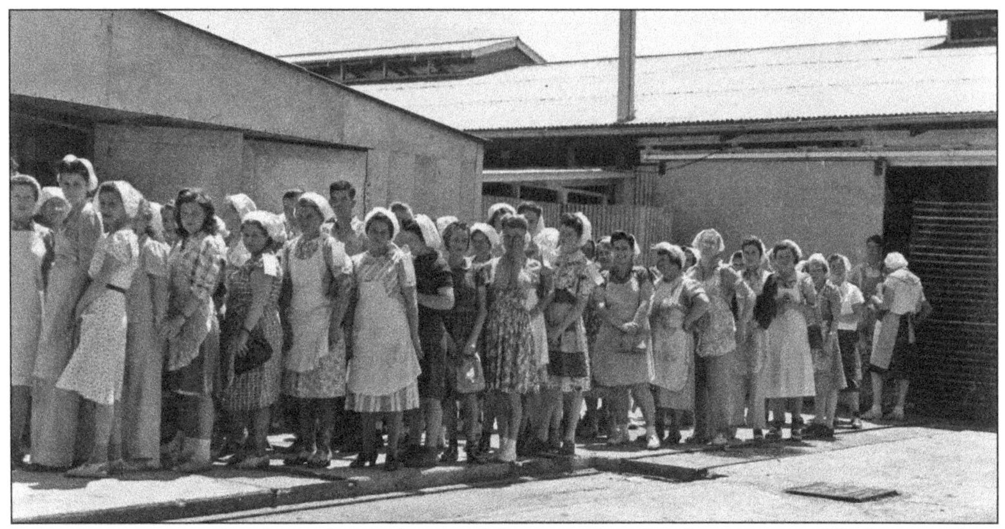

In 1945, women stand in line to begin their workday at an East San José cannery. Working mothers often faced balancing work with familial care responsibilities. Many women found caregivers or arranged shift schedules with their husbands to provide supervision of their children while they were at work. (Courtesy of History San José.)

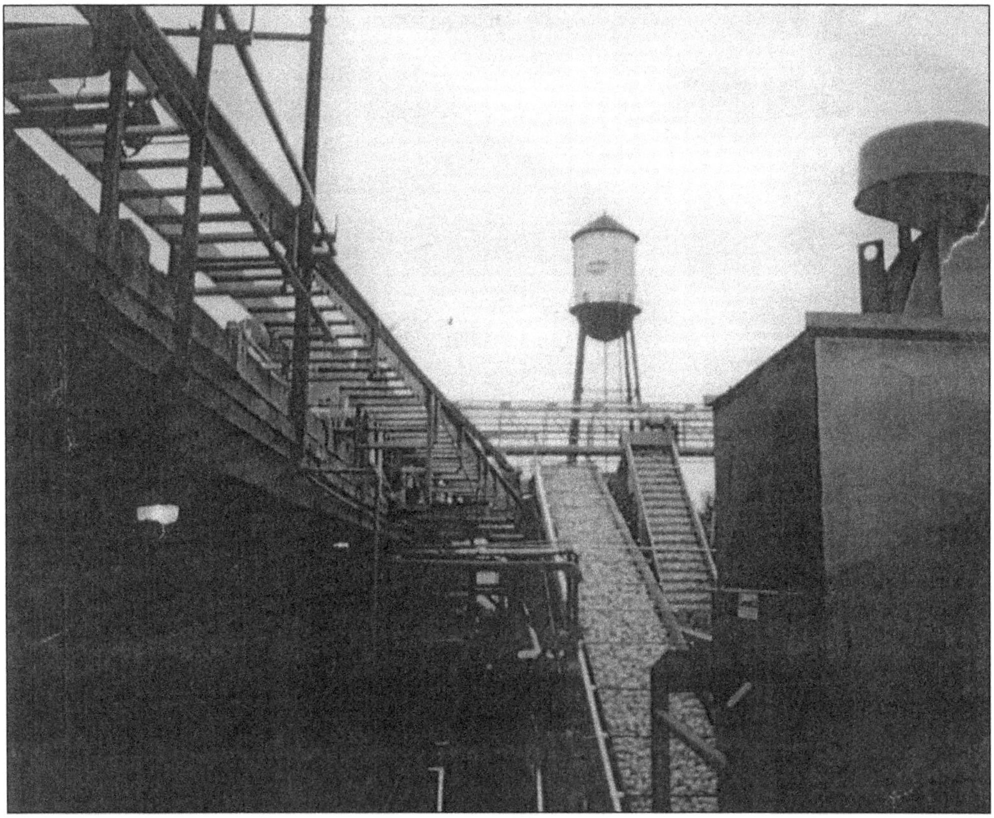

The image shows a conveyor belt filled with peaches, the tower, bridges, and walkways. The Del Monte Plant No. 3 was located on Auzerais Avenue. In 1999, the Del Monte Plant No. 3 closed. (Courtesy of History San José.)

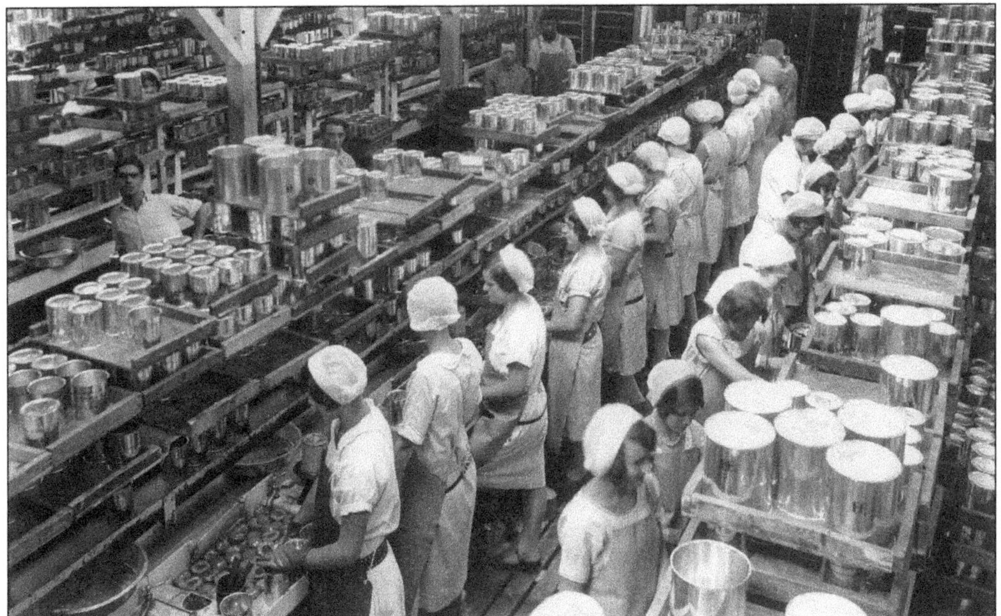

Women are lined up to fill cans with peaches. They are wearing the traditional uniform of cannery workers: a hair cap and an apron to cover their clothing. They are using rubber gloves to pick up slippery peaches that they are trimming and slicing. The men on the opposite side of the canning tables are organizing the cans for the women to fill. (Courtesy of History San José.)

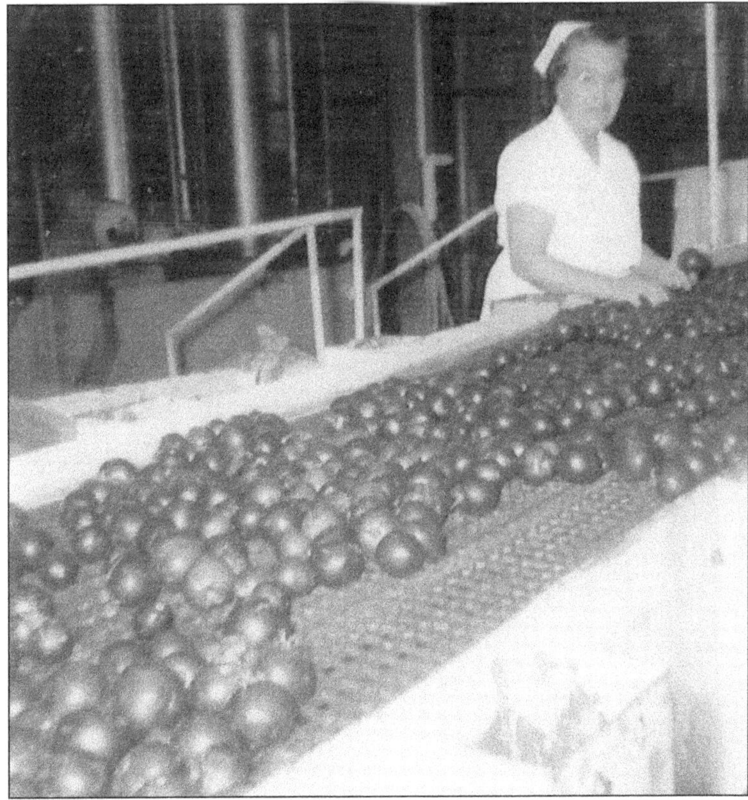

Dolores Palomo, originally from Del Rio, Texas, sorts tomatoes on a conveyor belt at a cannery in San José in 1971. (Courtesy of Pedro Palomo.)

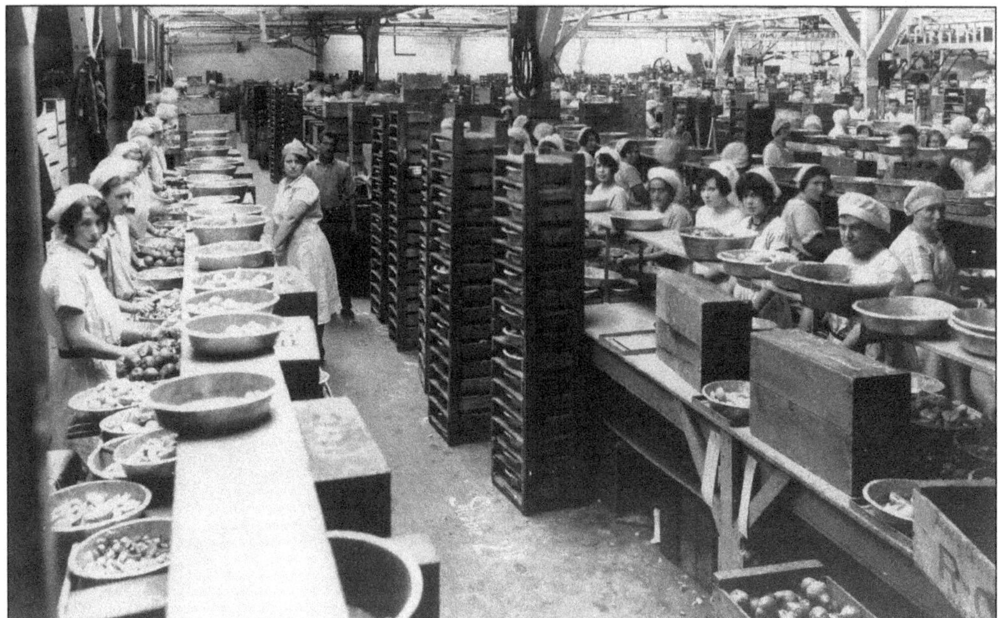

Women look at the camera but don't stop working as they are coring, halving, and peeling pears for canning at Richmond-Chase Company. Stacks of boxes with ripe fruit wait to be processed by the women. By the early 20th century, Mexicans began to replace Italian and Portuguese agricultural workers, packers, sorters, and cannery workers. (Courtesy of History San José.)

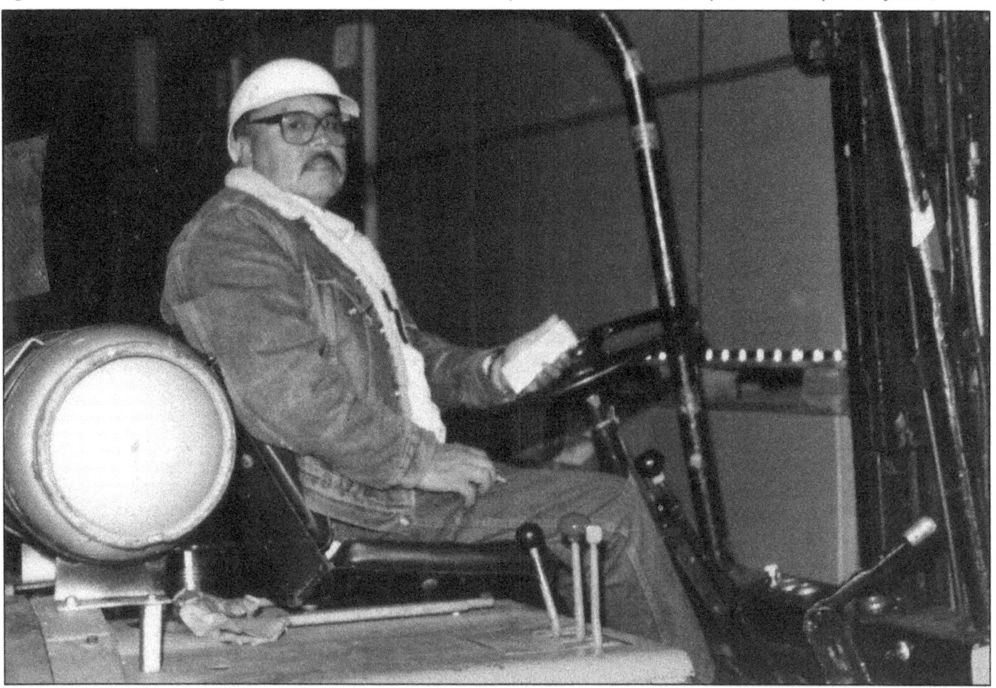

Ricardo Gutierrez sits atop a forklift in Del Monte Plant No. 3, moving pallets in the warehouse. Both Ricardo and his wife, Elida, worked at the cannery. They met while picking cotton in the fields of the San Joaquin Valley. Elida retired in 1996 after 44 years of service for Del Monte. (Courtesy of History San José.)

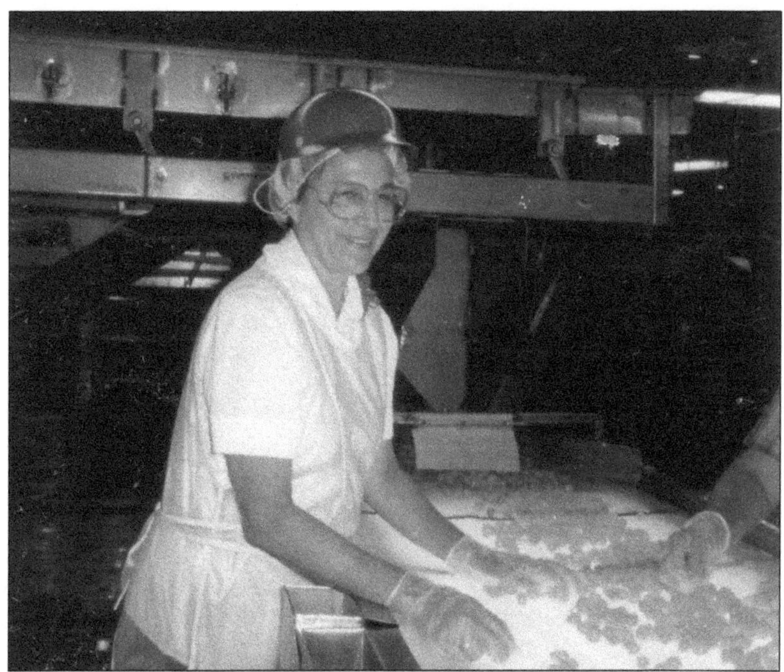

Beatrice Sanchez sorts yellow grapes for fruit cocktail in 1970 at Del Monte Plant No. 3. She also worked at Tri-Valley Cannery, sorting and canning peaches, pears, and cherries. On the weekends, she went dancing downtown at the Palomar and Starlight ballrooms with her husband, Julian. (Courtesy of History San José.)

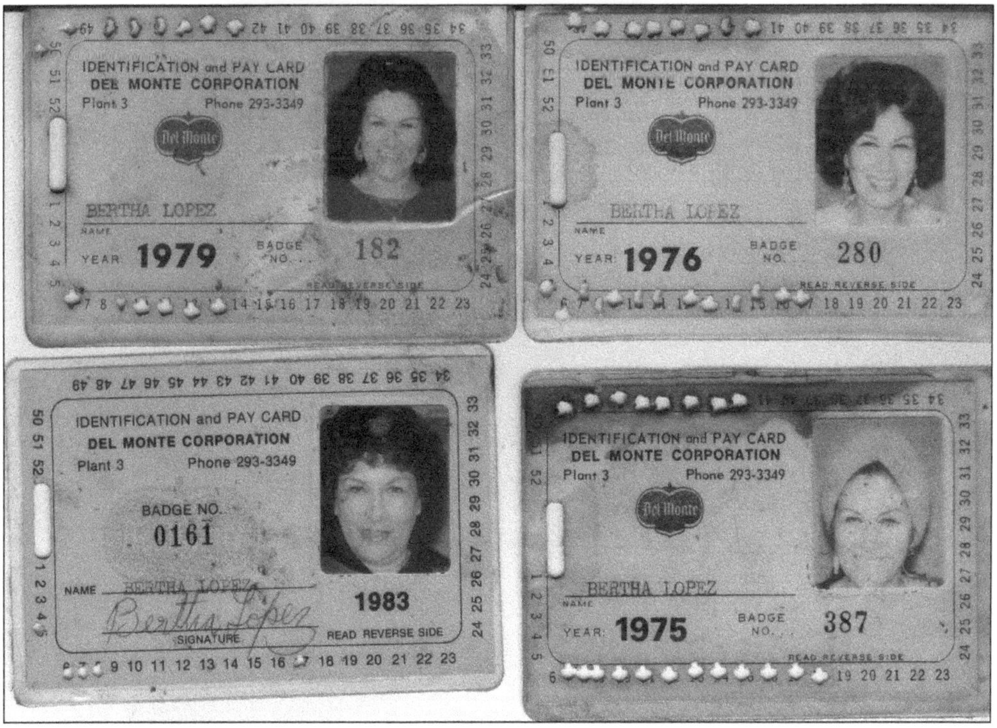

This image of Bertha Lopez's identification cards from Del Monte Plant No. 3 cannery shows the wear and tear of daily use. Some cannery women saved their earnings to purchase school clothes, books, and supplies for their children. Others saved up for a new washer or other household conveniences. Many were able to buy homes with the money they earned in the cannery. (Courtesy of History San José.)

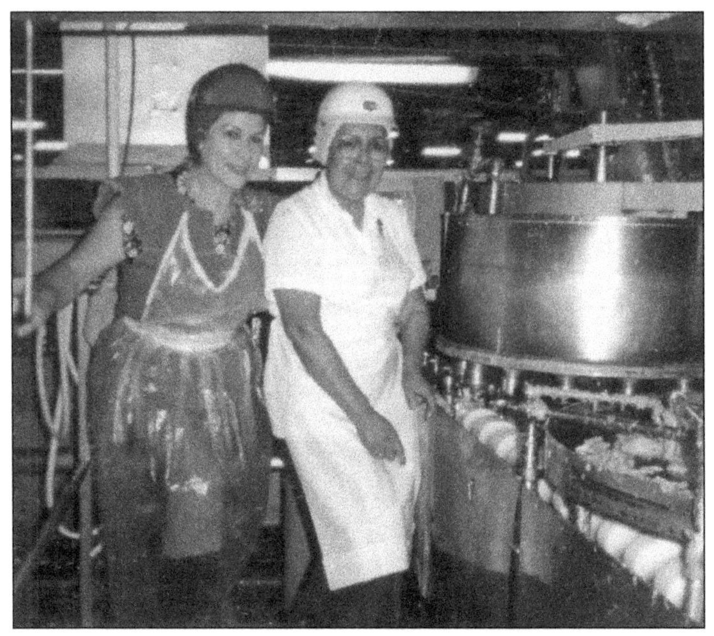

Cannery worker Bertha Lopez (left) and floor lady Rose Palomera(o) pose for a picture while working on the line. Lopez became active in her East San José community after a school principal ordered her daughter to wash her mouth out with Clorox bleach because she spoke Spanish in school. Through Lopez's efforts and with the support of other parents, the school principal was fired from his job for his mistreatment of Mexican students. (Courtesy of History San José.)

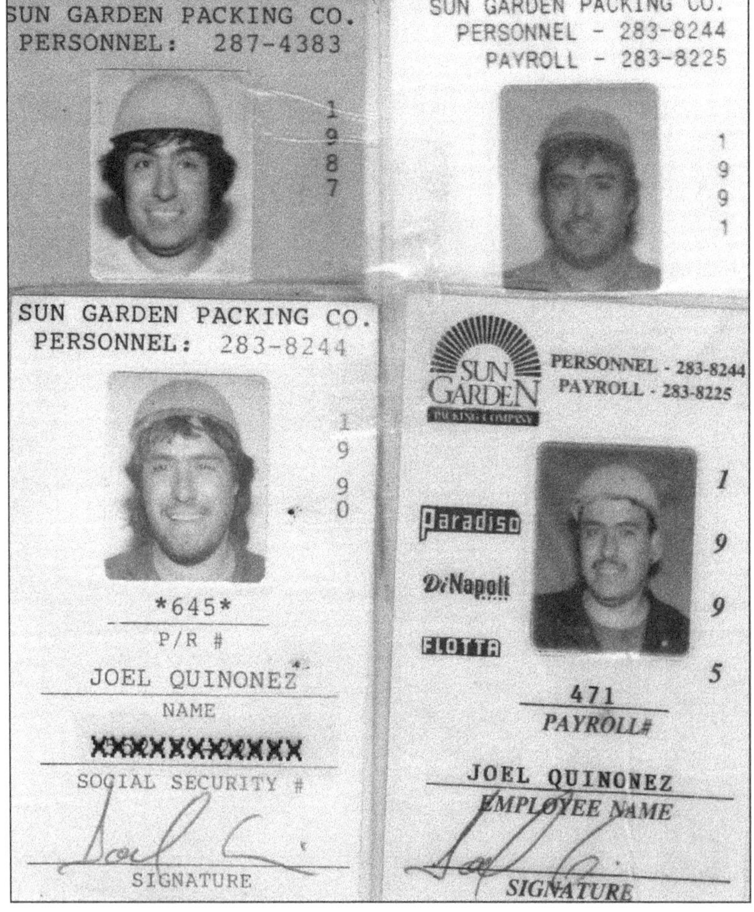

Sun Garden Packing Company employee Joel Quinonez was a mechanic. The San José cannery processed tomatoes and apricots. In 1996, Sun Garden closed its doors because of the competition with rival companies, which were located closer to the Central Valley crops for lower production costs and easier access to water. (Courtesy of Mabeel Garcia.)

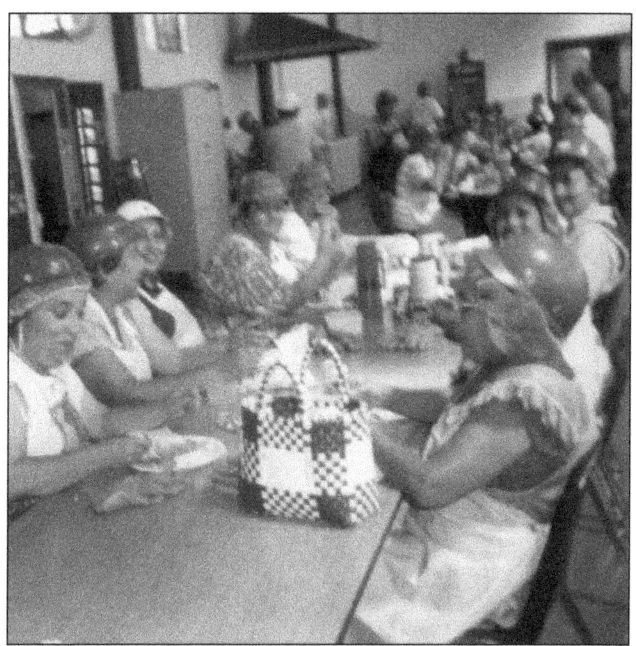

Del Monte Plant No. 3 cannery workers enjoy an end-of-the-season fiesta in the 1980s. Women wore hard hats for protection from falling metal cans on an overhead conveyer belt while they worked inside the cannery. During the harvest season from June to September, canneries operated virtually 24 hours per day, seven days a week. (Courtesy of History San José.)

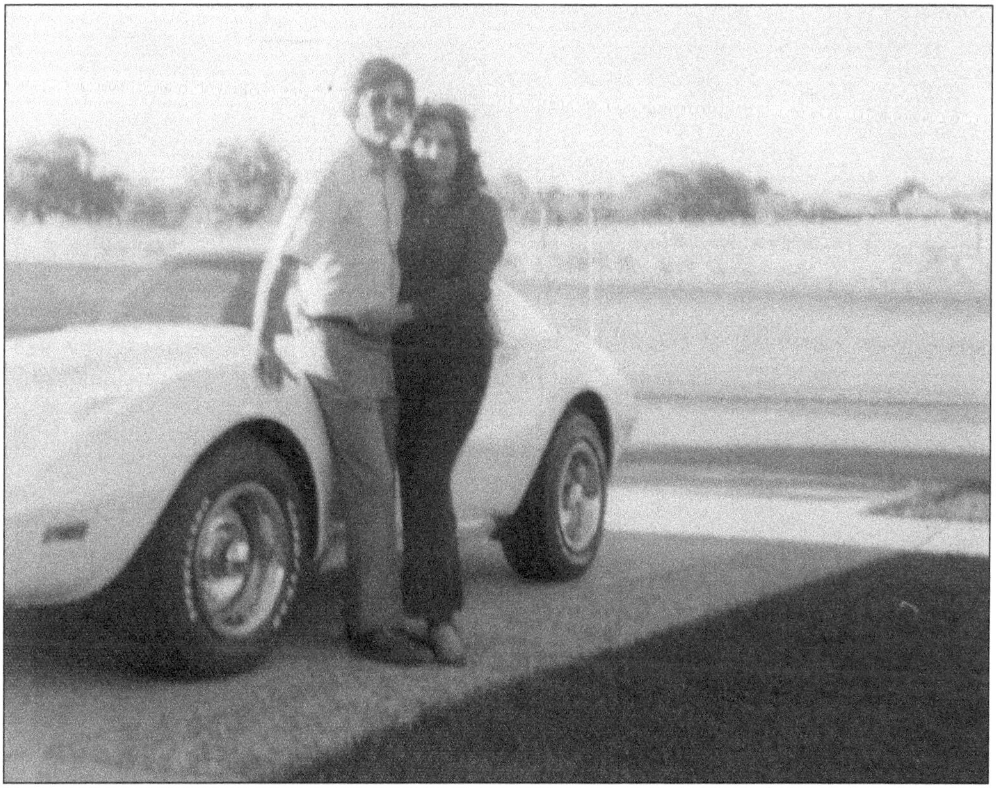

Moses and Connie Carrasco stand by their 1974 white Corvette on Aborn Road. For 16 years, Connie worked at Richmond-Chase Company in the summer and Stokely Cannery in the winter. With a dual income, the Carrascos were able to afford a home, furniture, and a Corvette. (Courtesy of Connie Carrasco.)

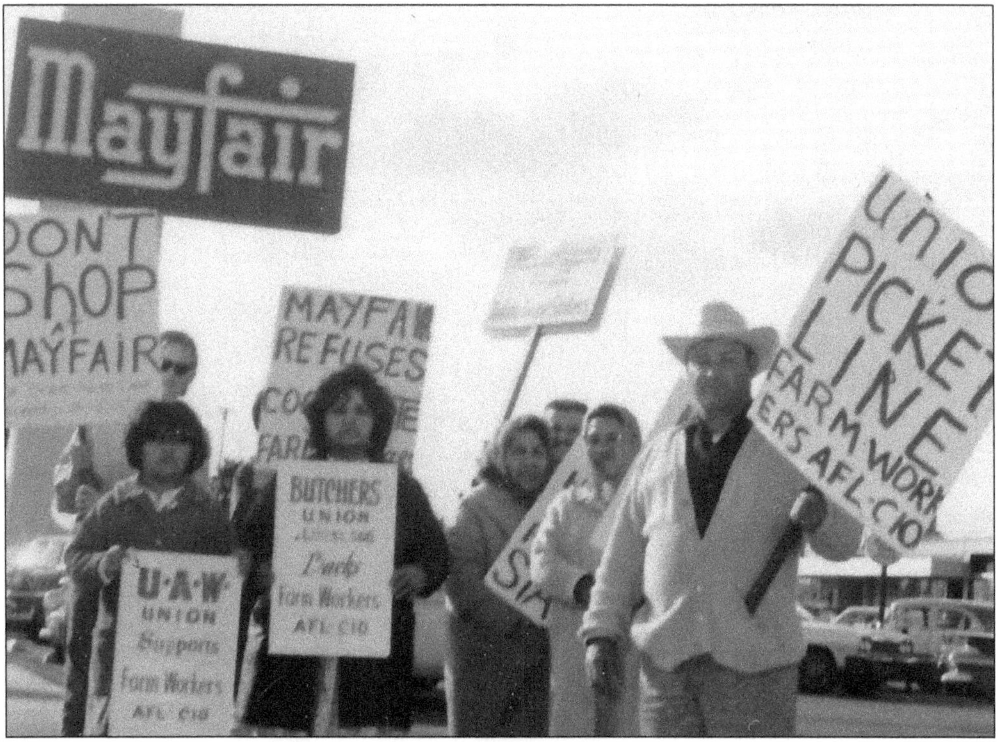

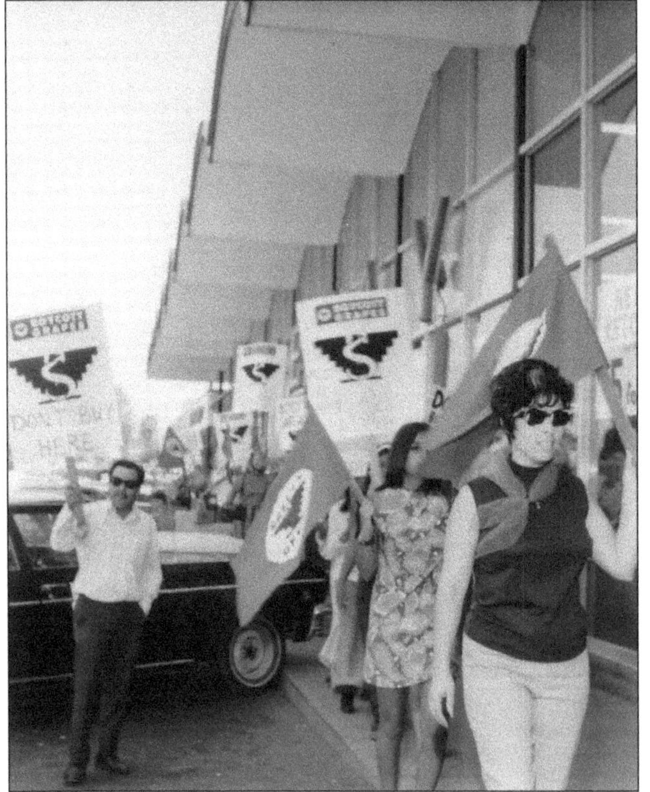

Mexicans in San José supported a strike and boycott of grapes grown in Delano, approximately three and a half hours south of San José. From 1965 to 1970, grape pickers in the city of Delano began a strike and boycott against grape growers led by San José's own Cesar Chavez and his counterpart Dolores Huerta. The strike consisted of Filipino and Mexican American grape pickers who formed the United Farm Workers union. Their grievances against growers included receiving low wages, enduring unsafe working conditions, and not having their union recognized as a bargaining agent. San José families, students, religious leaders, and other supporters joined the picket lines, as illustrated in the photographs. (Both courtesy of the California History Center.)

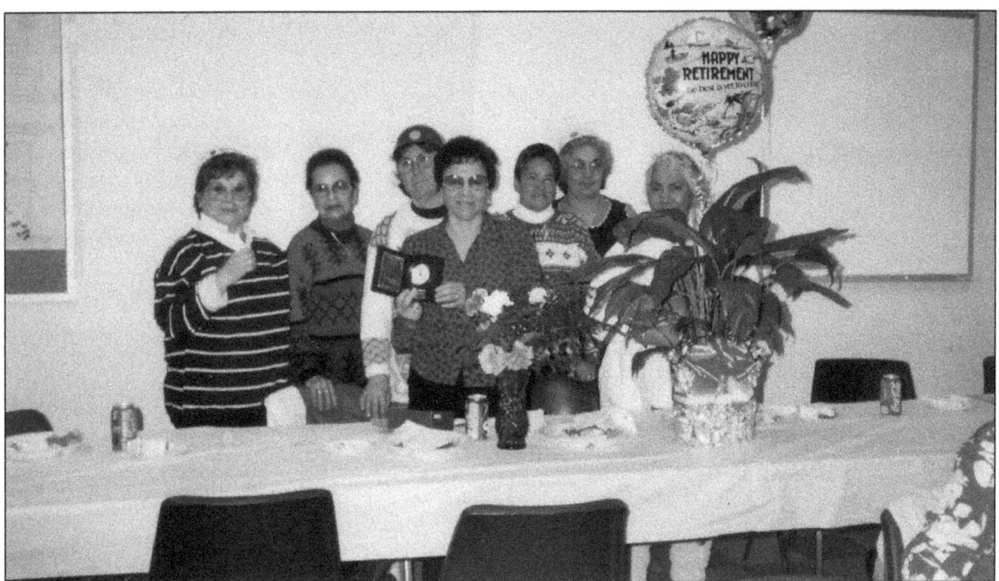

Beatrice Sanchez celebrates with her coworkers her retirement in 1996 from Del Monte Plant No. 3 after 25 years of service. Her typical work schedule was eight hours a day, six days a week at the canneries. Lunch breaks were 30 to 45 minutes long and often spent at nearby Paradiso's Italian delicatessen. (Courtesy of History San José.)

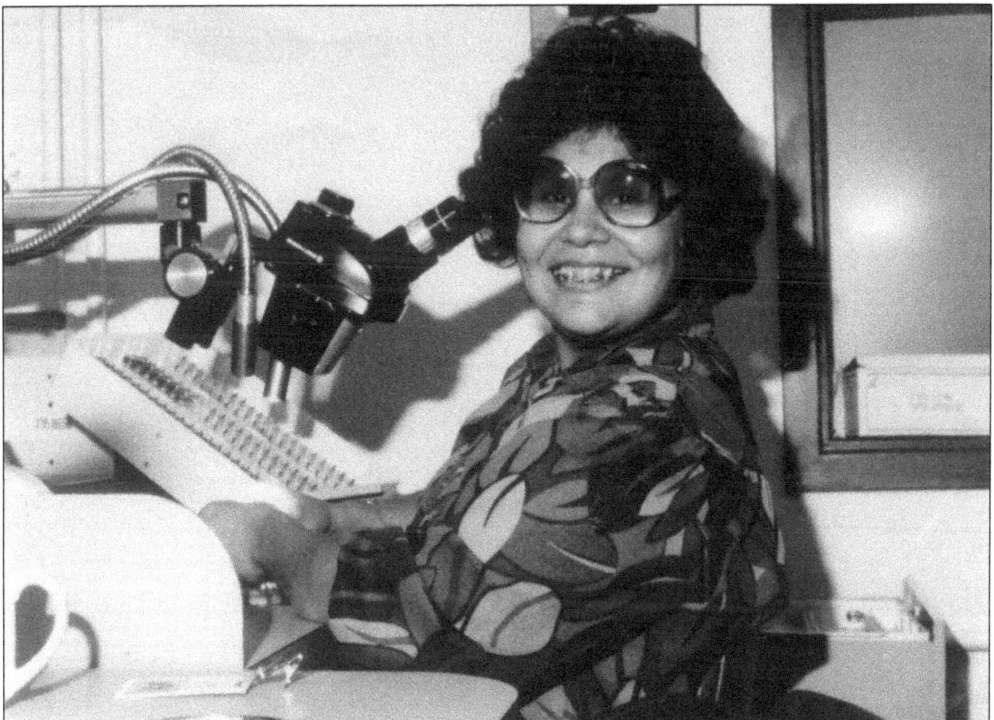

Mexican women switched out of working in the fields and canneries and into the electronics industry as assembly workers. In 1980, Vickie Romero worked at her station as a senior final inspector at IBM in Department 123, Building 5 on Cottle Road in South San José. Vickie retired from IBM in 1999 after 22 years of service. (Courtesy of Vickie Romero.)

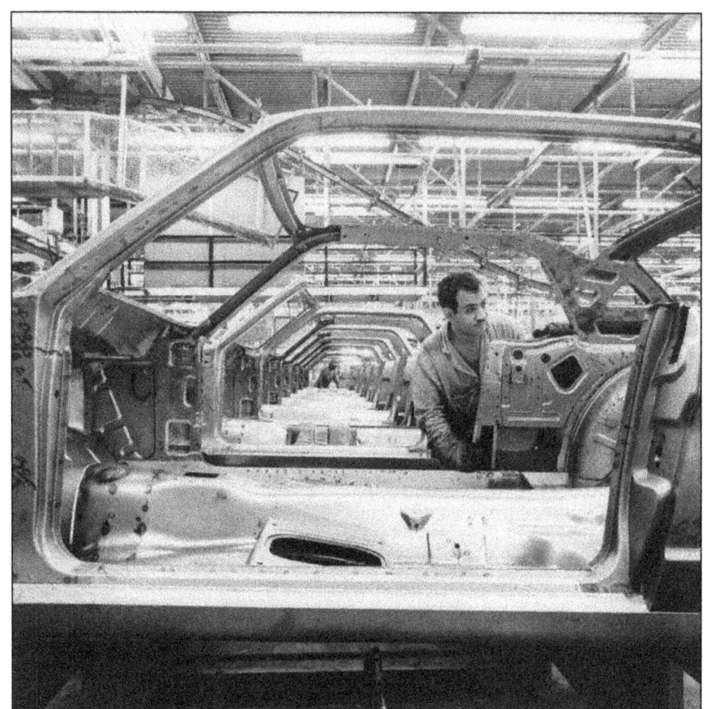

As an alternative to cannery work, manufacturing became a dominant industry for Mexican men and women. This man is manufacturing the frame of a Ford Mustang in an assembly line in 1964. (Photograph by Skeleton Photography, courtesy of the Santa Clara County Archives.)

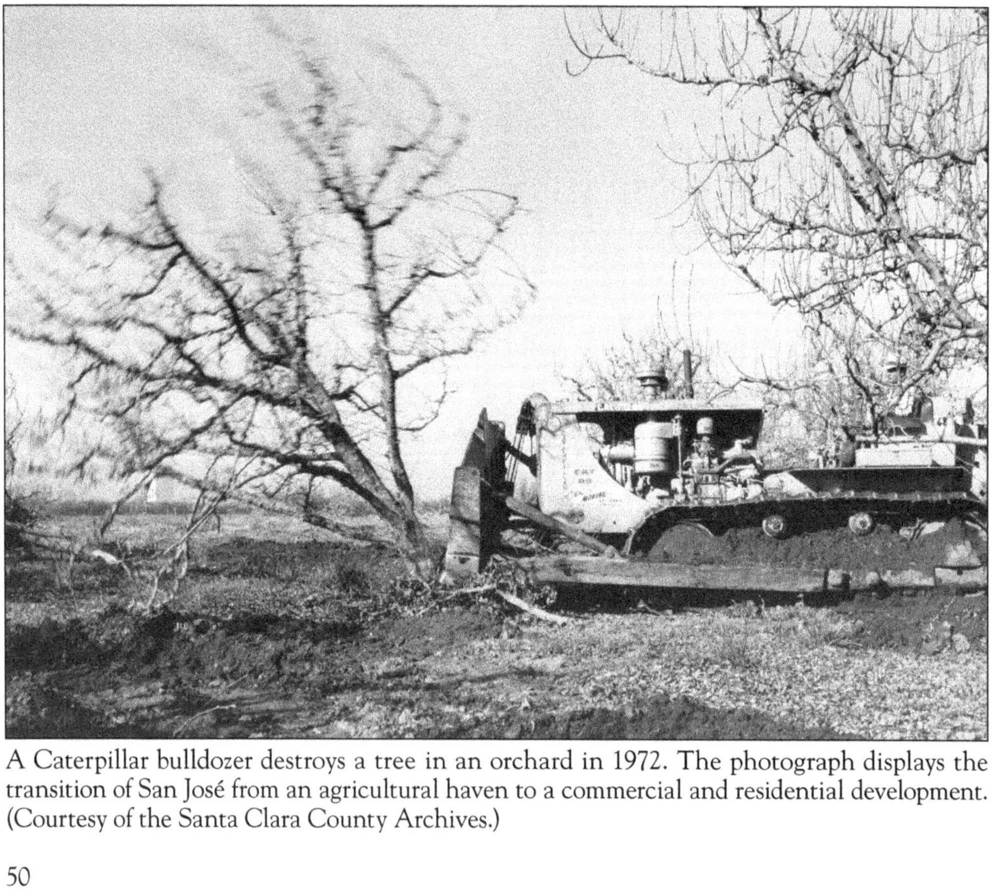

A Caterpillar bulldozer destroys a tree in an orchard in 1972. The photograph displays the transition of San José from an agricultural haven to a commercial and residential development. (Courtesy of the Santa Clara County Archives.)

Four

East San José

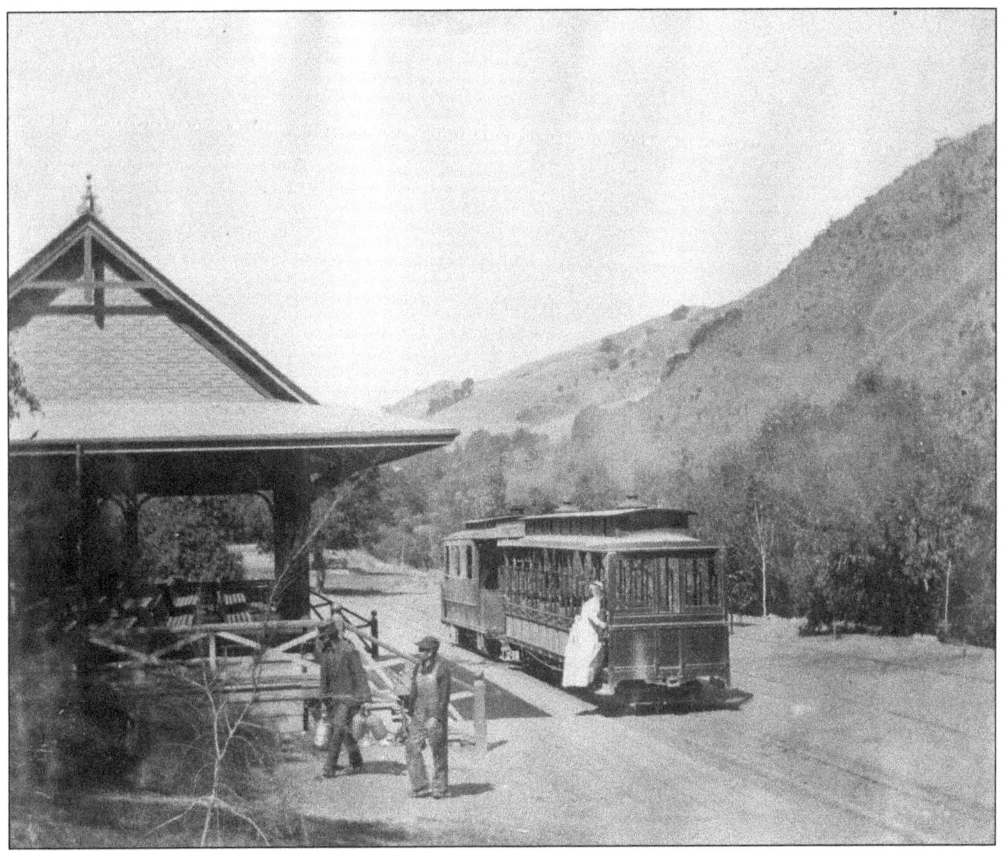

The San José Alum Rock Railroad, which was completed in the early 1900s, brought development to East San José, often called the Eastside. The tracks ran from Capitol Avenue to Alum Rock Park, named for the 200-foot-high rock of alum near its entrance. (Courtesy of History San José.)

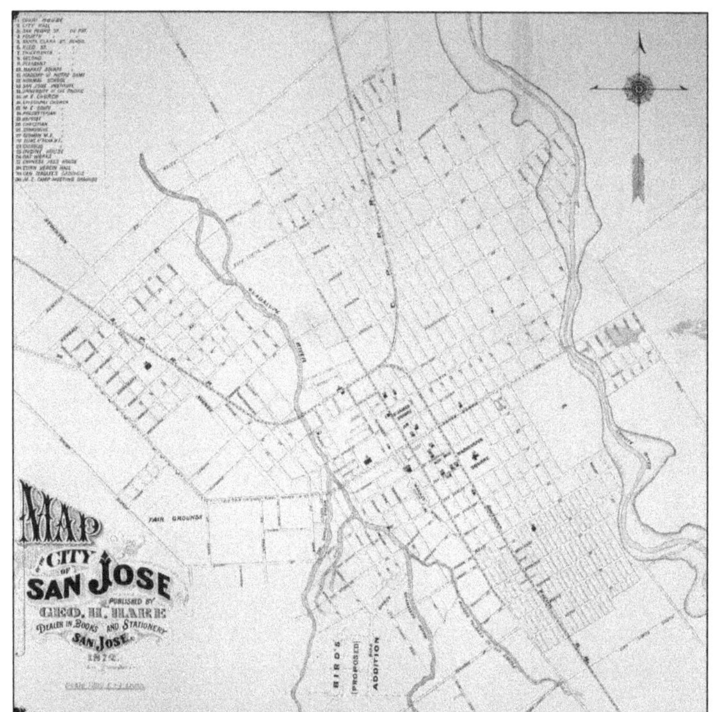

Abandoned before World War I by Euro-American farmers because of the area's poor soil, Eastside San José became home to Puerto Ricans arriving in the 1910s from the Hawaiian sugarcane fields. Mexicans began to settle in the Eastside in the early 1920s. Eastside offered the Mexican residents isolation, which allowed them to maintain their culture, but it also was a place of refuge, as many locations in San José practiced segregation, keeping Mexicans and other ethnic minorities from living in those areas. (Courtesy of History San José.)

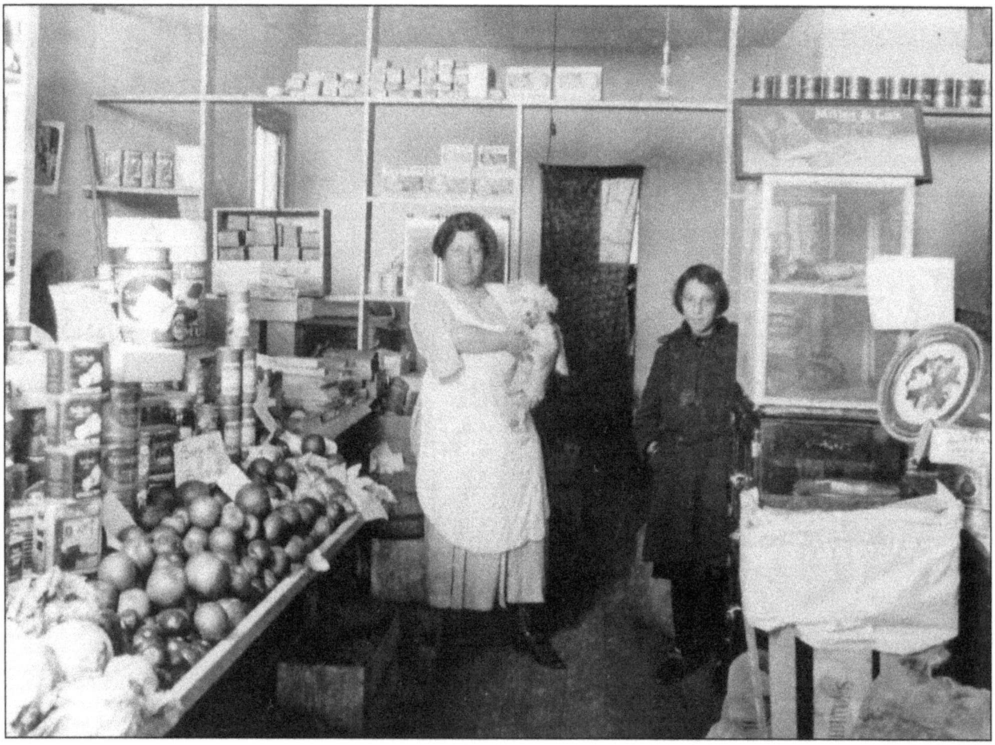

In this 1924 photograph are Augusta Chabolla Corbol and daughter Rosalie of the Chabolla family. The grocery store, operated by Francisco and Augusta Chabolla, was located on Twenty-second and Santa Clara Streets. (Courtesy of the Heritage Room, Evergreen Valley College.)

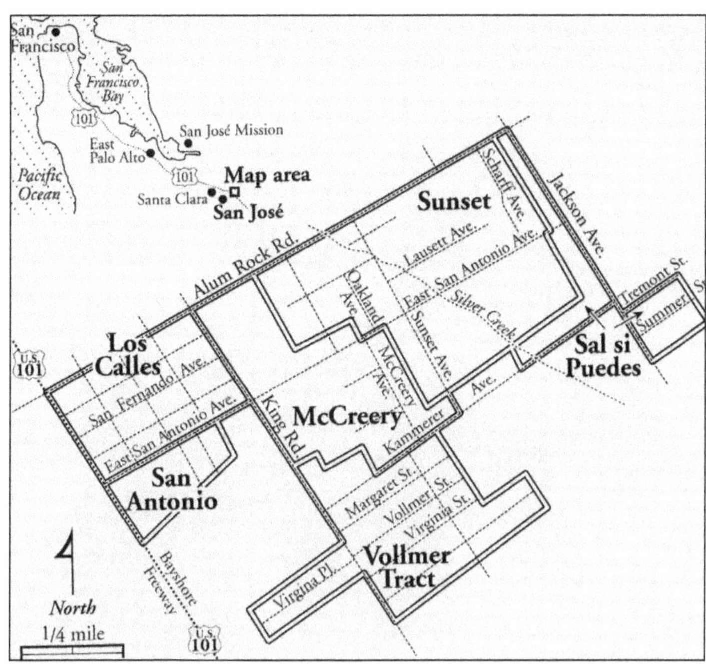

As a result of World War II, the Bracero Program, and Mexican migration, a substantial number of working-class Mexicans and Mexican Americans began to populate an area in Eastside's Mayfair district in the 1950s. By 1958, Alum Rock Avenue, Jackson Avenue, King Road, and Story Road became the informal boundaries of the Mayfair district. It consisted of two areas known by the residents as *Sal Si Puedes* (Leave if you can) and Little Egypt. (Courtesy of Princeton University Press.)

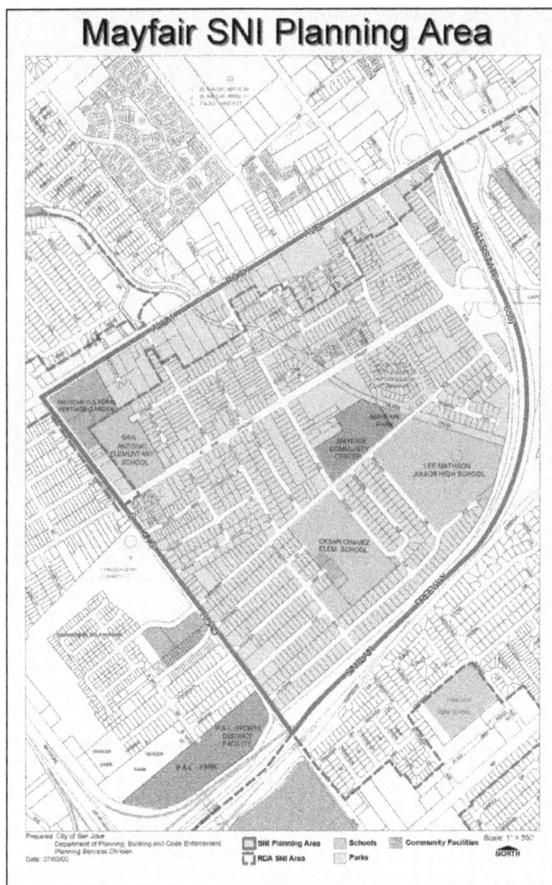

This modern map of the Mayfair district showcases three schools: San Antonio Elementary, Cesar Chavez Elementary, and Lee Mathson Middle School. Mayfair Park and the Mayfair Gardens lie at the heart of the Mayfair district. (Courtesy of the City of San José District 5.)

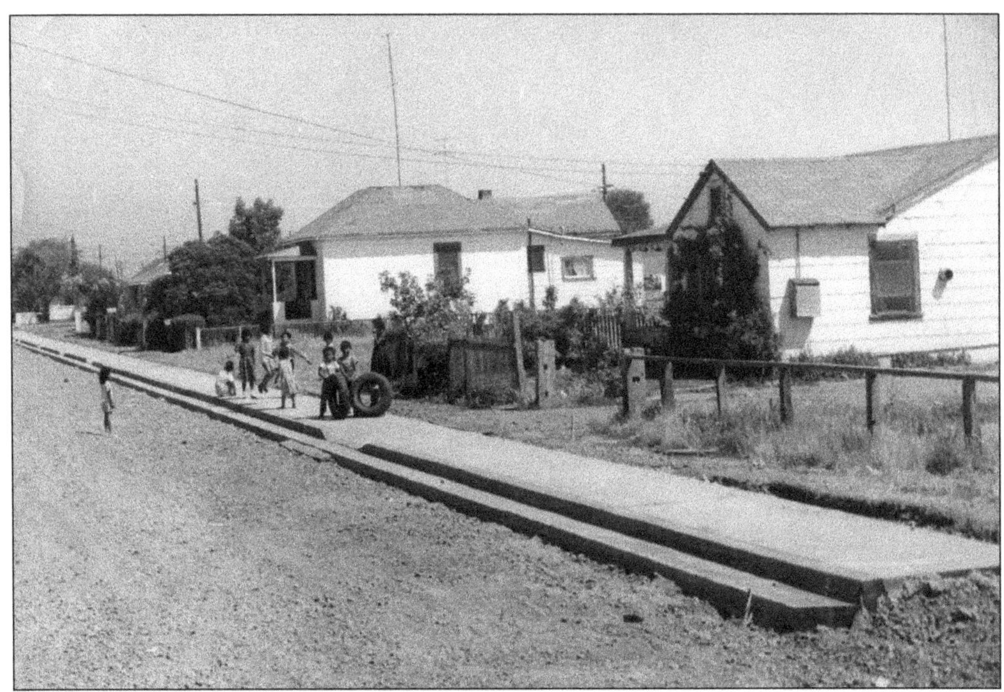

The photograph above shows children from Eastside rolling tires for fun. In a relatively underdeveloped neighborhood with unpaved streets and sidewalks and no playgrounds, children made toys with what was available to them. The photograph below of East San Antonio Street shows several workers setting up the foundation to pour cement for sorely needed sidewalks. Residents of East San Antonio Street pushed city and county officials to pave local streets, build sidewalks, and install outdoor streetlights during the 1950s. (Both courtesy of the Department of Special Collections and University Archives, Stanford University Libraries, Fred Ross Papers [M0812].)

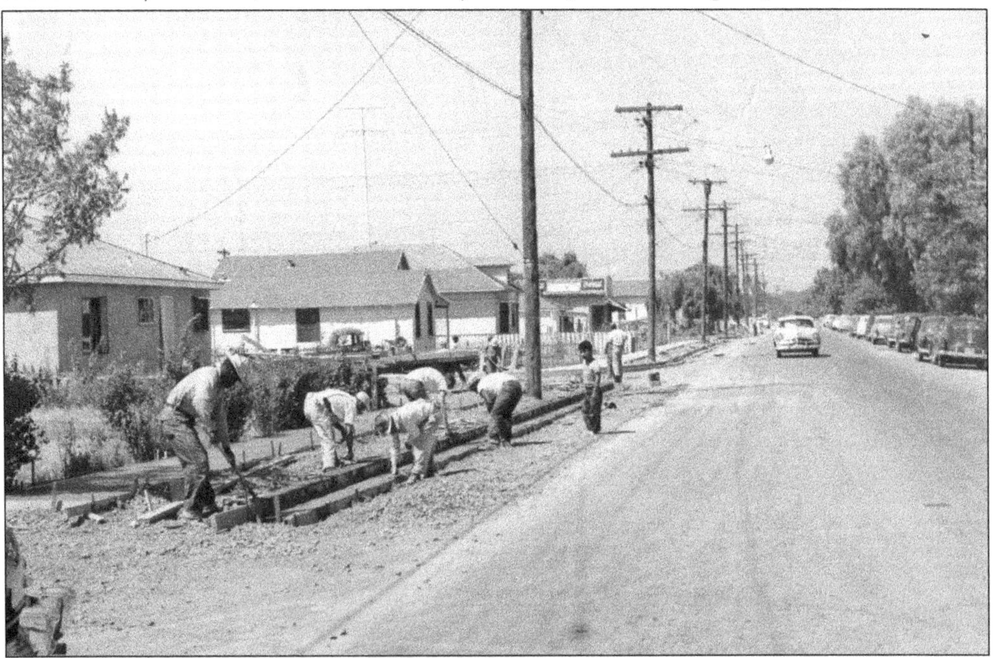

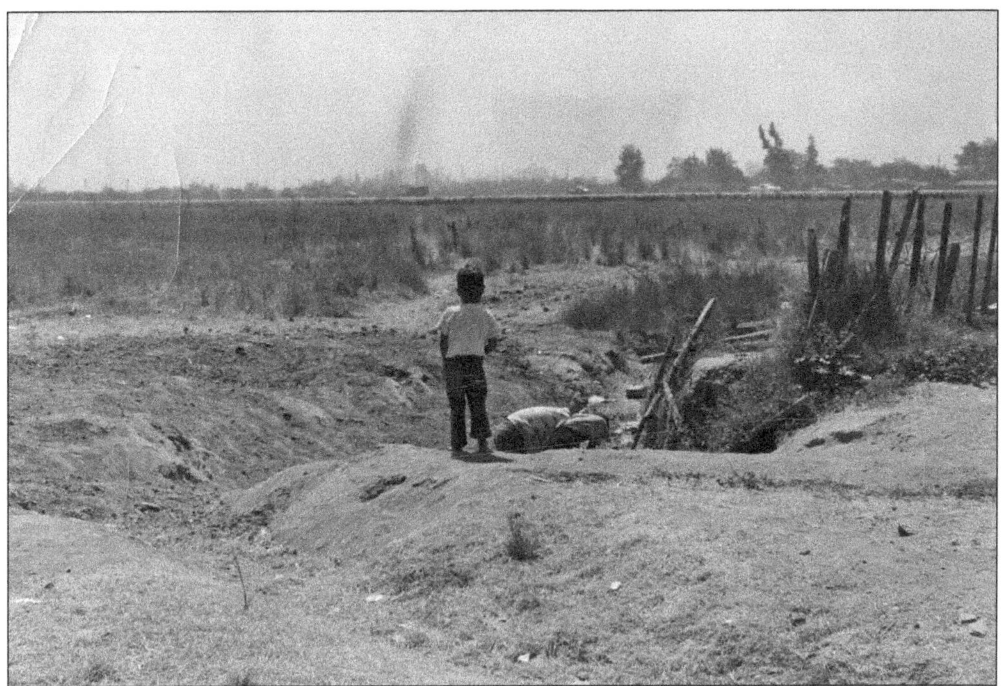

Parts of Eastside's Mayfair district lacked basic urban services in the late 1950s. In this image, three curious children play in a ditch at South Thirty-third Street. Often children were given free rein to play outdoors as neighbors and friends observed them and reported to their parents any wrongdoing. (Both courtesy of the Department of Special Collections and University Archives, Stanford University Libraries, Fred Ross Papers [M0812].)

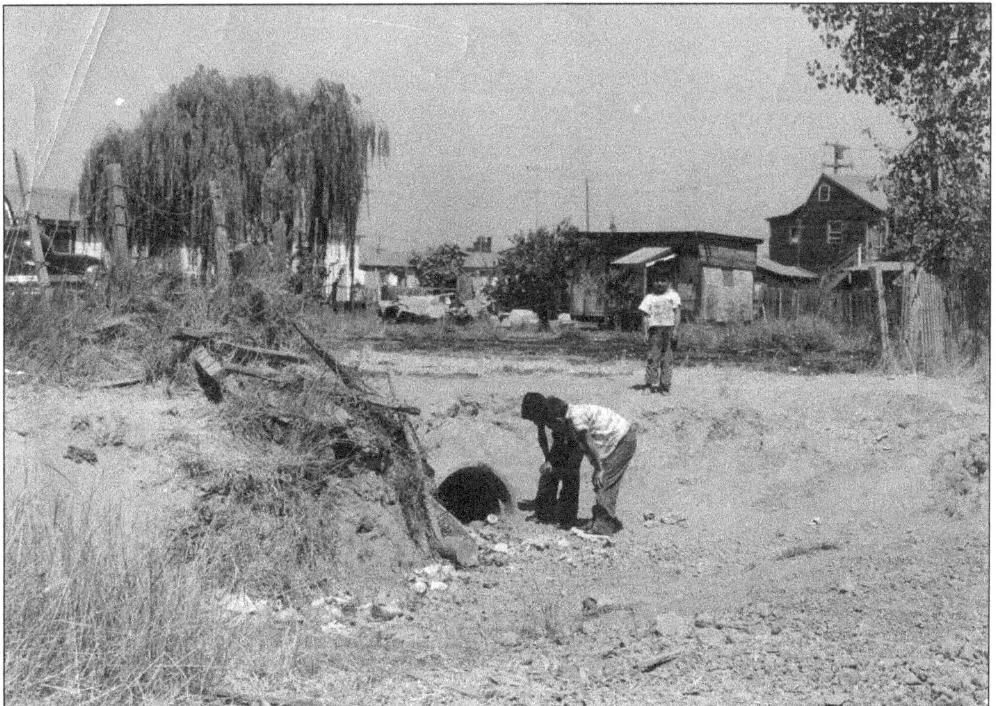

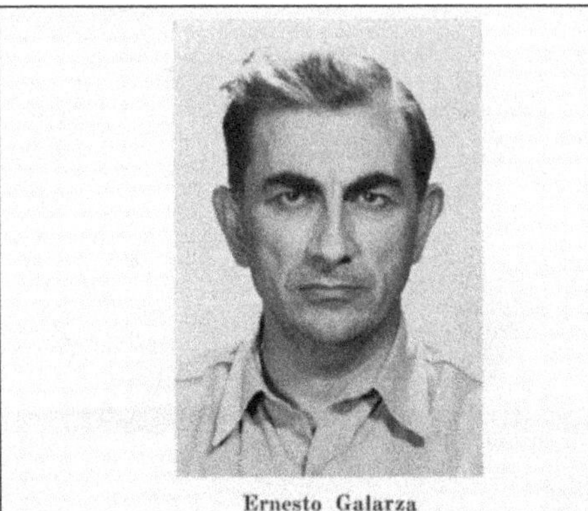

Ernesto Galarza

Secretary-Treasurer (1959)
National Agricultural Workers Union

Born in Mexico, Galarza is a naturalized American citizen. He came to the United States at the age of 4 with his family who were migratory farm workers following the crops from Texas to California. Educated in public schools of California, Occidental College, Los Angeles, Leland Stanford University, and received his Ph.D. at Columbia. Employed by the Pan-American Union, he resigned in 1947 to return to California as Research and Education Director for the Union. Educator, lecturer and author, his latest work is "Strangers In Our Fields," a study of the Mexican National employed in the United States.

Dr. Ernesto Galarza was a nationally recognized labor organizer, historian, and community activist. He was born in August 1905 in Jacotlan, Nayarit, Mexico. He attended Occidental College as an undergraduate student and earned a graduate degree from Stanford University and a doctorate in history and political science from Columbia University. After he settled in San José in 1948, he helped organize Mexicans and Mexican Americans for the National Farm Labor Union. While living in San José, Dr. Galarza researched and wrote about Chicanos in education, was an advocate for youth, and spoke up in defense of lowriders in the Eastside. (Courtesy of Department of Special Collections, Stanford University Libraries, Ernesto Galarza Papers [M0224].)

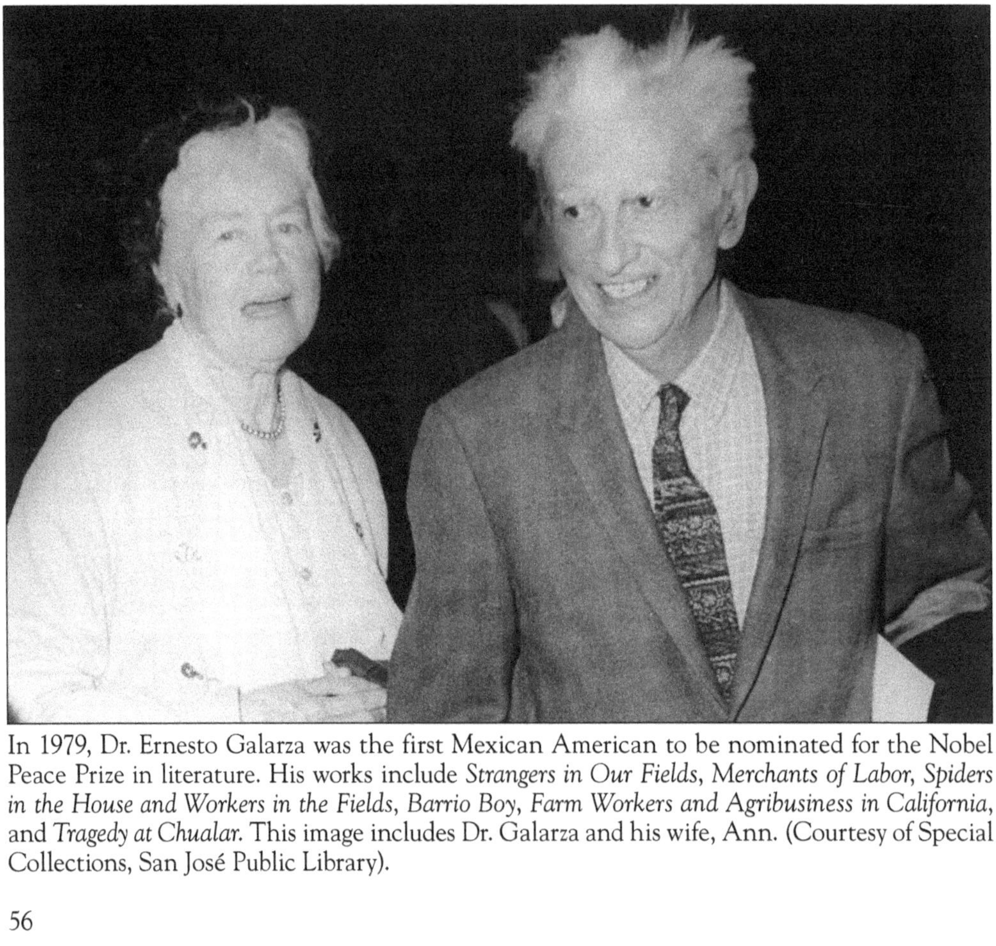

In 1979, Dr. Ernesto Galarza was the first Mexican American to be nominated for the Nobel Peace Prize in literature. His works include *Strangers in Our Fields*, *Merchants of Labor*, *Spiders in the House and Workers in the Fields*, *Barrio Boy*, *Farm Workers and Agribusiness in California*, and *Tragedy at Chualar*. This image includes Dr. Galarza and his wife, Ann. (Courtesy of Special Collections, San José Public Library).

From 1947 to 1952, Fred Ross worked with community organizer Saul Alinsky. Ross established the first Community Services Organization (CSO) in Los Angeles and the second in Eastside San José in 1952. He brought to his work a deep empathy for Mexicans and Mexican Americans. The CSO emerged as the state's leading Mexican American political action group in the 1950s. (Courtesy of Special Collections, San José Public Library.)

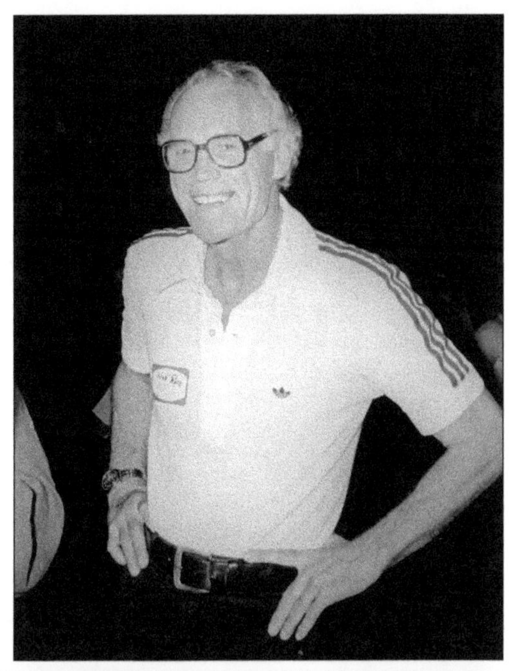

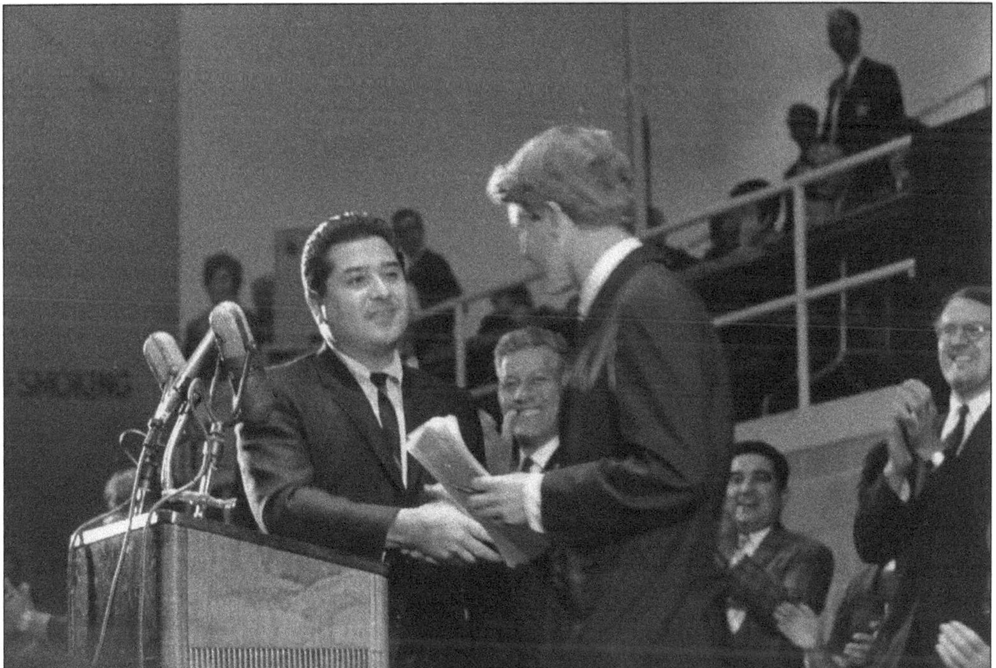

Herman Gallegos was the first elected president of the San José chapter of the CSO. While attending San José State University, he became involved in the CSO. He was committed to empowering Mexicans and Mexican Americans. Gallegos was later the founder and first executive director of the National Council of La Raza. In this 1968 photograph, Gallegos is shown on stage with Sen. Robert Kennedy at a Latin American Day Rally held at the University of San Francisco. (Courtesy of the Department of Special Collections and University Archives, Stanford University Libraries, Herman Gallegos Papers [M0821].)

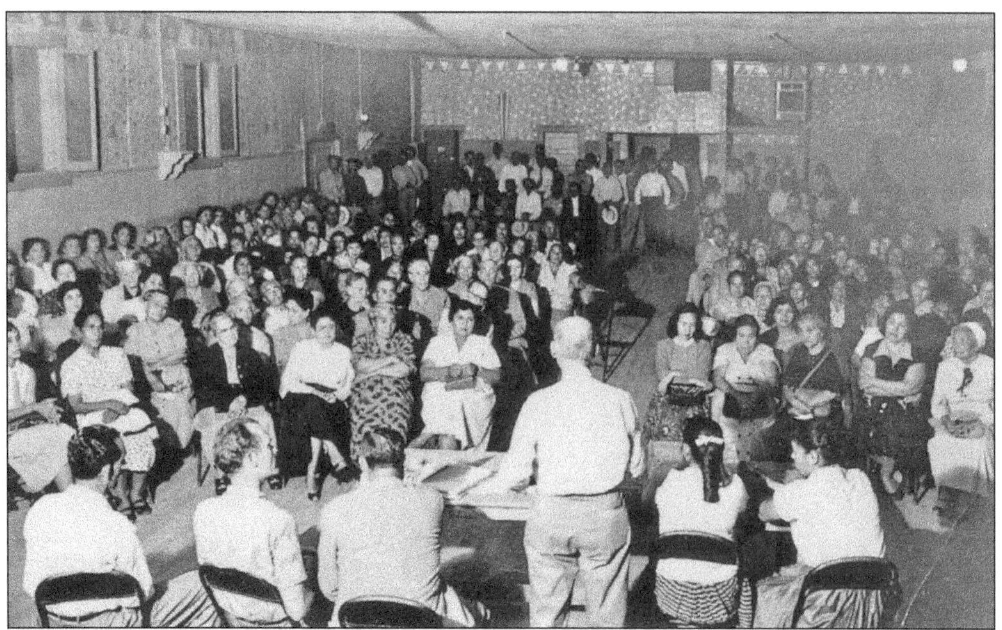

This photograph of a CSO gathering displays a large number of Mexicans and Mexican Americans in attendance. A significant majority of attendees are women. San José's CSO members encouraged the establishment of other CSO chapters throughout California due to their ties to other parts of the state. Spanish-language radio broadcasts also promoted the CSO throughout the American Southwest. (Courtesy of the Department of Special Collections and University Archives, Stanford University Libraries, Fred Ross Papers [M0812].)

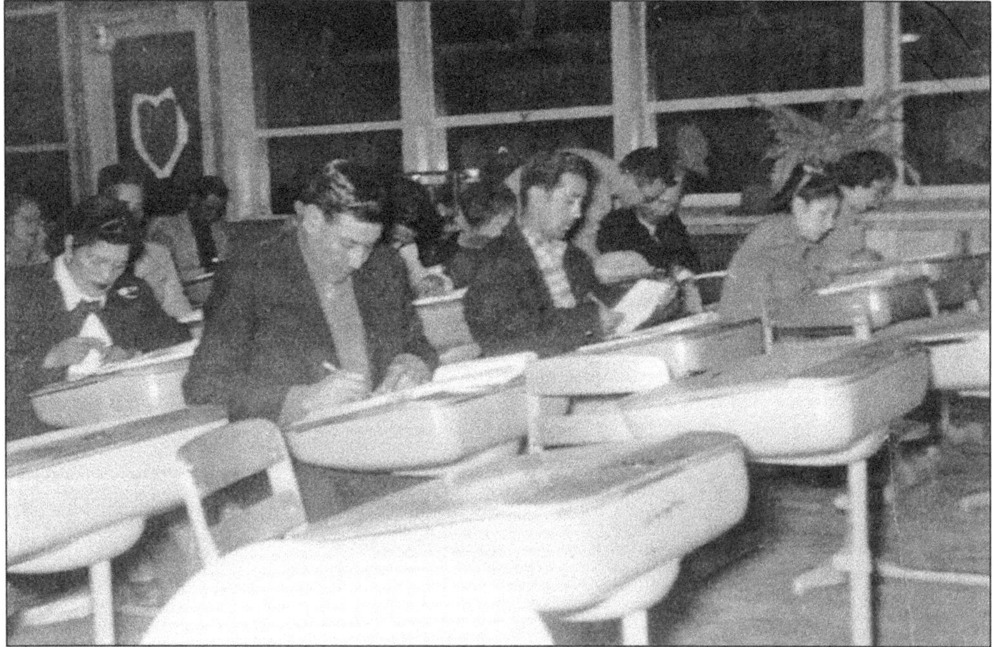

The San José chapter of the CSO offered English language classes to empower Mexicans to communicate effectively with people in positions of authority. (Courtesy of the Department of Special Collections and University Archives, Stanford University Libraries, Fred Ross Papers [M0812].)

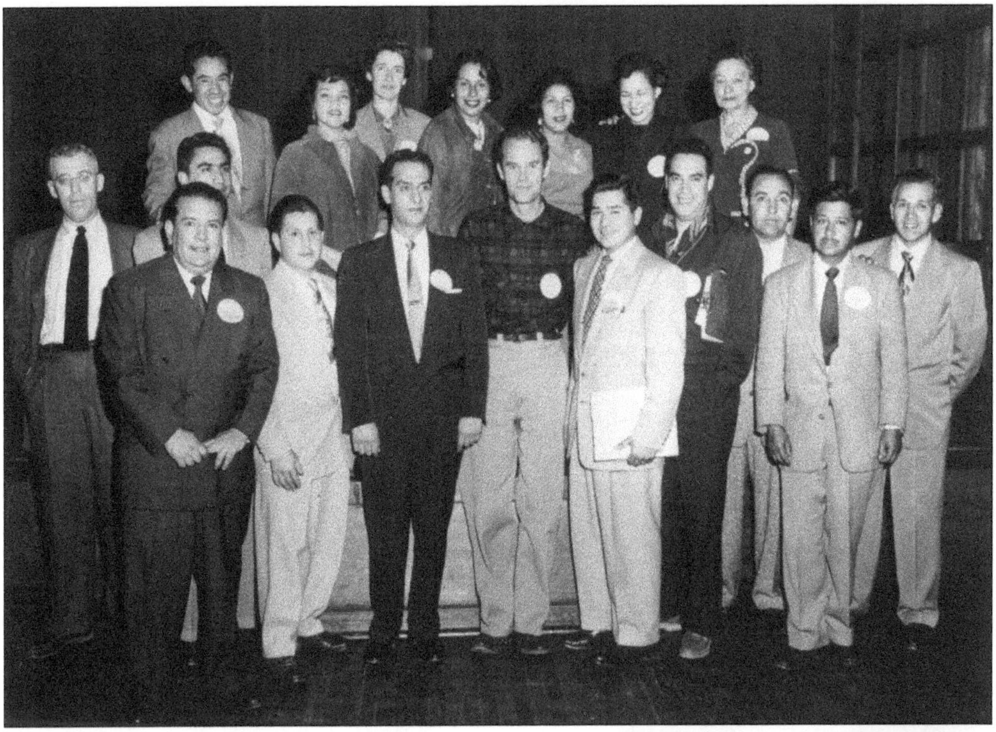

This image is a 1954 group photograph of the San José chapter of the CSO. On the far right is a young Cesar Chavez. Chavez was recruited by Fred Ross and received his training in organizing at the CSO. In 1956, there were 274 members in the San José chapter. Significantly, 189 of the members were women. (Courtesy of the Department of Special Collections and University Archives, Stanford University Libraries, Herman Gallegos Papers [M0821].)

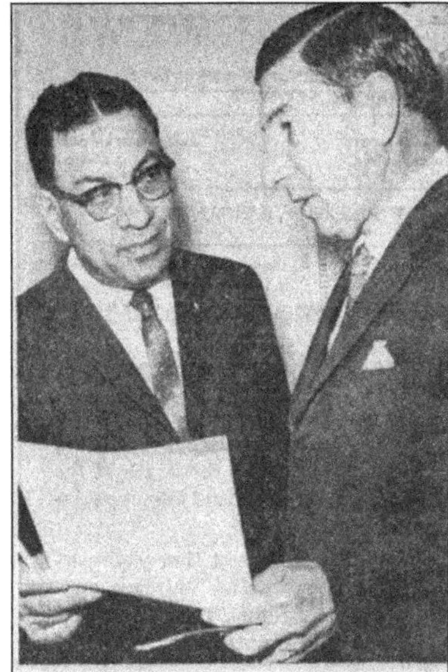

Big Job Lies Ahead

PROJECT DIRECTOR — L. M. Lopez (left), newly appointed director of the Community Council of Central Santa Clara County's new $33,376 Mexican - American Project, confers with Joseph Beck, vice-president of the council and chairman of its Mexican-American committee. Lopez, a former adviser to the mayor for Mexican-American affairs in Denver, will soon establish an office in East San Jose to start the two-year study.

The Mexican American Community Services Agency (MACSA), Inc., was established in 1964. In this 1964 photograph is Lino Lopez (left), the first director of MACSA. Sponsoring forums, discussion groups, lectures, and workshops, Lopez created an agency that helps Mexicans achieve representation in the community and politics. MACSA expanded its services to the Eastside community by providing health and day care, housing, educational programs for senior citizens, and other family services. (Courtesy of Department of Special Collections, Stanford University Libraries, Ernesto Galarza Papers [M0224].)

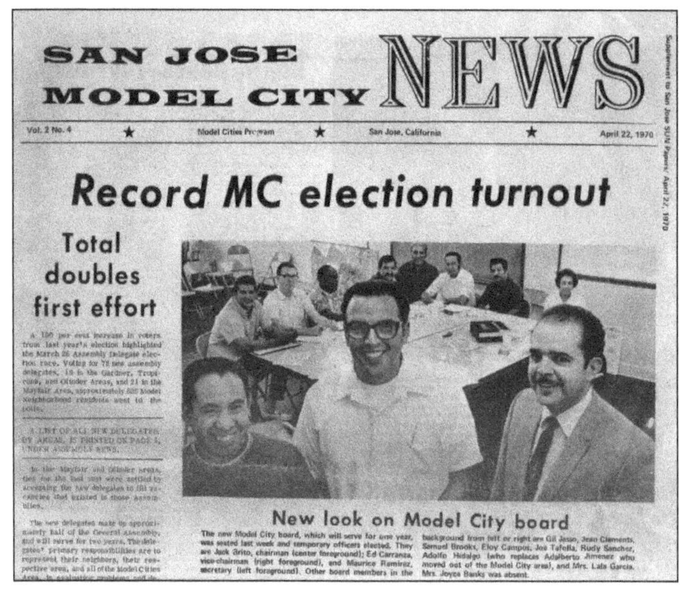

SAN JOSE MODEL CITY NEWS

Vol. 2 No. 4 ★ Model Cities Program ★ San Jose, California ★ April 22, 1970

Record MC election turnout

Total doubles first effort

New look on Model City board

The new Model City board, which will serve for one year, was seated last week and temporary officers elected. They are Jack Brito, chairman (center foreground); Ed Carranza, vice-chairman (right foreground), and Maurice Ramirez, secretary (left foreground). Other board members in the background from left or right are Gil Jasso, Jean Clements, Samuel Brooks, Eloy Campos, Joe Tafolla, Rudy Sanchez, Adolfo Hidalgo (who replaces Adalberto Jimenez who moved out of the Model City area), and Mrs. Lala Garcia. Mrs. Joyce Banks was absent.

Model Cities was established in 1969 as an extension of Pres. Lyndon Johnson's vision of a Great Society. The program enlisted young college graduates to build and maintain physical, social, and economic programs to improve the quality of life for residents. Activist Jack Brito (center foreground) was the chairman of the Model City board. (Courtesy of the Chicano Collection, Cultural Heritage Center, Dr. Martin Luther King Jr. Library, San José State University.)

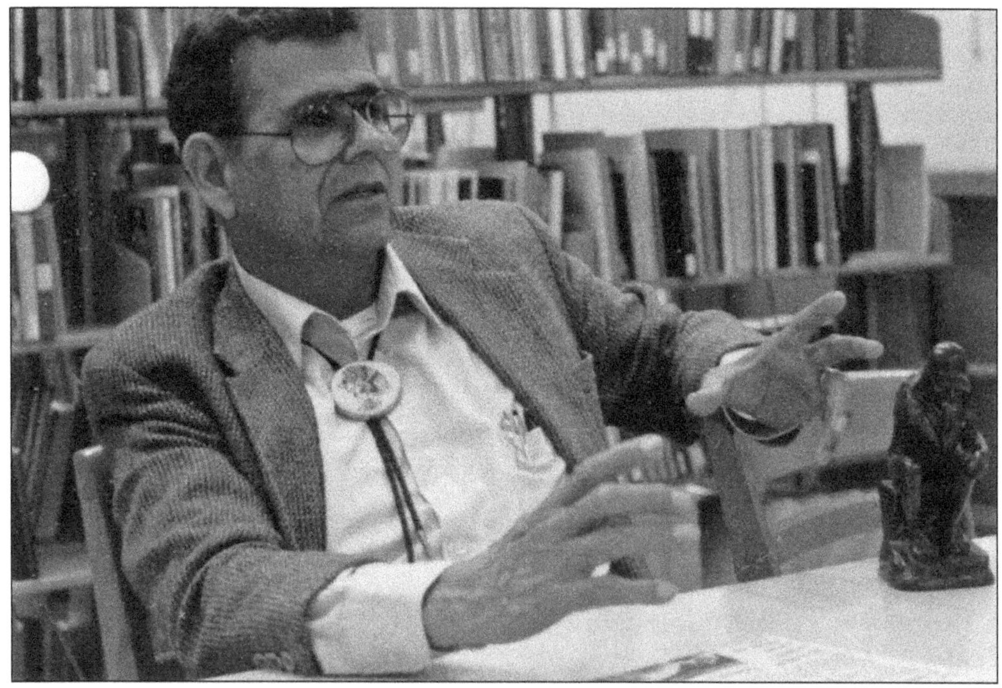

José Villa made his mark as a leader while a resident of San José. In addition to his membership in the Model Cities program, Villa played a leadership role with the CSO. He was also a professor and chairman of the Mexican American Graduate Studies Department and the School of Social Work at San José State University. (Courtesy of the Chicano Collection, Cultural Heritage Center, Dr. Martin Luther King Jr. Library, San José State University.)

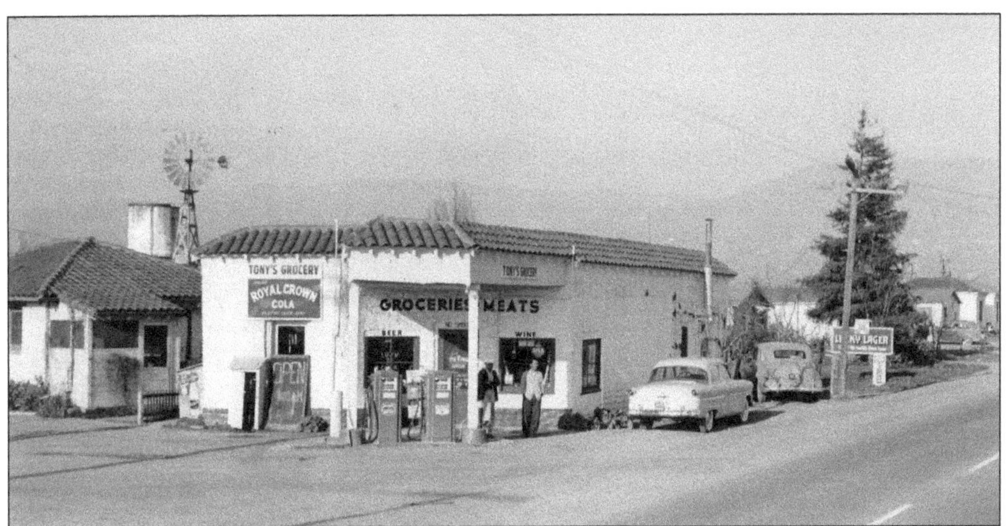

Tony's Grocery was located on the northeast corner of Capitol Avenue and Story Road. It is the present-day site of a gas station and car wash. The photograph was taken by Del Carlo Photography in April 1954. (Courtesy of the Santa Clara County Archives.)

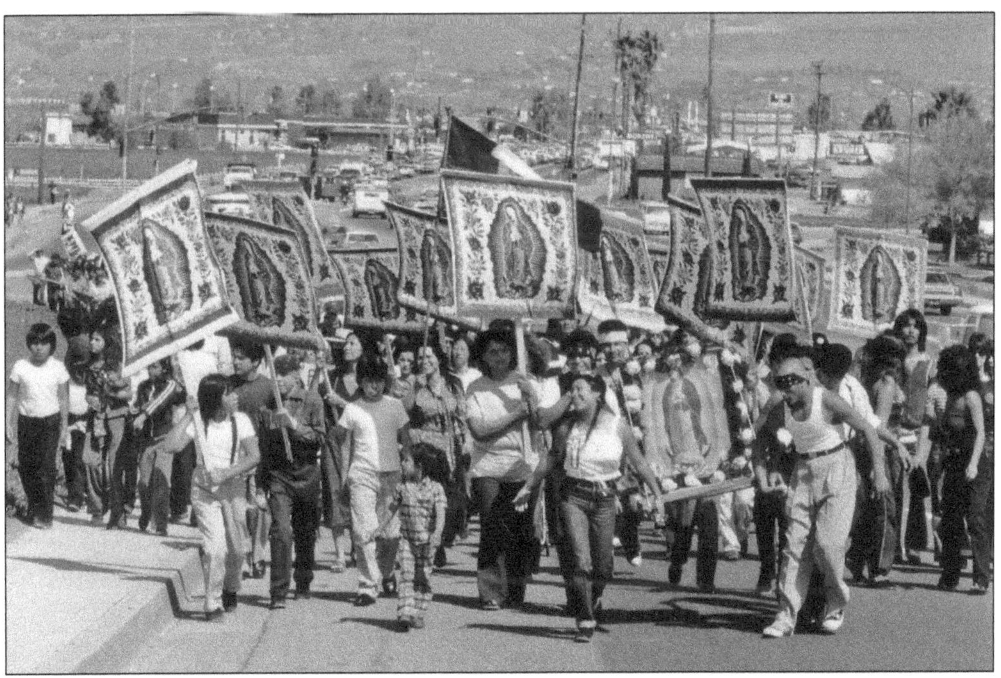

Students of W. C. Overfelt High School, their family members, and community supporters marched on Story Road in response to the lack of Mexican American instructors and curriculum addressing Mexican American history and culture at the school in the late 1970s. The marchers carried flags of La Virgen de Guadalupe, a revered religious figure for Mexicans and Mexican Americans. (Photograph by and courtesy of Paul Ortiz.)

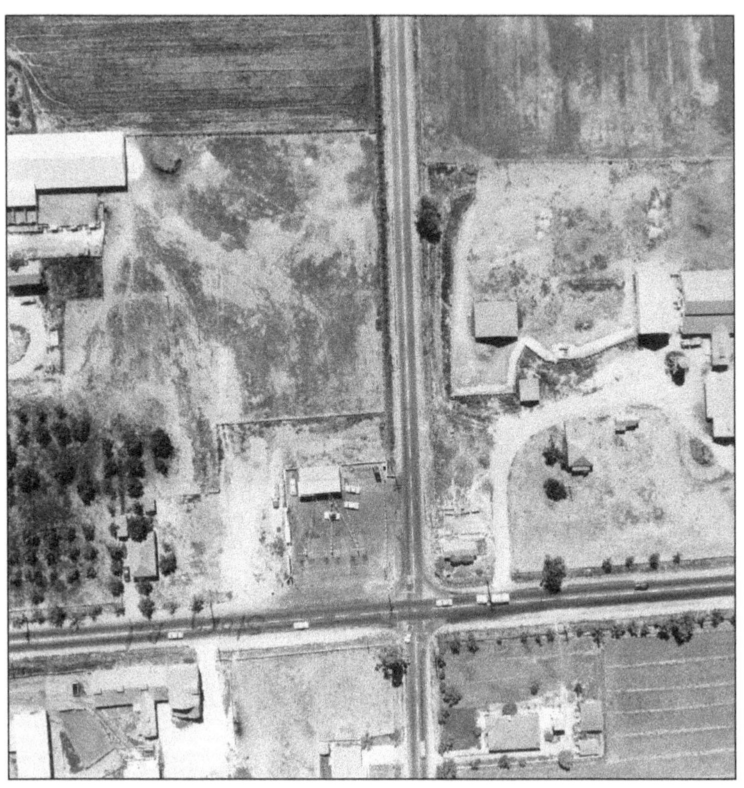

This aerial photograph was taken in August 1956 for the County of Santa Clara. It illustrates the crossroads at King and Story Roads. King Road was named after Andrew Lewis King, a native of Virginia who came to San José in 1851. The roads became an important epicenter of Eastside, with business activity by day and cruising by night. (Courtesy of the Santa Clara County Archives.)

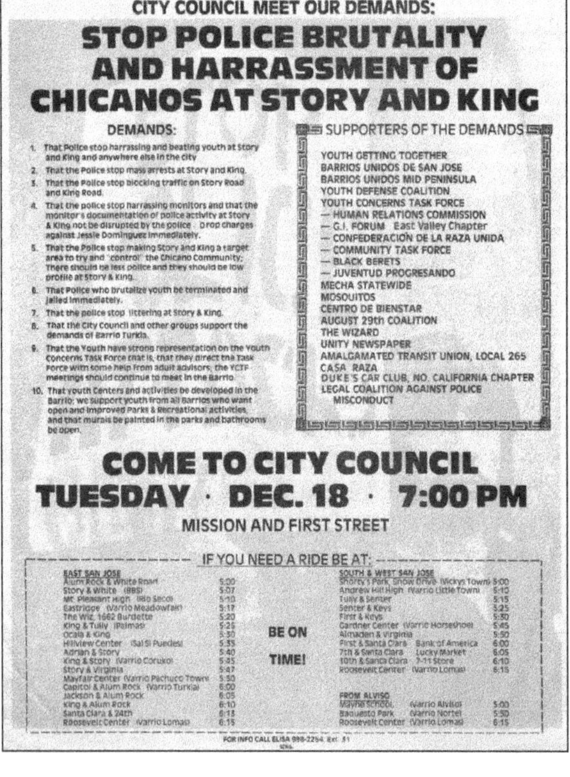

CITY COUNCIL MEET OUR DEMANDS:

STOP POLICE BRUTALITY AND HARRASSMENT OF CHICANOS AT STORY AND KING

DEMANDS:

1. That Police stop harrassing and beating youth at Story and King and anywhere else in the city
2. That the Police stop mass arrests at Story and King.
3. That the Police stop blocking traffic on Story Road and King Road.
4. That the police stop harrassing monitors and that the monitor's documentation of police activity at Story & King not be disrupted by the police. Drop charges against Jessie Dominguez immediately.
5. That the Police stop making Story and King a target area to try and "control" the Chicano Community; There should be less police and they should be low profile at Story & King.
6. That Police who brutalize youth be terminated and jailed immediately.
7. That the police stop littering at Story & King.
8. That the City Council and other groups support the demands of Barrio Turkia.
9. That the Youth have strong representation on the Youth Concerns Task Force that is, that they direct the Task Force with some help from adult advisors; the YCTF meetings should continue to meet in the Barrio.
10. That youth Centers and activities be developed in the Barrio; we support youth from all Barrios who want open and improved Parks & Recreational activities, and that murals be painted in the parks and bathrooms be open.

SUPPORTERS OF THE DEMANDS

YOUTH GETTING TOGETHER
BARRIOS UNIDOS DE SAN JOSE
BARRIOS UNIDOS MID PENINSULA
YOUTH DEFENSE COALITION
YOUTH CONCERNS TASK FORCE
— HUMAN RELATIONS COMMISSION
— G.I. FORUM East Valley Chapter
— CONFEDERACION DE LA RAZA UNIDA
— COMMUNITY TASK FORCE
— BLACK BERETS
— JUVENTUD PROGRESANDO
MECHA STATEWIDE
MOSQUITOS
CENTRO DE BIENSTAR
AUGUST 29th COALITION
THE WIZARD
UNITY NEWSPAPER
AMALGAMATED TRANSIT UNION, LOCAL 265
CASA RAZA
DUKE'S CAR CLUB, NO. CALIFORNIA CHAPTER
LEGAL COALITION AGAINST POLICE MISCONDUCT

COME TO CITY COUNCIL

TUESDAY · DEC. 18 · 7:00 PM

MISSION AND FIRST STREET

IF YOU NEED A RIDE BE AT:

EAST SAN JOSE

Alum Rock & White Road	5:00
Story & White (BBS)	5:07
Mt. Pleasant High (Rio Seco)	5:10
Eastridge (Varrio Meadowfair)	5:17
The Wiz, 1662 Burdette	5:20
King & Tully (Palmas)	5:25
Ocala & King	5:30
Hillview Center (Sal Si Puedes)	5:35
Adrian & Story	5:40
King & Story (Varrio Coruko)	5:45
Story & Virginia	5:47
Mayfair Center (Varrio Pachuco Town)	5:50
Capitol & Alum Rock (Varrio Turkia)	6:00
Jackson & Alum Rock	6:05
King & Alum Rock	6:10
Santa Clara & 24th	6:13
Roosevelt Center (Varrio Lomas)	6:15

BE ON TIME!

SOUTH & WEST SAN JOSE

Shorty's Park, Snow Drive (Vickys Town)	5:00
Andrew Hill High (Varrio Little Town)	5:10
Tully & Senter	5:15
Senter & Keys	5:25
First & Keys	5:30
Gardner Center (Varrio Horseshoe)	5:45
Almaden & Virginia	5:50
First & Santa Clara Bank of America	6:00
7th & Santa Clara Lucky Market	6:05
10th & Santa Clara 7-11 Store	6:10
Roosevelt Center (Varrio Lomas)	6:15

FROM ALVISO

Mayne School, (Varrio Alviso)	5:00
Baquesto Park (Varrio Norte)	5:50
Roosevelt Center (Varrio Lomas)	6:15

FOR INFO CALL ELISA 998-2254 Ext. 51

In the heyday of cruising in customized cars in the late 1970s and early 1980s, Mexican residents and visitors from throughout California cruised at the intersection of King and Story Roads. Yet police brutality and harassment against Mexican Americans or Chicano youth was a serious problem as this flyer demonstrates. Residents, with the support of organizations, unions, businesses, and newspapers, were encouraged to attend a San José City Council meeting and propose a list of demands to stop the harassment by the San José police force. (Courtesy of the Chicano Collection, Cultural Heritage Center, Dr. Martin Luther King Jr. Library, San José State University.)

The mural *Mexicatlan* was painted by master muralist Yermo Aranda along with members of the East San José community. It was painted in August 2002 on a building on Sunset and Alum Rock Roads. It was a joint effort by Mayfair Si, a community based organization in the Mayfair area. Portrayed on the right side of the mural is Cesar Chavez, whose home is a few blocks away. (Photograph by and courtesy of Ernie de la Torre.)

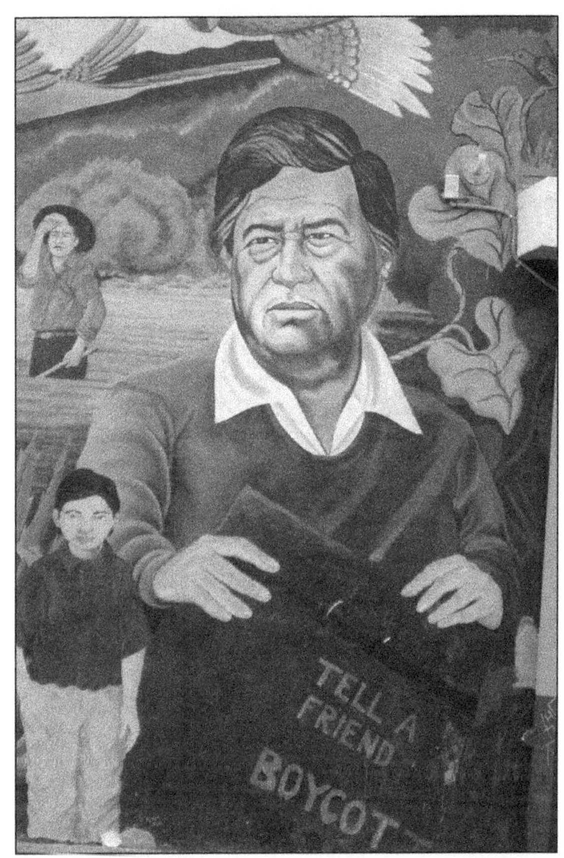

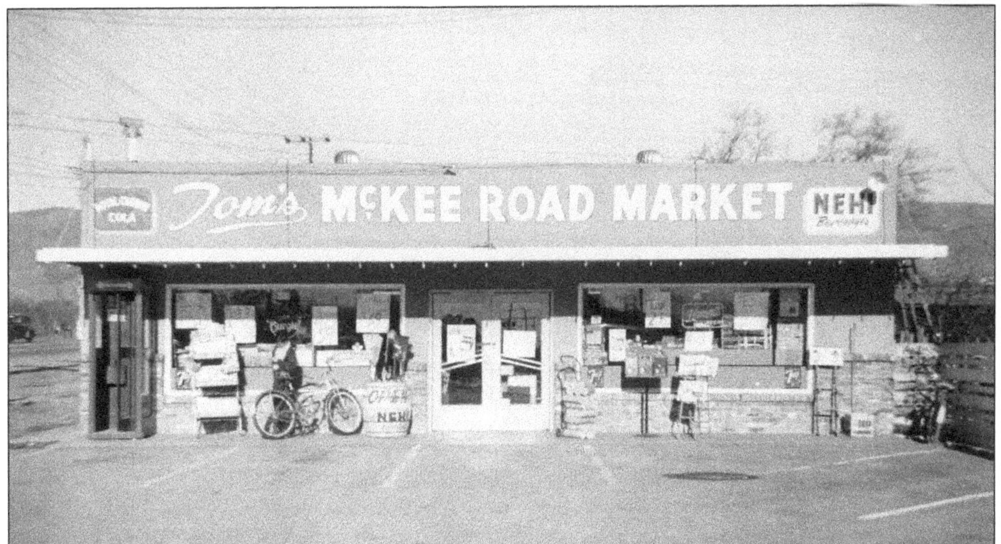

This photograph of the McKee Market was taken in the 1950s. It currently is the site of a liquor store, which sits on the corner of Capitol Avenue and McKee Road. McKee Road was named after Joseph Olcott McKee, who was originally from Connecticut and arrived in San José in 1849. McKee was the first to transport fresh fruit from San José to the San Francisco market via the docks at the city of Alviso north of San José. (Courtesy of the Santa Clara County Archives.)

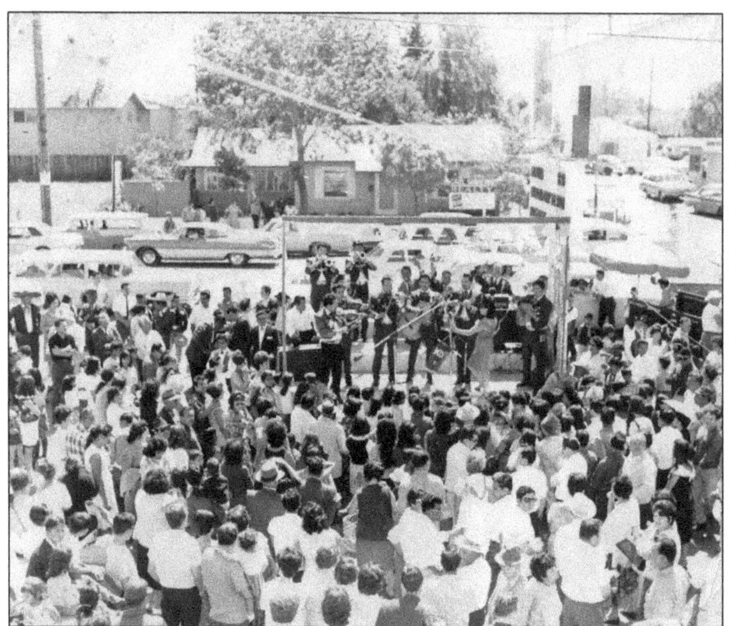

Outdoor entertainment was provided by Mariachis at the Pink Elephant retail strip in 1968 as a promotion for Spanish radio station KOFY. By 1970, the Mayfair district in Eastside had the largest concentration of Mexicans in all Santa Clara County. The total population was 6,300, of which 64 percent were Mexican American, 15 percent white, 15 percent African American, and 6 percent other. (Courtesy of the Jesus Valenzuela family.)

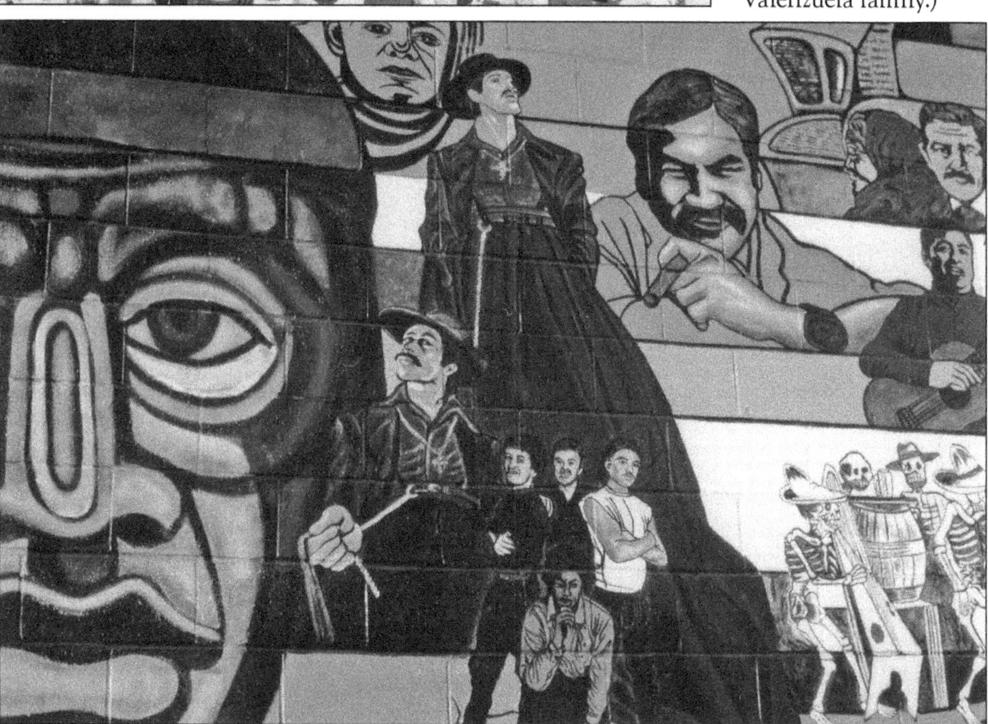

This mural is titled *Mural de la Raza* and was painted by Frank Torres in 1985. It was sponsored by the Eastside San José Council and the Eastside Youth Center. The mural is located on the side of a building at Story Road near Jackson Street. The mural portrays Luiz Valdez, a playwright, filmmaker, and founder of the theater group Teatro Campesino. Valdez was an East San José resident and a graduate of James Lick High School and San José State University. El Pachuco, a character in Valdez's feature film *Zoot Suit*, is included in the mural. (Photograph by and courtesy of Paul Ortiz.)

Five

CHICANO AND YOUTH MOVEMENTS

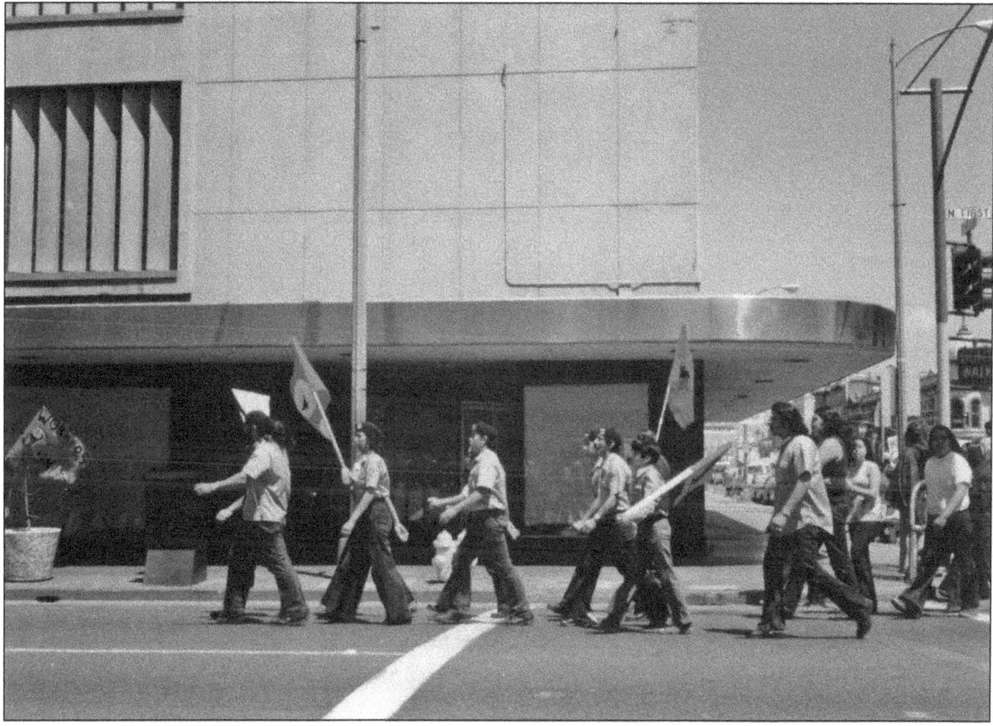

In the late 1960s and 1970s, Mexican American youth began to identify themselves as Chicanos. They felt unrepresented in their education, in the curriculum at their schools and colleges, and in their communities. Often the first in their families to attend college, many Chicanos united on issues of social justice. They supported civil rights movements such as the Delano, California, grape pickers' strike led by Cesar Chavez, Dolores Huerta, Gil Padilla, and union members of the National Farm Workers Association (NFWA), a precursor to the United Farm Workers (UFW) union. Chicano youth, students, and community members supported the union's non-violent strikes, pilgrimages, marches, and international boycott of grapes grown in Delano. Taken in the 1970s, this image shows marchers, including members of the Brown Berets, on North First Street in downtown San José, carrying the UFW flag. (Courtesy of the Chicano Collection, Cultural Heritage Center, Dr. Martin Luther King Jr. Library, San José State University.)

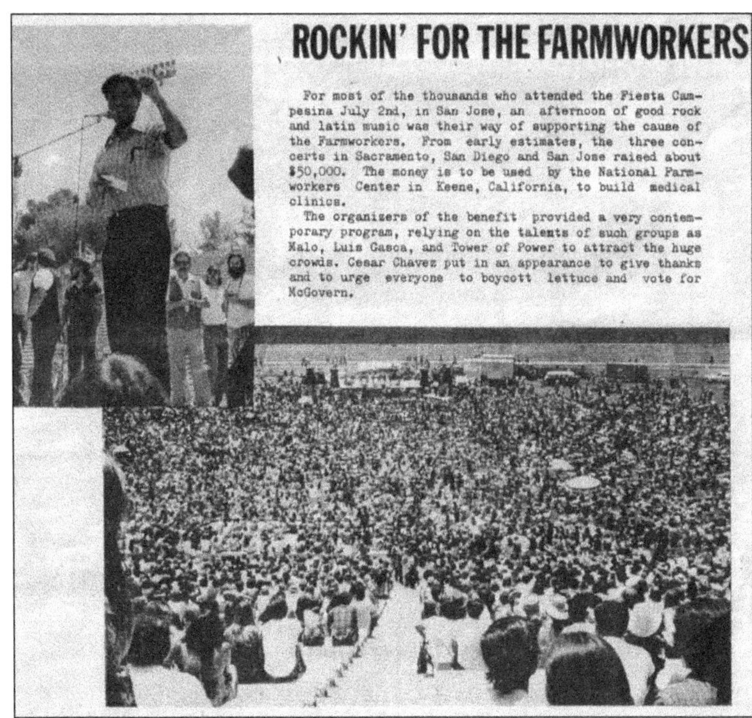

ROCKIN' FOR THE FARMWORKERS

For most of the thousands who attended the Fiesta Campesina July 2nd, in San Jose, an afternoon of good rock and latin music was their way of supporting the cause of the Farmworkers. From early estimates, the three concerts in Sacramento, San Diego and San Jose raised about $50,000. The money is to be used by the National Farmworkers Center in Keene, California, to build medical clinics.

The organizers of the benefit provided a very contemporary program, relying on the talents of such groups as Malo, Luis Gasca, and Tower of Power to attract the huge crowds. Cesar Chavez put in an appearance to give thanks and to urge everyone to boycott lettuce and vote for McGovern.

Cesar Chavez and the UFW held numerous rallies, concerts, and demonstrations in San José. In this photograph taken in the early 1970s, Chavez addresses the crowd gathered at the Fiesta Campesina. (Courtesy of the Chicano Collection, Cultural Heritage Center, Dr. Martin Luther King Jr. Library, San José State University.)

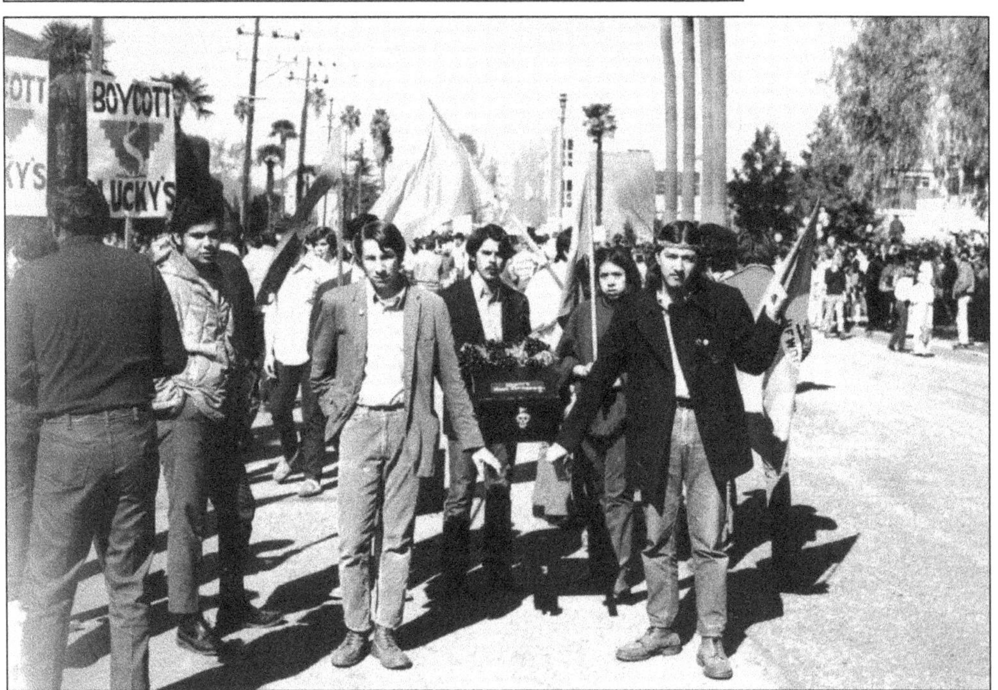

In the early 1970s, a boycott of Lucky's supermarket and grapes grown in California's San Joaquin Valley during the Delano grape strike was supported by Mexican American youth. From left to right are San José State University students Mauro Chavez, Adrian Vargas, Juan Olivarez, Abby Delgado, and Sid Flores. (Courtesy of the Chicano Collection, Cultural Heritage Center, Dr. Martin Luther King Jr. Library, San José State University.)

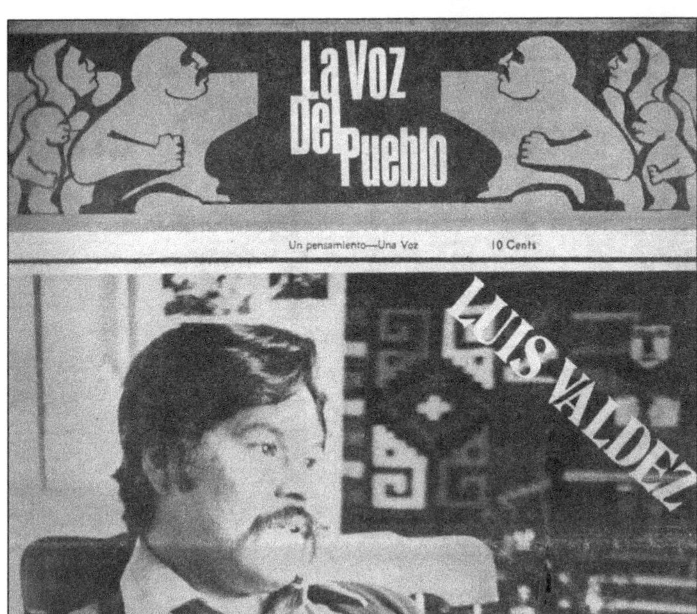

In 1964, the first organizational effort in the nation to bring attention to the needs of Mexican American students was the Student Initiative at San José State University. The Student Initiative was organized by Armando Valdez. *La Voz del Pueblo* was a barrio newspaper from the Chicano movement period. (Courtesy of the Chicano Collection, Cultural Heritage Center, Dr. Martin Luther King Jr. Library, San José State University.)

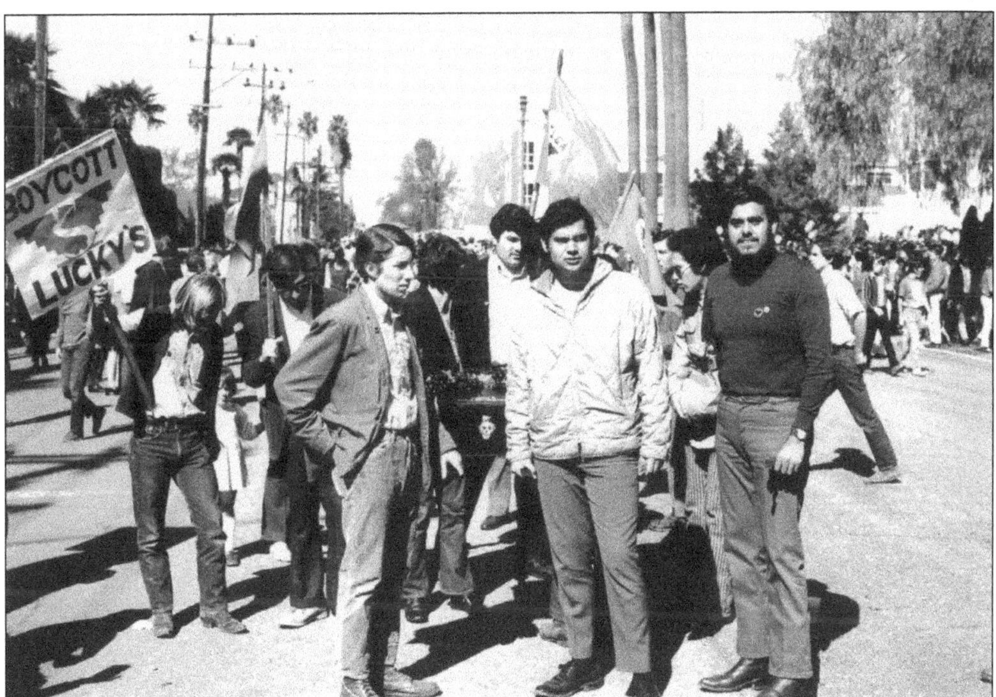

In 1967, the Student Initiative at San José State University changed its name to the Mexican American Student Confederation (MASC). This photograph includes students of MASC marching at a 1970s demonstration in support of the farm workers strike. From left to right are student organizers Adrian Vargas, Mauro Chavez, and Ramon Martinez. (Courtesy of the Chicano Collection, Cultural Heritage Center, Dr. Martin Luther King Jr. Library, San José State University.)

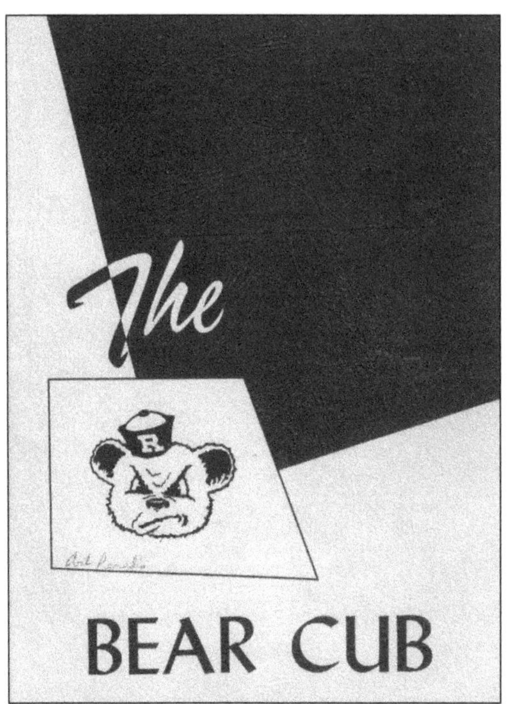

This image is a Roosevelt Junior High School yearbook. In 1967, Roosevelt Junior High School students walked out of school to address issues of racism and institutional discrimination. Educators José Carrasco and Consuelo Rodriguez co-organized the walkout, one of the first documented walkouts by Mexican American students in the United States. (Courtesy of Art Peredia.)

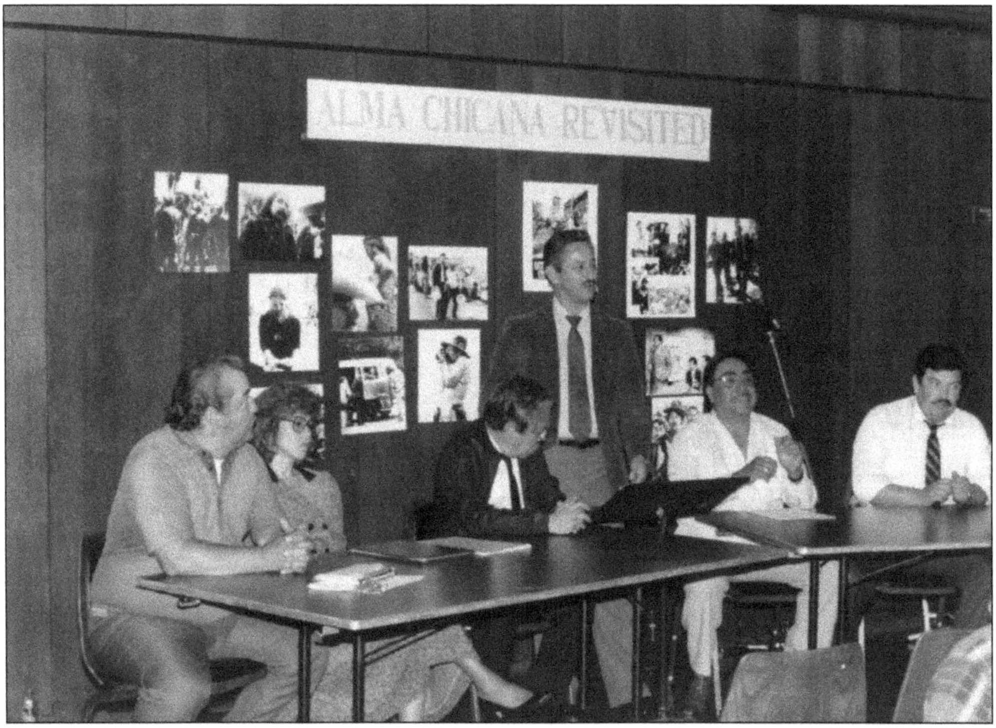

Pictured in this photograph from the 1980s are Consuelo Rodriguez (second from the left) and José Carrasco (speaking at the podium), co-organizers of the Roosevelt Junior High School student walkout in 1967. (Courtesy of the Chicano Collection, Cultural Heritage Center, Dr. Martin Luther King Jr. Library, San José State University.)

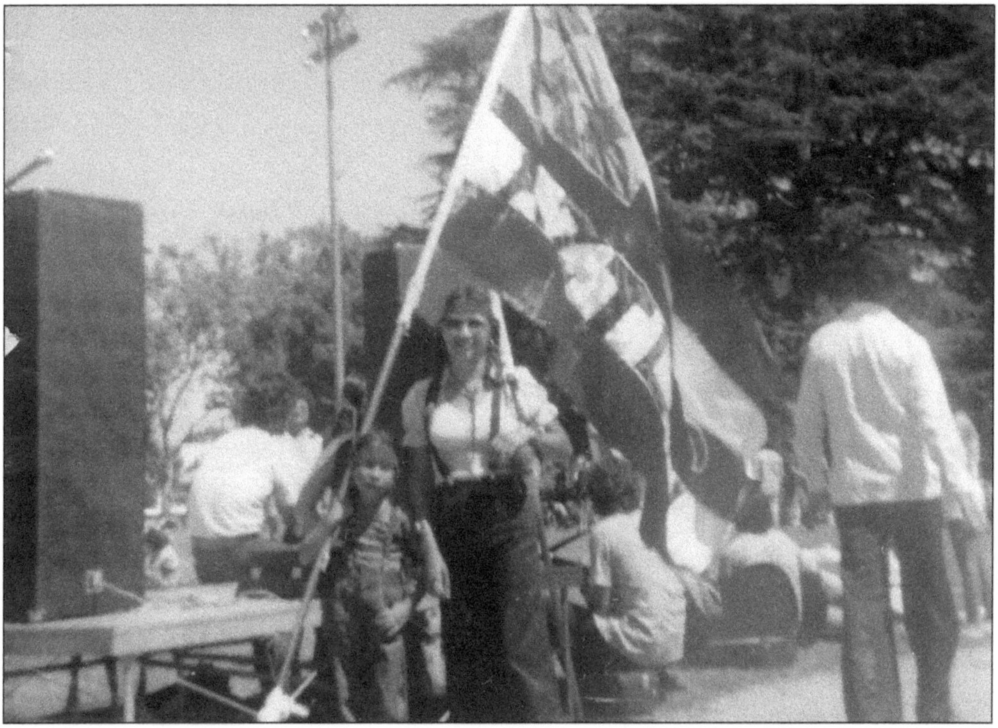

On a demonstration march, graduate of James Lick High School Elaine Ortiz (right) and Christina Alvarado pose with a flag of Aztlan in Backesto Park on Thirteenth and Empire Streets in 1978. Aztlan was the name of the legendary ancestral home in the American Southwest of the Aztec people. The march began at Five Wounds Catholic Church and ended in Backesto Park. (Courtesy of Elaine Ortiz-Kristich.)

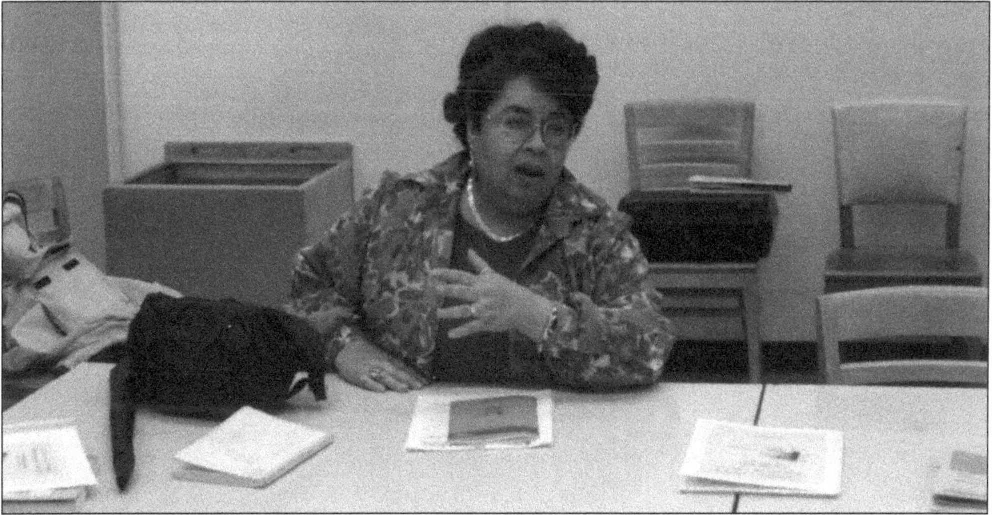

United People Arriba (UPA) was an Eastside San José organization that began in 1967 with the student protests at Roosevelt Junior High School. Sofía Mendoza, a community leader, encouraged UPA in 1968 to broaden its action beyond educational grievances to include other community issues. (Courtesy of the Chicano Collection, Cultural Heritage Center, Dr. Martin Luther King Jr. Library, San José State University.)

CHICANO COMMENCEMENT 1971

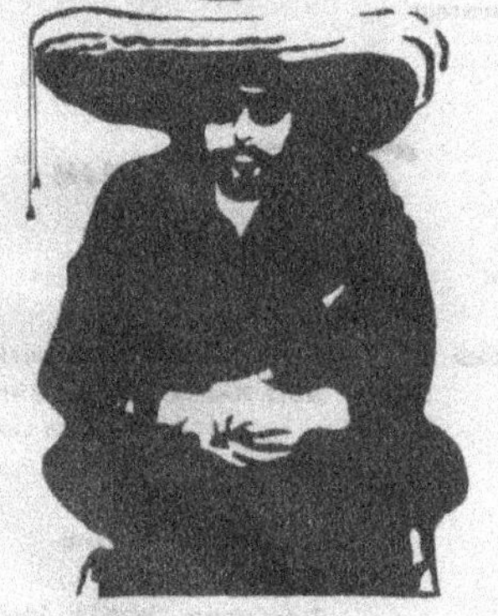

"No culture is deprived, it is only classified as deprived because it does not correspond to the middle – class culture of this country".

Pete Mesa, Principal San Jose High School

The concept of creating a Chicano commencement for graduating Mexican Americans was implemented by students and faculty in 1968 at San José State University. The Chicano Commencement came to fruition in 1970. The keynote speaker was Dr. Fernando Torres-Gil, a graduate of San José State University, an organizer of the event, and a community activist. The 1971 Chicano Commencement included in its program community members Fr. Anthony Soto, Dr. José Carrasco, and Sofía Mendoza and a performance by the theater group El Teatro de la Gente, "The People's Theatre." (Both courtesy of the Chicano Collection, Cultural Heritage Center, Dr. Martin Luther King Jr. Library, San José State University.)

Welcome! to our first annual Chicano Commencement. This event was initiated with the purpose of presenting independent commencement exercises worthy of our students and the community. In the past, the gabacho denied and ignored our right to be equally represented in their one-sided anglo oriented graduating ceremonies. Today graduating Chicano students assert their unity and pride by participating in a commencement relevant and representative of their efforts and the interest of the community.

The Program

1:00 P.M.	Opening prayer by Father Soto
SPEAKERS:	Jose Carrasco (Master of Ceremonies) Sophie Mendoza – Community worker and member of United People Arriba
	Music by Teatro de la Gente
	Tony Quintero – Boalt Law School graduate U.C. Berkeley
	Graduate Students of 1971
2:30 P.M.	Mariachis, Mexican food, and cerveza in the patio

Bienvenidos a nuestra primera graduación Chicana.

Esta función se inicio con el propósito de presentar una graduación independiente y a la vez digna de nuestros alumnos y de la comunidad.

Anteriormente, el gabacho a tratado de no hacernos caso. Aun, nos ha negado el derecho de ser digno y verdaderamente representados en estas funciones prejuiciosas. Actualmente, los alumnos chicanos posgraduantes manifiestan su unidad y orgullo participando en una función de graduación relativa y representativa de sus esfuerzos propios y de interes a la comunidad.

Programa

1:00 P.M.	Benedición por el Rev. Padre Anthony Soto
MAESTRO DE CEREMONIAS:	Jose Carrasco
ORADORES:	Sophie Mendoza Tony Quintero Graduados de la clase de 1971
MUSICA:	Teatro de la Gente
2:00 P.M.	Mariachis, Comida Mexicana y cerveza en el patio.

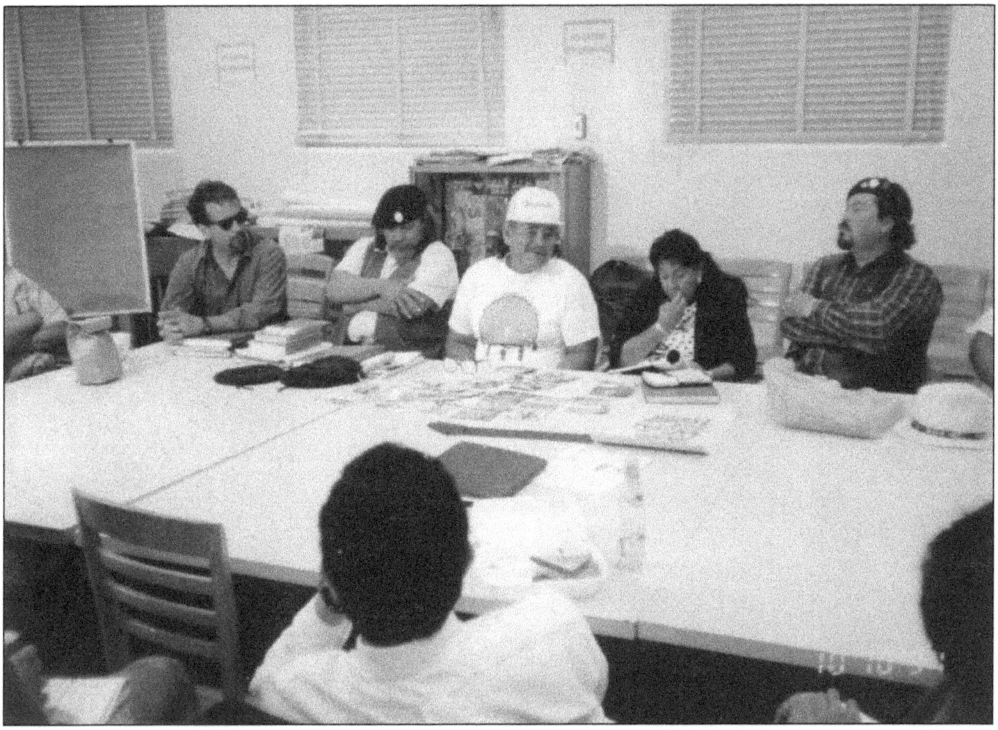

The Black Berets for Justice in San José was the first chapter in the country. This 1993 photograph was taken at a seminar in the Chicano Library Resource Center at San José State University. The Black Beret members are, second from left to right, Henry Dominguez, Chemo Candelaria, Theresa Candelaria, and Luis Viniegra. (Courtesy of the Chicano Collection, Cultural Heritage Center, Dr. Martin Luther King Jr. Library, San José State University.)

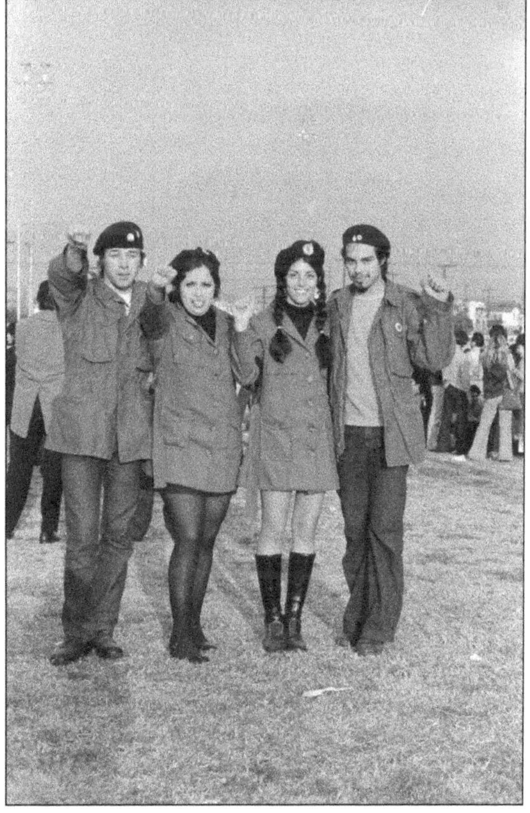

In this early-1970s photograph taken at a San José rally are Daniel Arroyo (left), a San José Black Beret; two unidentified Brown Beret female members (center) from the Bay Area; and Black Beret member Joel Viniegra (right). Both organizations were dedicated to achieving equality and justice for Mexicans and other people of color. (Courtesy of the Chicano Collection, Cultural Heritage Center, Dr. Martin Luther King Jr. Library, San José State University.)

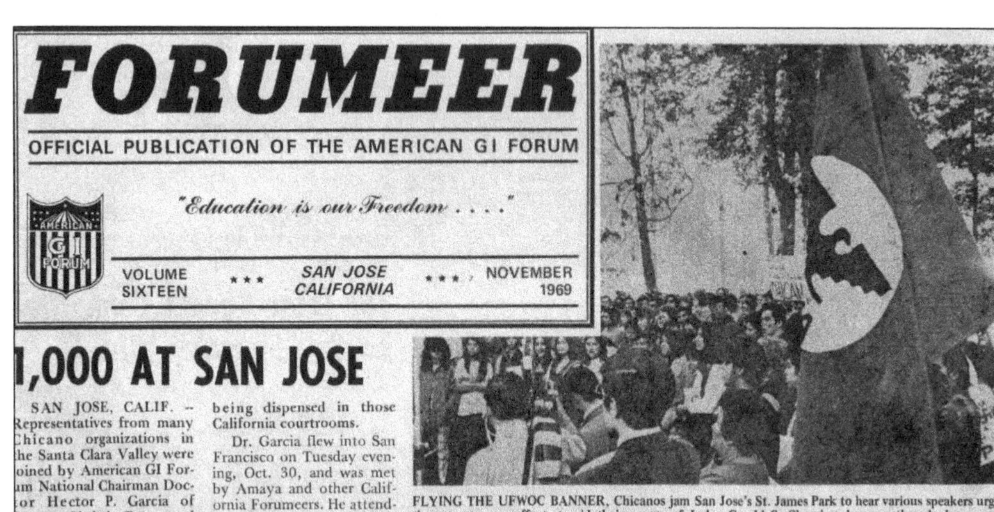

FORUMEER

OFFICIAL PUBLICATION OF THE AMERICAN GI FORUM

"Education is our Freedom . . . ."

AMERICAN GI FORUM

VOLUME SIXTEEN ★★★ SAN JOSE CALIFORNIA ★★★ NOVEMBER 1969

1,000 AT SAN JOSE

SAN JOSE, CALIF. -- Representatives from many Chicano organizations in the Santa Clara Valley were joined by American GI Forum National Chairman Doctor Hector P. Garcia of Corpus Christi, Texas and California State Chairman

being dispensed in those California courtrooms.

Dr. Garcia flew into San Francisco on Tuesday evening, Oct. 30, and was met by Amaya and other California Forumeers. He attended a 9 PM press conference at the Project SER head-

FLYING THE UFWOC BANNER, Chicanos jam San Jose's St. James Park to hear various speakers urge them to step up efforts to rid their courts of Judge Gerald S. Chargin who recently asked a young Mexicano to commit suicide.

While presiding over a case of incest in 1969, Santa Clara County judge Gerald S. Chargin told an accused Mexican American defendant that he should commit suicide and made racist remarks about Mexicans. In response to Chargin's racist comments, Mexicans and others held a rally at St. James Park in downtown San José. The rally was attended by over 1,000 angry people. Judge Chargin was eventually censured by the California Supreme Court and removed of his duties. (Courtesy of Department of Special Collections, Stanford University Libraries, Ernesto Galarza Papers [M0224].)

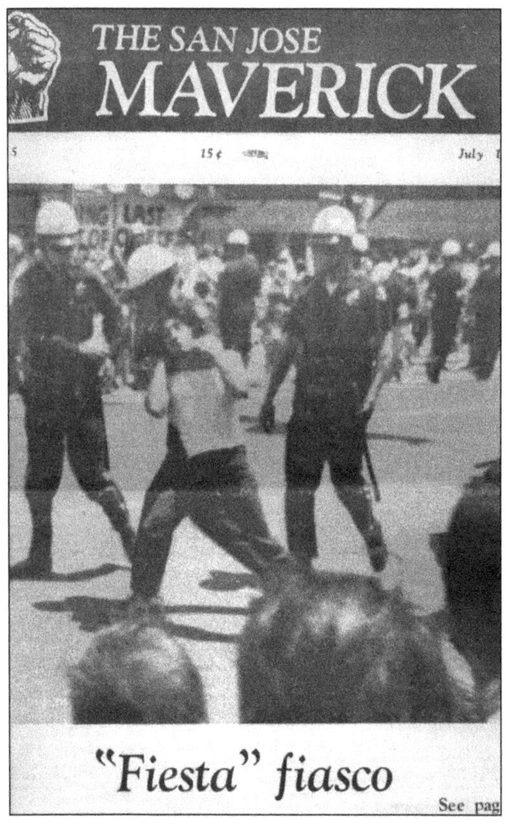

THE SAN JOSE MAVERICK

15¢ July

"Fiesta" fiasco

See pag

On June 1, 1969, the City of San José attempted to revive an old parade highlighting the Spanish history in San José called the Fiestas de Las Rosas. Many viewed the parade as an insult to Mexicans who had liberated themselves from Spain in 1821. Mexicans demonstrated against the parade and suffered harassment, beatings, and arrest by San José police officers. (Courtesy of the Chicano Collection, Cultural Heritage Center, Dr. Martin Luther King Jr. Library, San José State University.)

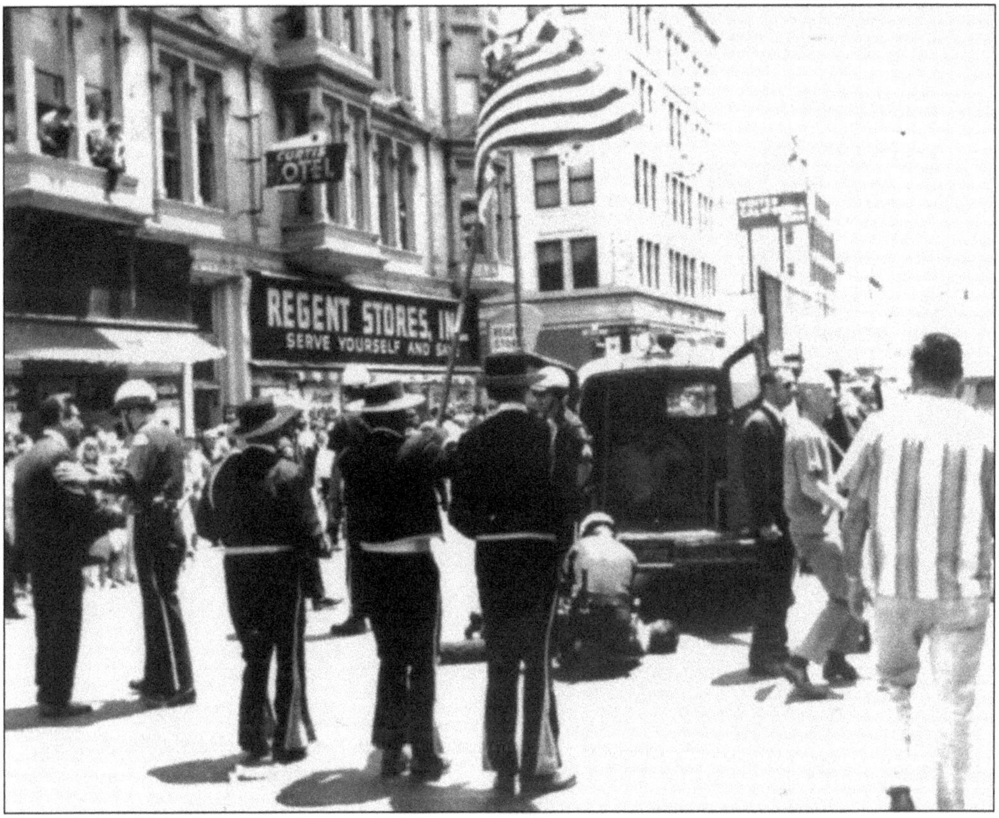

Three Fiestas de las Rosas parade participants are dressed in Spanish attire while a man on the left is trying to negotiate with a San José police officer. Mexican protestors are being placed in a paddy wagon. The parade became known as the "Fiesta Fiasco." (Courtesy of the Chicano Collection, Cultural Heritage Center, Dr. Martin Luther King Jr. Library, San José State University.)

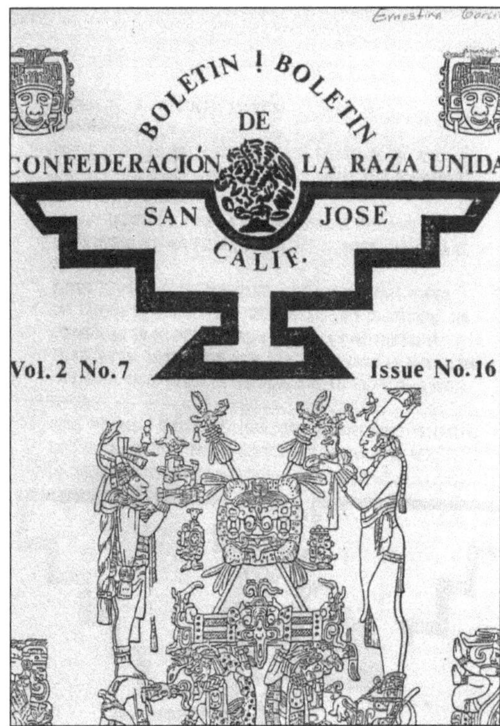

As a result of the Fiesta Fiasco, Mexican and Mexican American individuals and groups united in 1969 under La Confederación de La Raza Unida (CLRU) to protest the Fiesta de las Rosas. The CLRU also took a leadership role in approaching government officials on redevelopment and gentrification, which were lacking in Mexican communities. The image is the cover of a CLRU newsletter. (Courtesy of the Chicano Collection, Cultural Heritage Center, Dr. Martin Luther King Jr. Library, San José State University.)

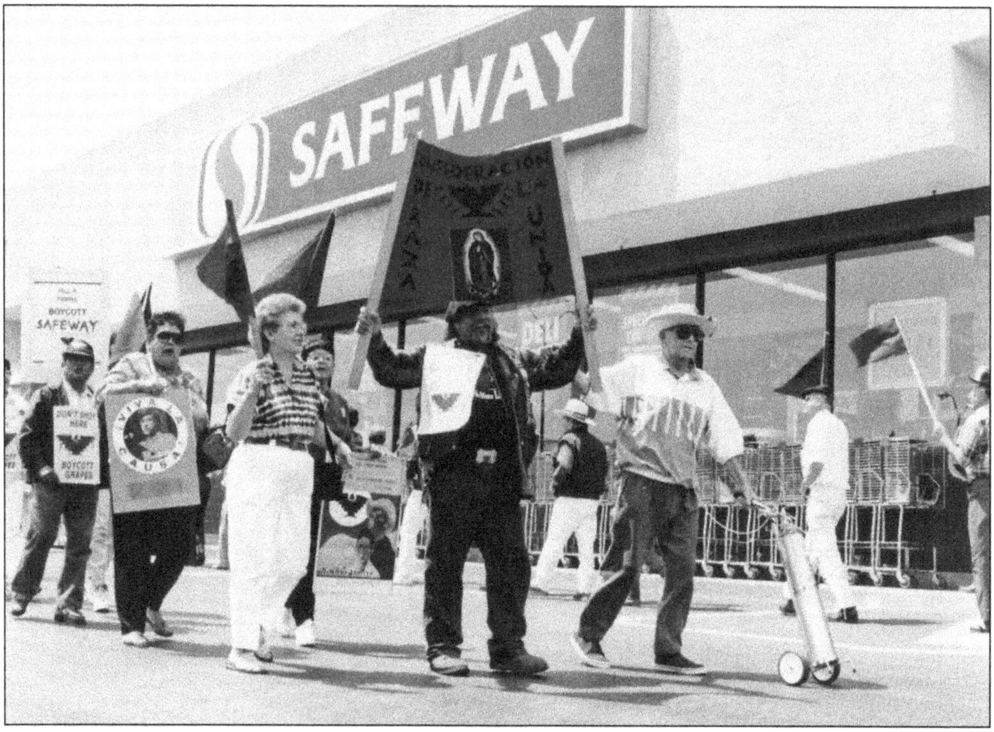

In the early 1970s, members of the CLRU organization supported the National Association of Farm Workers union's boycott of Safeway grocery stores for selling grapes picked by non-union members. Second from left is Ernestina Garcia, one of the organization's leaders. Holding the sign of La Virgen de Guadalupe is Henry Dominguez, a member of the Black Berets and a student of San José City College. (Photograph by Mary Andrade, courtesy of *La Oferta* newspaper.)

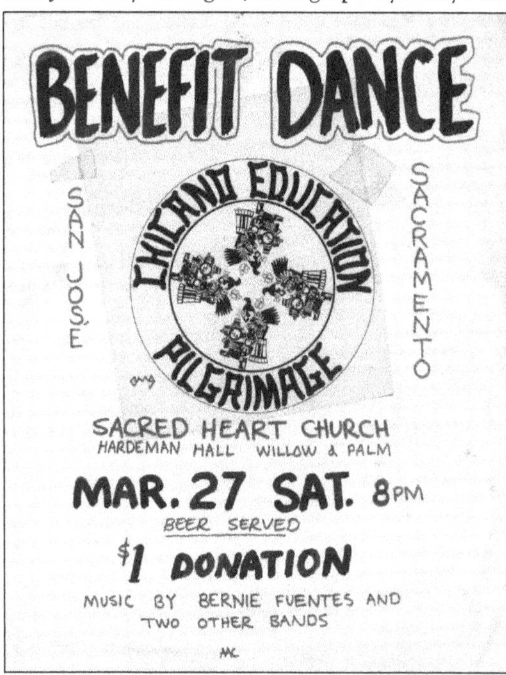

On April 9, 1974, over 200 Mexican and Chicano San José State University educators, student leaders, and community members marched from San José to Sacramento to press their demands for equal education for Mexican children. The march organizers claimed that taxpayers were deceived by educators and politicians into believing that their tax money was well spent on equal education. This flyer advertises the benefit dance held to help fund and support the educational pilgrimage. (Courtesy of the Chicano Collection, Cultural Heritage Center, Dr. Martin Luther King Jr. Library, San José State University.)

This poem from the Chicano movement by San José State University student Richard Olivas captures the Chicano students' frustration. Students felt alienated and ignored at schools by faculty, administrators, and school board members. Students also criticized history courses that excluded the contributions of Mexicans in the United States' history. (Courtesy of the Chicano Collection, Cultural Heritage Center, Dr. Martin Luther King Jr. Library, San José State University.)

I'm sitting in my history class,
he instructor commences rapping,
I'm in my US history class,
And I'm on the verge of napping.

Mayflower landed on Plymouth R
Tell me more! Tell me more!
Thirteen colonies settled.
Man, I've heard it all before.

What did he say?
Dare I ask him to reiterate?
Oh, why bother
It sounded like he said
George Washington's my father.

I'm reluctant to believe it,
I suddenly raise my mano.
If George Washington is my father,
Why wasn't he Chicano?

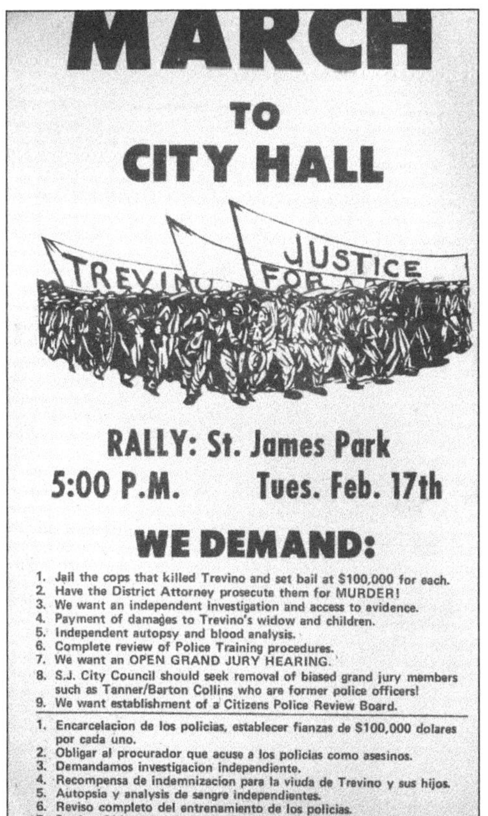

The controversial killing of Danny Trevino, a resident of San José, by the San José police in 1974 sparked a massive demonstration and a march by Chicano activists and their supporters. The incident occurred when Trevino was sitting in his parked car with his girlfriend and was shot by a San José Police Department officer. This image is of a flyer announcing one of the many rallies protesting this alleged instance of police brutality. (Courtesy of the Chicano Collection, Cultural Heritage Center, Dr. Martin Luther King Jr. Library, San José State University.)

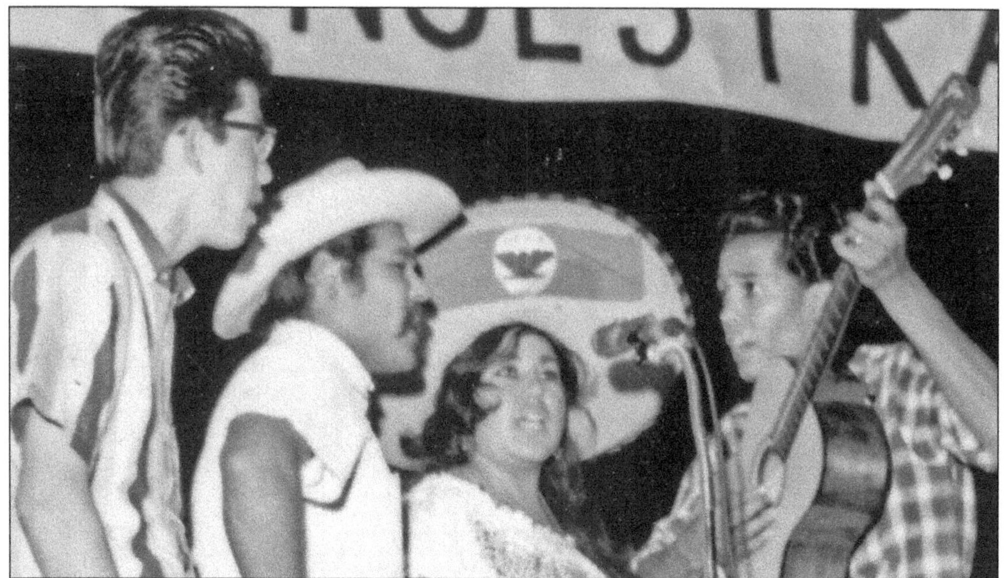

In 1965, San José resident Luis Valdez (second from left) joined Cesar Chavez and the United Farm Workers union in the fields of Delano. Utilizing his theatrical skills he developed in part as a student at San José State University, Valdez organized a group of actors to perform plays for striking farm workers. His theater group became El Teatro Campesino, "The Farmworkers Theatre." In 1971, the headquarters for El Teatro Campesino was established in San Juan Bautista, 45 minutes south of San José. (Courtesy of the California History Center.)

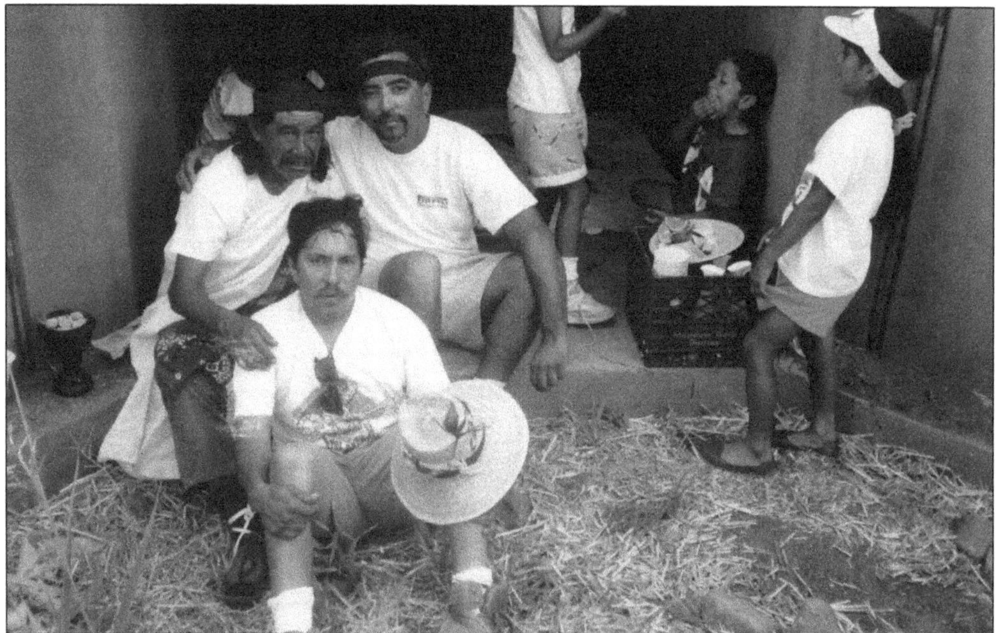

Mexican experts and maestros come to San José to share their indigenous traditions. Maestro Andres Segura is one such individual. He oversaw the Mexica ceremony at the unveiling of the statue of Quetzalcoatl at Plaza de Cesar Chavez in downtown San José. In this photograph are Andres Segura (left) with Arturo Huitzilin Mata (center) and Louie Rocha (right). (Courtesy of Huitzilin Mata.)

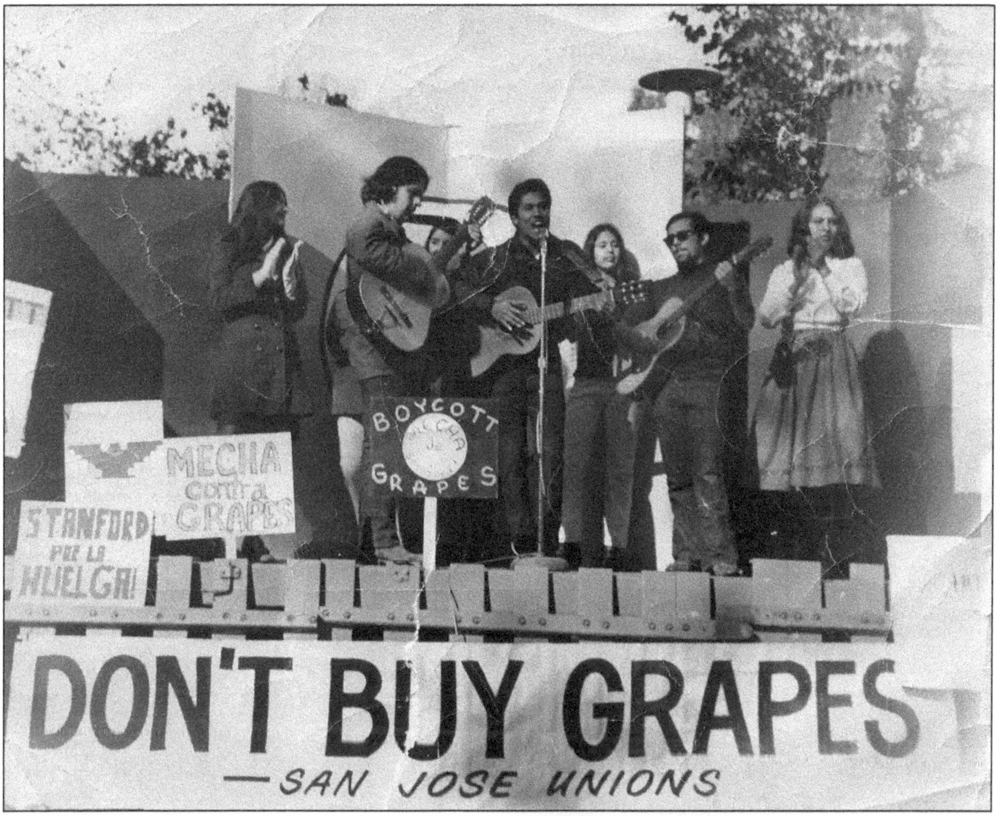

In the photograph is Teatro Urbano, "Urban Theatre," of San José. The members are, from left to right, Gracie Soto, Felipe Rodriguez, Armida Valdez (background), Danny Valdez, Debora Rodriguez, Manuel Martinez, and Yolanda Perez. Teatro Urbano performs music and *actos*, "acts," at a United Farm Workers union rally at St. James Park in 1969. (Courtesy of Phillip Rodriguez.)

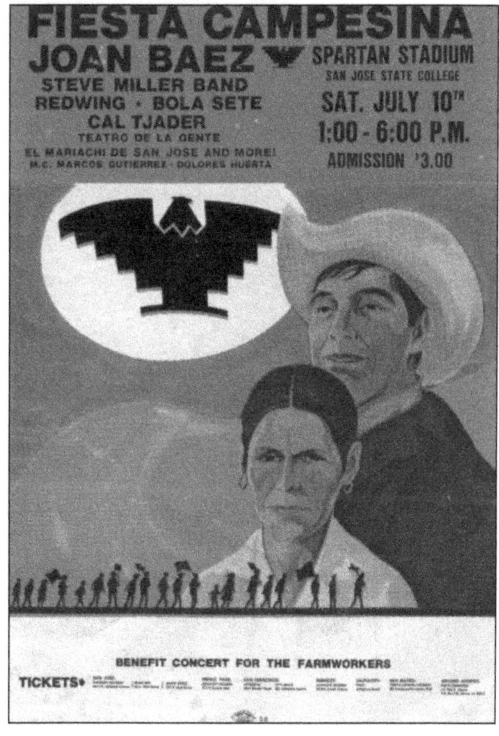

This flier is of the Fiesta Campesina, meaning "Farmworker Fiesta." Performers included San José's own Teatro de la Gente, "People's Theater." Teatro de La Gente began informally between 1969 and 1970 and was incorporated as a nonprofit in 1973. (Courtesy of the Chicano Collection, Cultural Heritage Center, Dr. Martin Luther King Jr. Library, San José State University.)

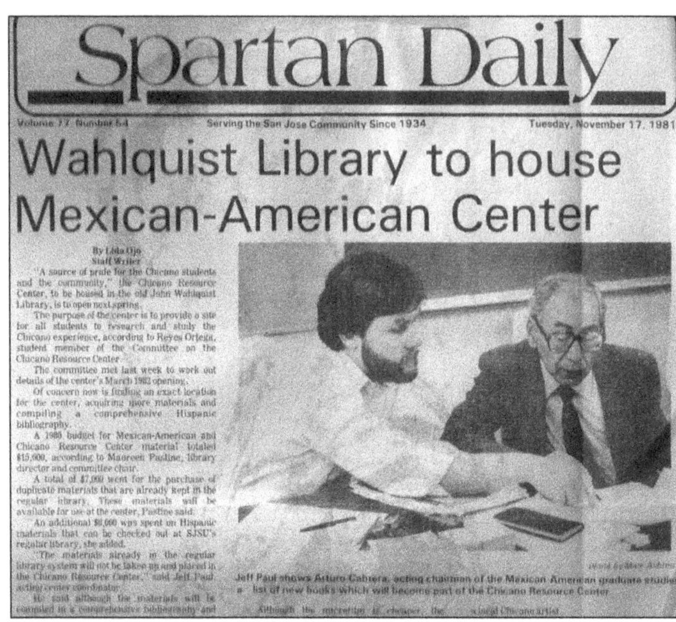

Spartan Daily

Volume 77, Number 54 — Serving the San Jose Community Since 1934 — Tuesday, November 17, 1981

Wahlquist Library to house Mexican-American Center

By Lida Ojo
Staff Writer

"A source of pride for the Chicano students and the community," the Chicano Resource Center, to be housed in the old John Wahlquist Library, is to open next spring.

The purpose of the center is to provide a site for all students to research and study the Chicano experience, according to Reyes Ortega, student member of the Committee on the Chicano Resource Center.

The committee met last week to work out details of the center's March 1982 opening.

Of concern now is finding an exact location for the center, acquiring more materials and compiling a comprehensive Hispanic bibliography.

A 1980 budget for Mexican-American and Chicano Resource Center material totaled $15,000, according to Maureen Pastine, library director and committee chair.

A total of $7,000 went for the purchase of duplicate materials that are already kept in the regular library. These materials will be available for use at the center, Pastine said.

An additional $8,000 was spent on Hispanic materials that can be checked out at SJSU's regular library, she added.

"The materials already in the regular library system will not be taken up and placed in the Chicano Resource Center," said Jeff Paul, acting center coordinator.

He said although the materials will be compiled in a comprehensive bibliography and

Jeff Paul shows Arturo Cabrera, acting chairman of the Mexican American graduate studies, a list of new books which will become part of the Chicano Resource Center.

In 1982, the Committee of the Chicano Resource Center (CRC), led by San José State University student Reyes Ortega, worked to create the CRC at San José State University. Pictured in the university's student newspaper, the *Spartan Daily*, are CRC center coordinator Jeff Paul (left) and Dr. Arturo Cabrera, chairman of the Mexican American Graduate Studies Department. (Courtesy of the Chicano Collection, Cultural Heritage Center, Dr. Martin Luther King Jr. Library, San José State University.)

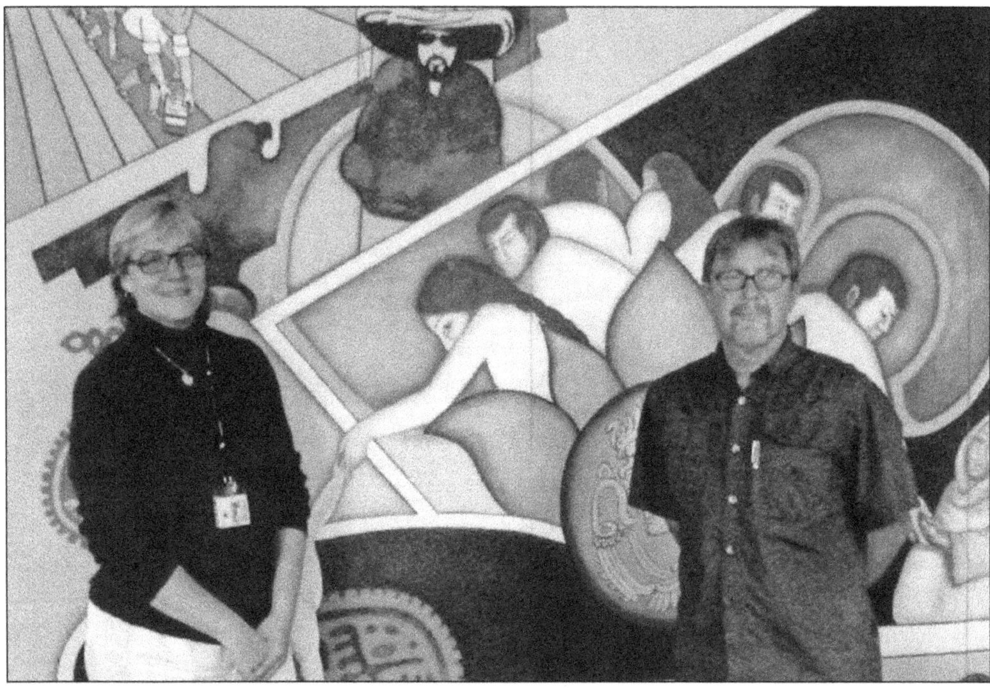

This mural is titled *Politec*. It is a multi-colored three-panel mural and is located at the Dr. Martin Luther King Jr. San José Public Library. It was painted in 1980 by Etta Mascarenas, Marta Delgado, Lupe Carranza, Rosalida Jaimes, Isabel Najera, and Manuele Paz. Standing in front of the mural are Kathryn Blackmer Reyes, the librarian and director, and Jeff Paul, the project manager of Librarians for Tomorrow. (Courtesy of the Chicano Collection, Cultural Heritage Center, Dr. Martin Luther King Jr. Library, San José State University.)

Six

Leadership and Organizations

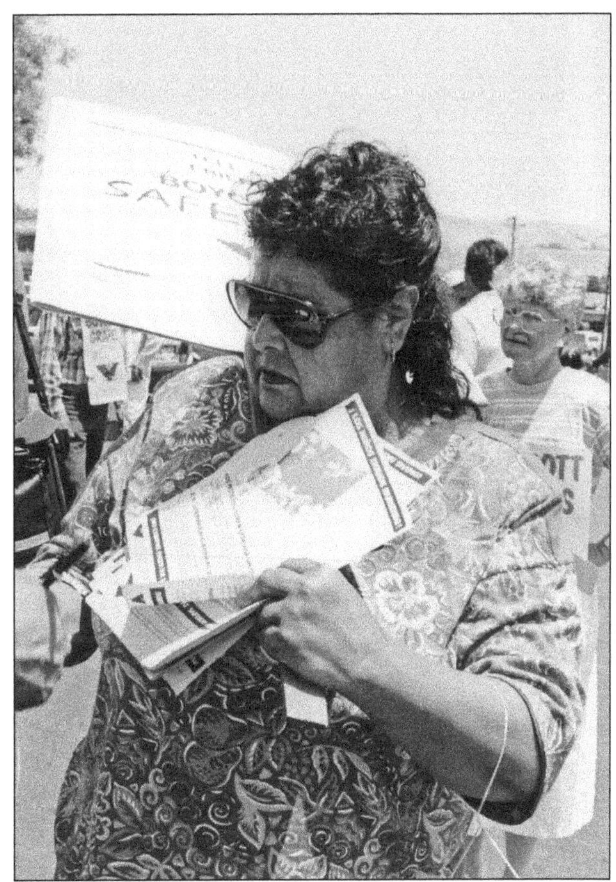

Ernestina Garcia is a lifelong activist fighting for social justice for Mexican Americans in San José and Milpitas, 10 miles east of San José. Garcia established Parents Pro-Estudiantil, an organization that challenged institutional racism in education. On one occasion, the organization challenged the Milpitas school system. When her children showed her their school yearbook, she noticed that for the Mexican high school students who missed picture day, the yearbook staff left empty boxes with the students' names. Inside each empty box was an image of a sleeping Mexican with a large sombrero and the caption, "Out Asleeping Again." Garcia and Parents Pro-Estudiantil recruited the support of several Mexican American organizations from San José to force the school district to eliminate the yearbook practice and to make other meaningful changes in its policies. (Photograph by Mary Andrade, courtesy of *La Oferta* newspaper.)

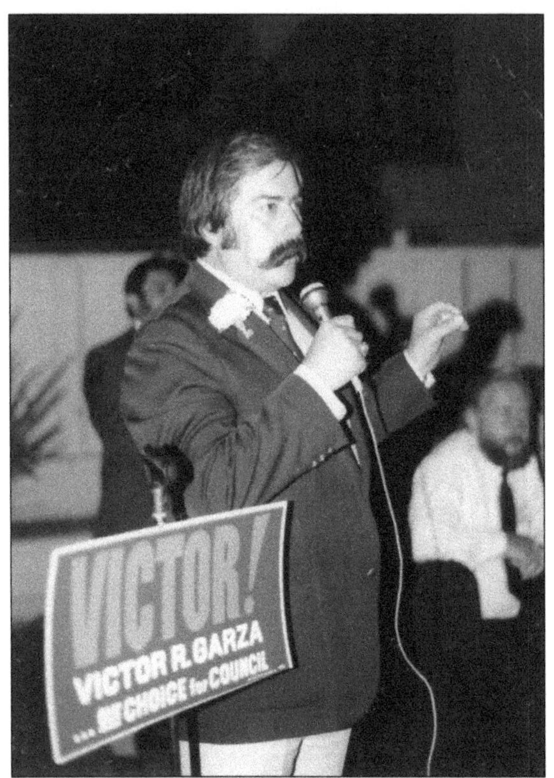

Originally from Eagle Pass, Texas, Victor Garza has served the San José community since the 1960s. Garza served two terms as the commander of the San José Chapter of the G.I. Forum, was a founding member of the Enlace Mentor Advisory Council at Evergreen Valley College, and was the founder and chair of La Raza Roundtable of Santa Clara County, an umbrella organization concerned with issues facing the Latino community. This photograph shows Victor as a candidate for the San José City Council. In 1998, Garza was invited by the White House to participate in Pres. Bill Clinton's Initiative on Race and Poverty. (Courtesy of Victor Garza.)

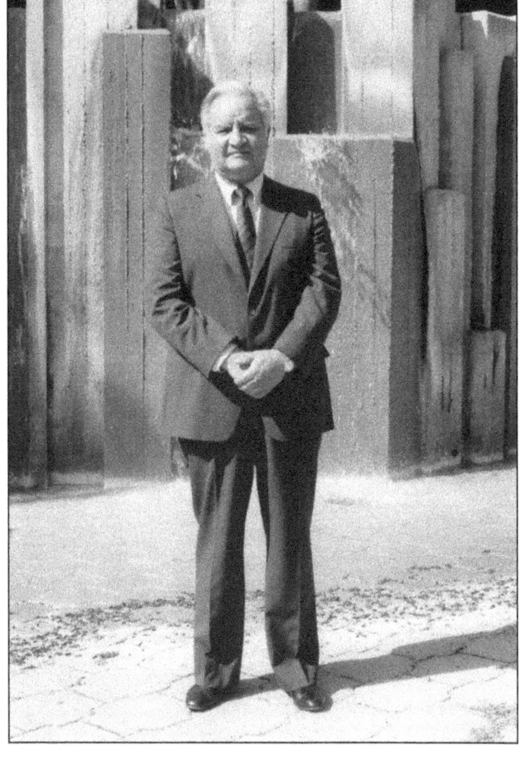

San José police officer Dan Campos spoke out against the barriers keeping ethnic minorities and women off of the police force. For example, for many years, candidates could not become San José police officers until they climbed over an 8-foot wall. Campos successfully fought to remove this policy, leading to an increase in diverse police officers. (Photograph by Mary Andrade, courtesy of *La Oferta* newspaper.)

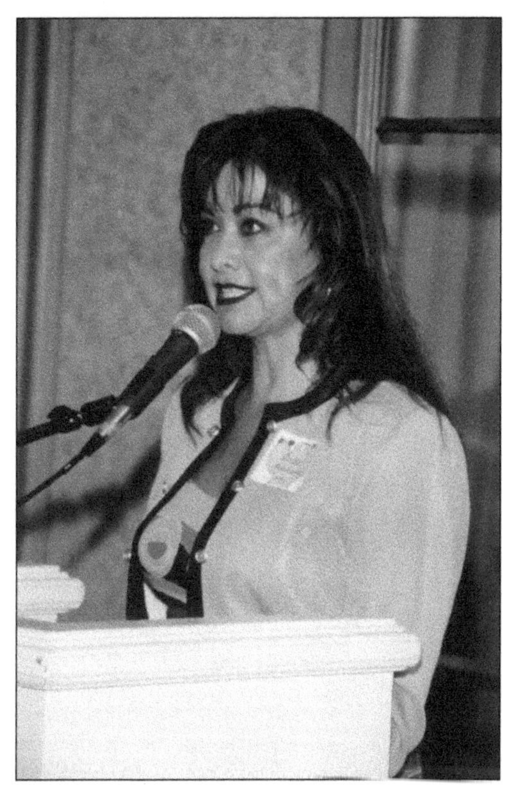

Rose Amador speaks at the Capital Club in honor of California lieutenant governor Cruz Bustamante's visit to San José in 1998. Amador has been the president and CEO of the Center for Training Careers, Inc., since 1982. Since her youth, she has been very active in the Mexican and Native American communities. She was inspired by the volunteerism of her father, Monico Amador. In 1967, he was first director of the Mexican American Opportunity Center and the founder of the Bay Area Construction Opportunity Program in San José. In the 1980s, he was regional director of Housing Urban Development in Santa Clara County. (Courtesy of Victor Garza.)

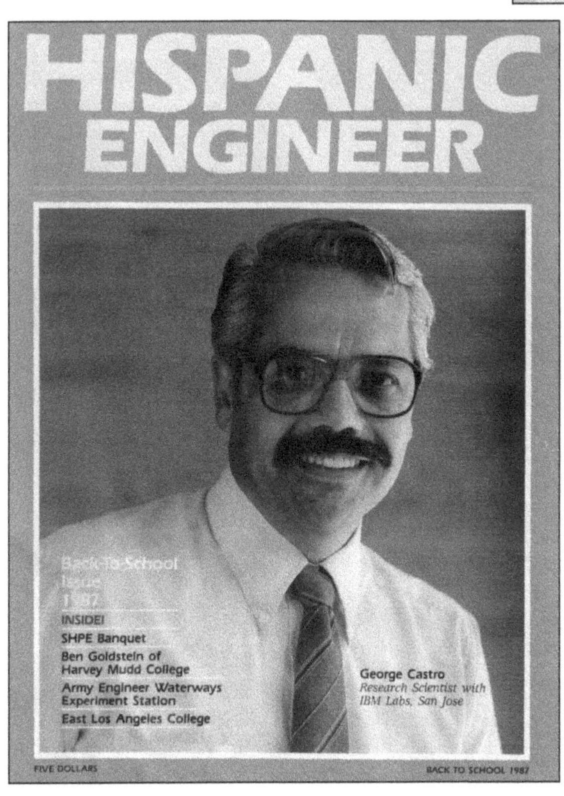

In 1987, *Hispanic Engineer* magazine recognized Dr. George Castro, who was employed at IBM as an outstanding research scientist. After a successful career at IBM, he joined the administration at San José State University as an associate dean of the College of Sciences until his retirement in 2004. In addition to his academic and professional accomplishments, he is dedicated to improving the education of Mexican youth, as demonstrated by his volunteering efforts at Joseph George Elementary School and the Enlace Program at Evergreen Valley College. A member of several distinguished professional societies and national committees, he also cofounded the Society for the Advancement of Chicanos and Native Americans in Science. In 1999, he received the Presidential Award for Excellence in Science Mathematics and Engineering Mentoring. (Courtesy of George Castro.)

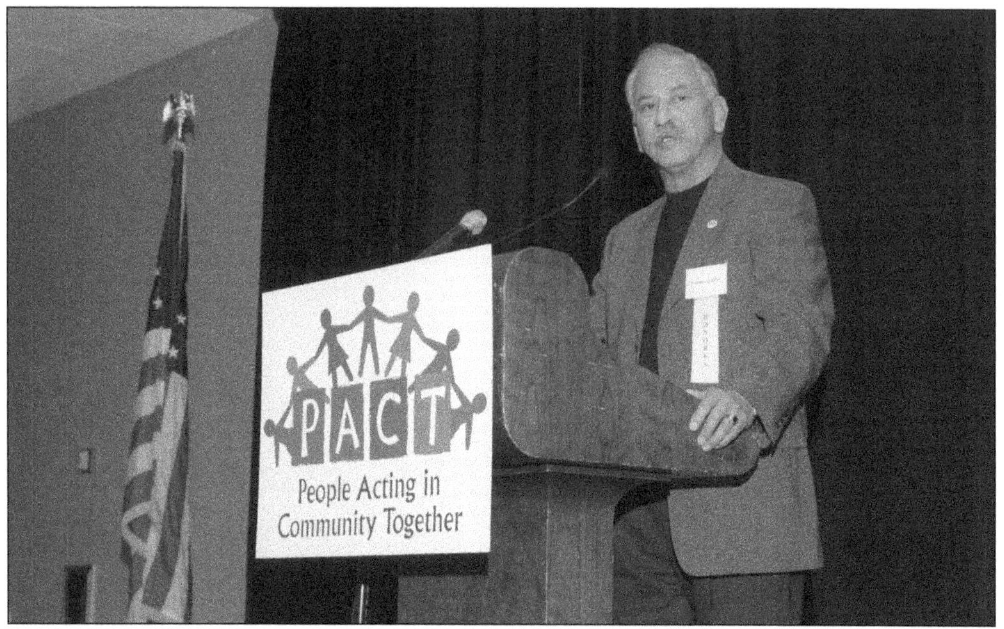

A professor at San José State University and a graduate of Stanford University, Dr. José Carrasco encouraged Mexican American students to succeed in their education. He promoted several projects, such as San José State University's Chicano Commencement and the Mexican American Studies Department, for which he was chair. As a community organizer, Dr. Carrasco helped establish PACT (People Acting in Community Together). (Courtesy of People Acting in Community Together.)

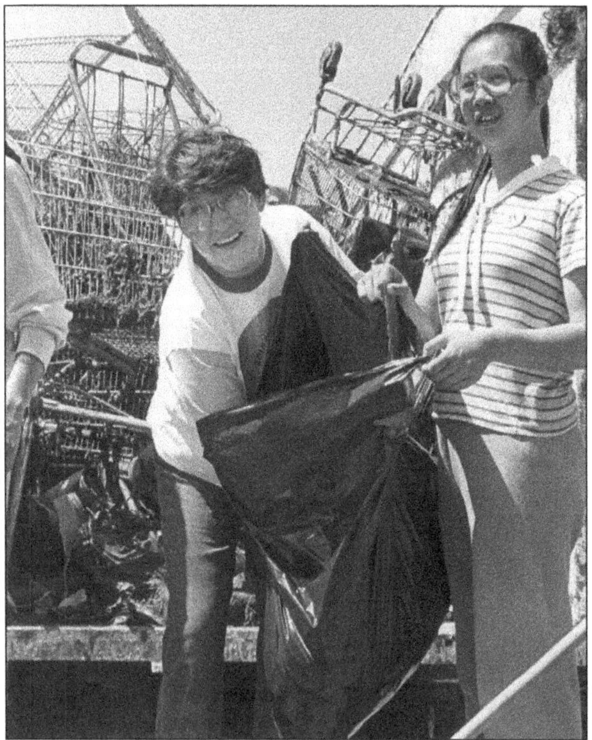

A graduate of San José High School and an East San José resident, Blanca Alvarado served three terms as a member of the Santa Clara County Board of Supervisors and was elected chairperson of the board in 1998. She was the first Mexican American woman in the nation to be elected as chairperson of a board of supervisors. In 1980, she was elected to the San José City Council, representing the newly created fifth district of East San José. That same decade, she began the initial steps toward creating a Mexican cultural center in San José to uplift Eastside San José's Mayfair district. With her husband, José, she helped organize the Mexican community alongside labor leader Cesar Chavez in the 1950s. (Photograph by Mary Andrade, courtesy of *La Oferta* newspaper.)

Jesus Valenzuela speaks into his microphone at the KSJO radio station in 1948. Valenzuela began his radio broadcasting career in 1937 in Santa Barbara, California. He moved to San José in 1948 and worked for KSJO. Valenzuela was nicknamed El Amo del Microfono, "the master of the microphone." His radio program was called *Hora Artistica*. (Courtesy of the Jesus Valenzuela family.)

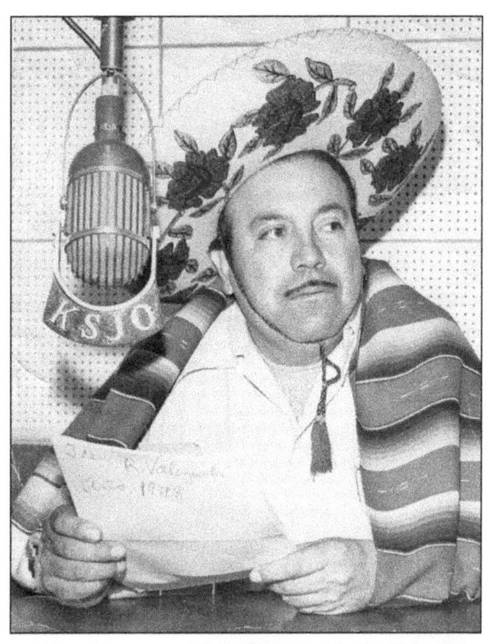

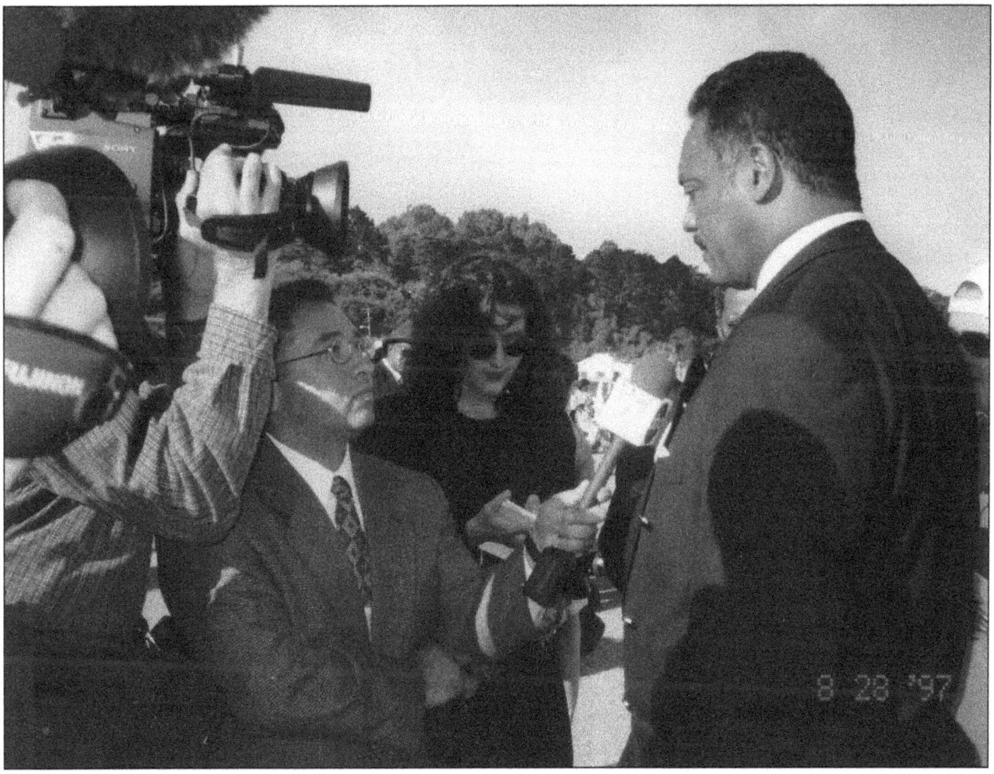

KNTV Channel 11 news reporter Damian Trujillo interviews Rev. Jesse Jackson in 1997. Trujillo is also the host and producer of *Comunidad del Valle*, a show that highlights the Latino community in San José. He has served as master of ceremonies for countless fund-raising events. A graduate of San José State University, he was raised in Greenfield, California, and worked with his family in the agricultural fields to help contribute to the family's income. (Courtesy of Damian Trujillo.)

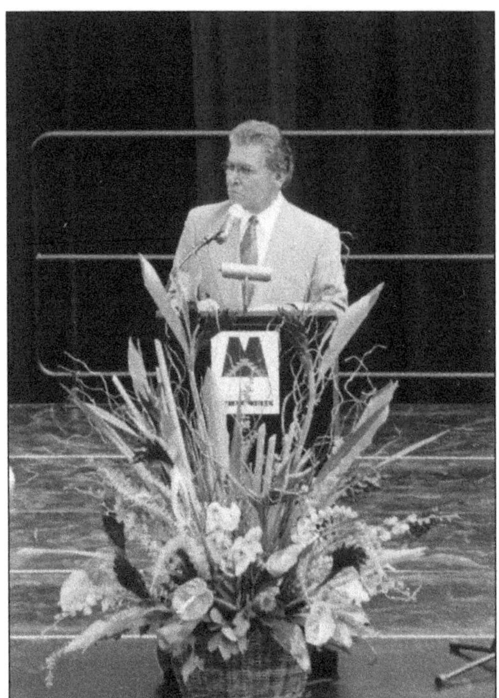

Master of Ceremonies Rigo Chacon speaks at the opening of the Mexican Heritage Plaza in 1999. The recipient of three Emmy awards, Chacon was a news reporter, starting in 1974, for ABC television Channel 7 for 29 years. In addition to news reporting, he saw a need to raise money for scholarships, so he created Abrazos and Books in 1990, providing scholarships for more than 400 students. Chacon attended San José High School and San José State University. In 2007, the National Association of Hispanic Journalists inducted him into its Hall of Fame. (Photograph by Mary Andrade, courtesy of *La Oferta* newspaper.)

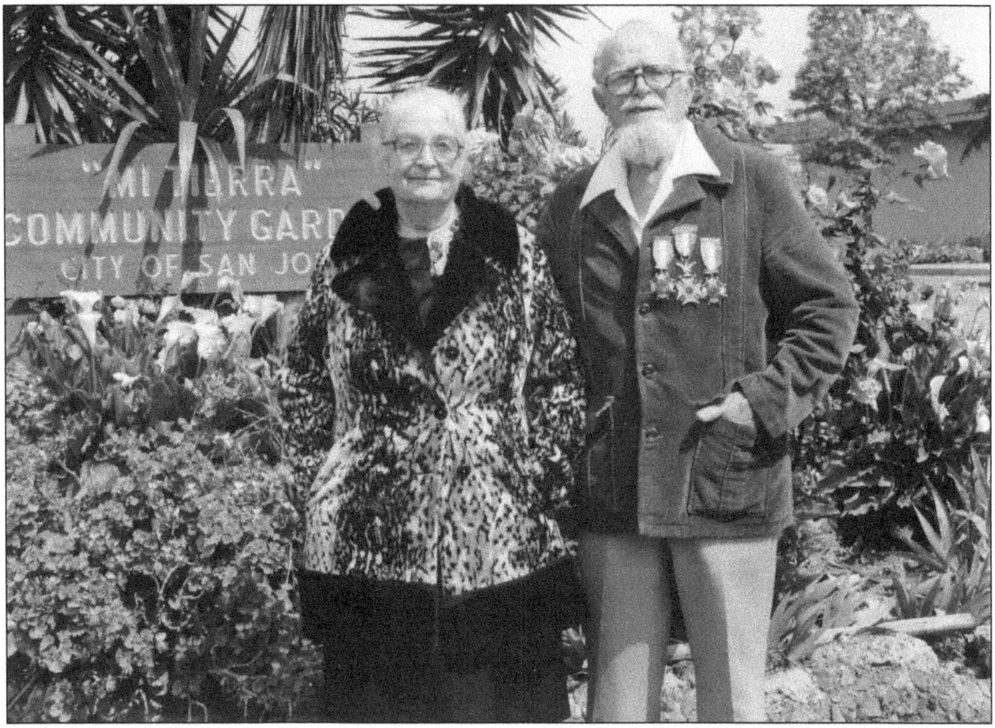

Both Artemio and Carmen Carranza were born in Mexico and grew up during the Mexican Revolution of 1910–1920. The Carranzas were instrumental in obtaining 4.3 acres from the City of San José's Parks and Recreation Department in 1975 for a community garden called Mi Tierra, "my land." (Photograph by Mary Andrade, courtesy of *La Oferta* newspaper.)

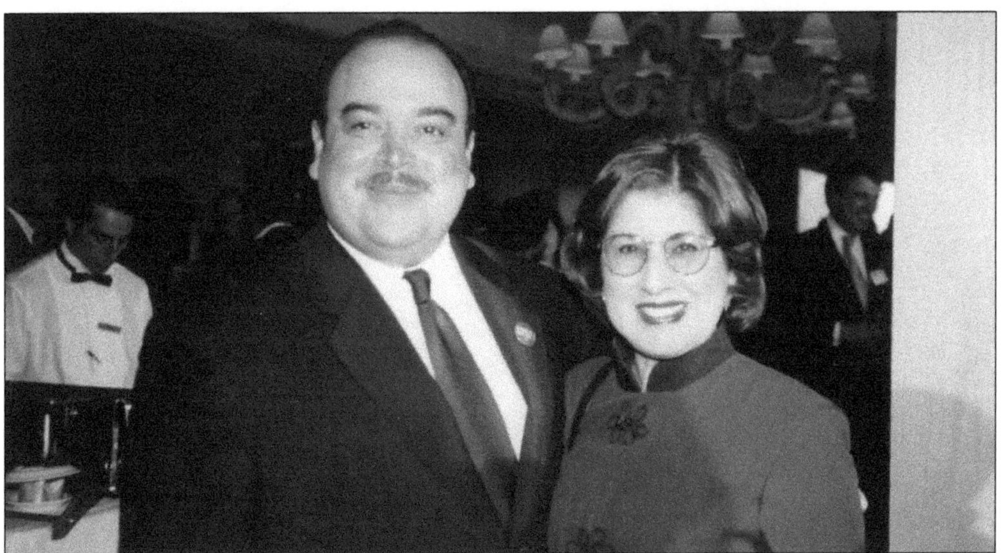

As a young single mother, Teresa Guerrero Daley (right) graduated from San José State University and Lincoln Law School. She served as the independent police auditor for the City of San José, where her work received national recognition. She is a former president of both La Raza Lawyers of Santa Clara County and La Raza Lawyers of San Mateo County. In 2007, she was chairperson of the Hispanic Foundation of Silicon Valley board. She became a superior court judge in Santa Clara County in 2004. (Courtesy of Victor Garza.)

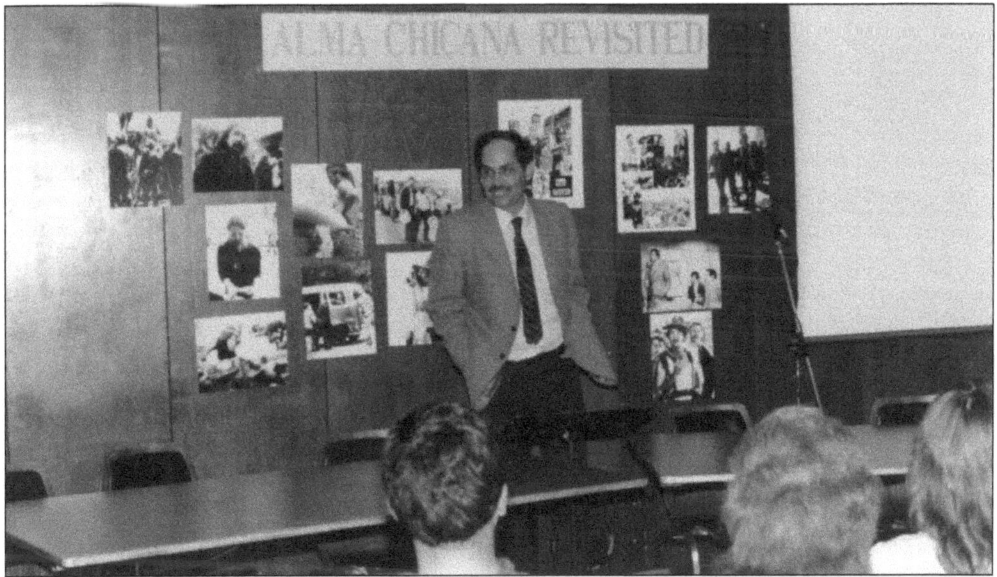

In this image, Dr. Mauro Chavez speaks to an audience at San José State University about Alma Chicana, an oral history project begun at San José State University in the late 1980s. Along with Dr. José Carrasco and Jeff Paul, he was a co-principal investigator of Alma Chicana. A community activist and an educational reformer, he cofounded the Enlace Program of Evergreen Valley College. In 2006, the Student Center at Evergreen Valley College was named after Dr. Chavez to recognize his contributions to the campus and the San José community. (Courtesy of the Chicano Collection, Cultural Heritage Center, Dr. Martin Luther King Jr. Library, San José State University.)

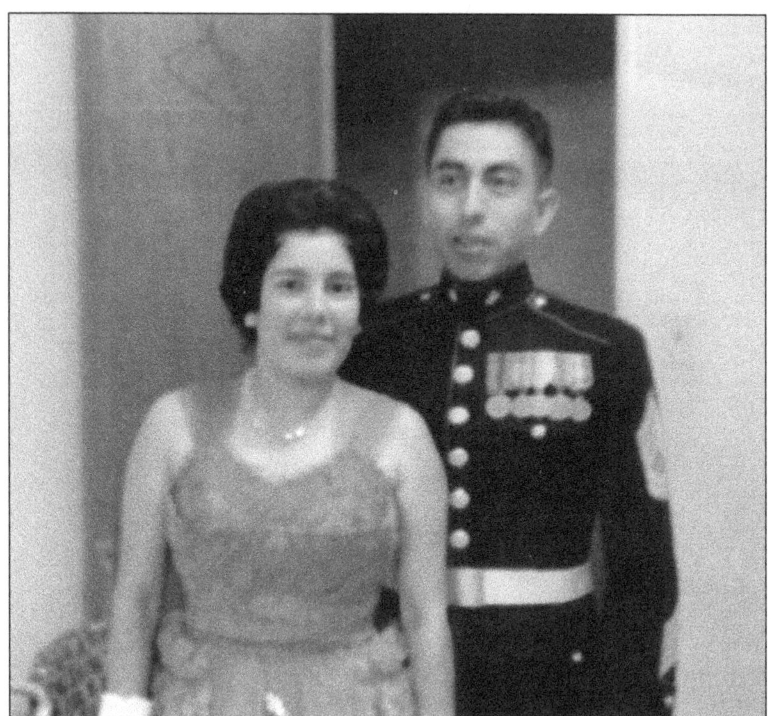

Serving in the marines during World War II and in the Vietnam War, Rafael Jimenez poses in 1962 with his wife, Dolores. Rafael worked for four years for the State of California and 15 years for the City of San José. During his tenure, he was the director of the Santa Clara County Housing Authority and a member of the Mexican Chamber of Commerce. (Courtesy of Rafael Jimenez.)

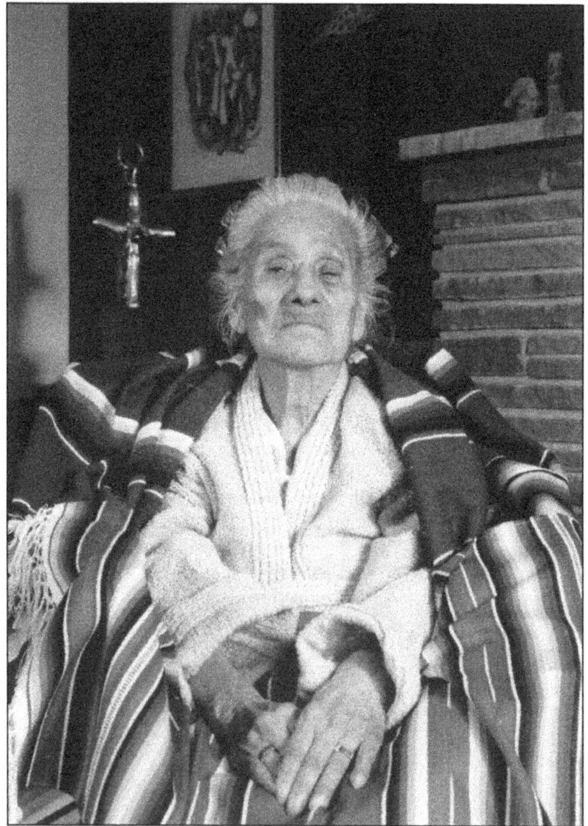

Born in Mexico in 1902, Jerónima Marquez became a soldier during the Mexican Revolution. She displayed her leadership skills by serving in a high-ranking position in General Pancho Villa's army. By 1917, she left Mexico for the United States. She settled in San José and had four children. (Photograph by Mary Andrade, courtesy of *La Oferta* newspaper.)

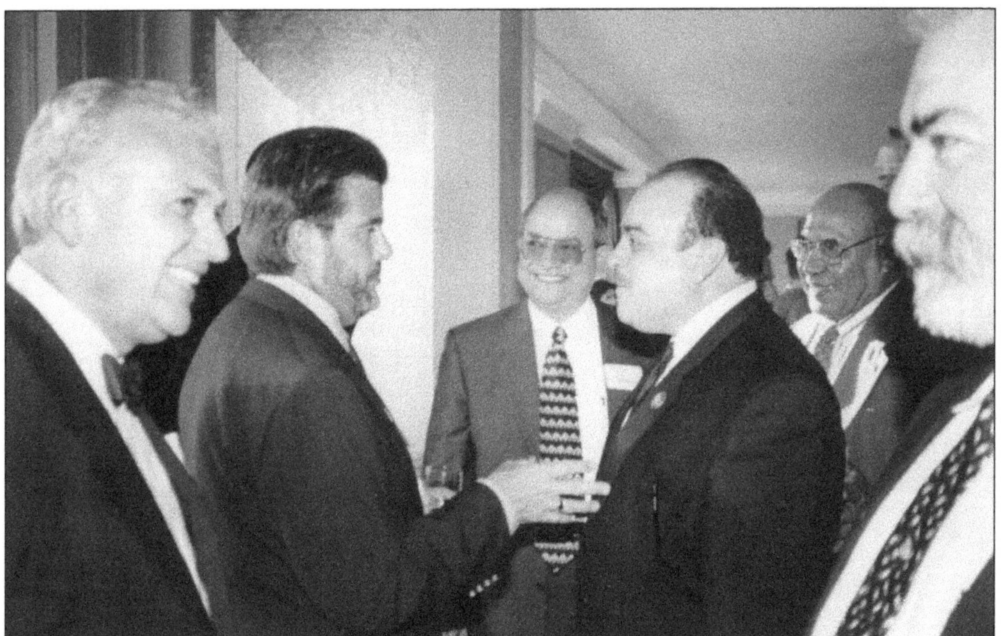

In a 1998 who's who photograph, speaking to California lieutenant governor Cruz Bustamante are community leaders, from left to right, attorney Fernando Zazueta; president of San José State University, Bob Koret; public defender of Santa Clara County, José Villarreal (back); Cruz Bustamante; publisher of *El Observador* newspaper, Hilbert Morales (back); and political activist Victor Garza (far right). (Courtesy of Victor Garza.)

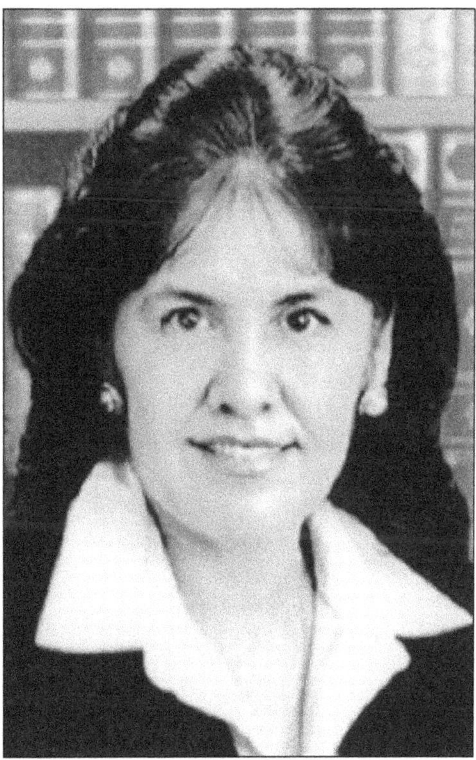

Jessie Serna was frustrated with the high number of minorities and the poor in the criminal justice system. This led her to earn a law degree. She was the lead attorney in the California Supreme Court case of *Rudy Ochoa v. County of Santa Clara* for the medical neglect of a 13-year-old Mexican American boy who died at juvenile hall despite his family's plea for medical attention. She is a member and former president of the Santa Clara County Trial Lawyers Association and is one of the founding members of the La Raza Lawyers of Santa Clara County. (Courtesy of Jessie Serna.)

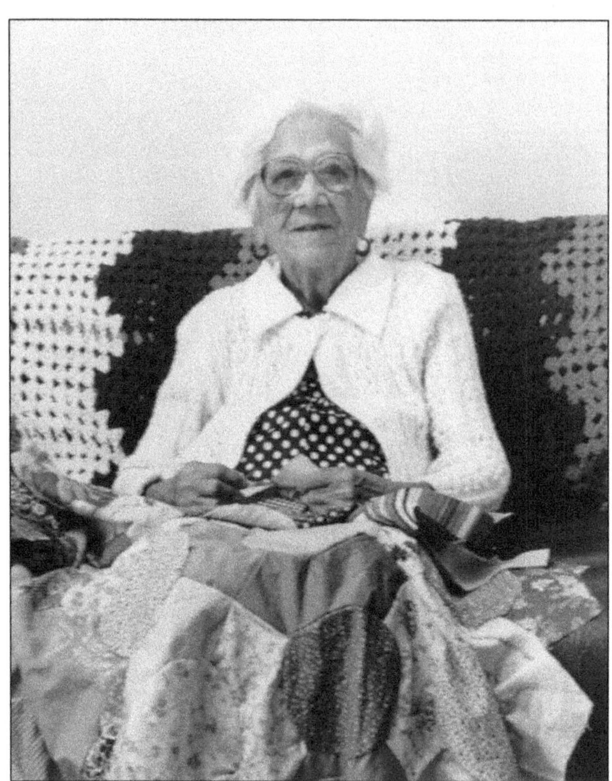

Juana Chavez, mother of labor leader and humanitarian Cesar Chavez, moved to East San José in 1939 after working in the fields with her family in Yuma, Arizona. In her 70s, she marched to Sacramento with her son and striking Mexican farm workers. The home where she raised her family was designated as a San José Historical Landmark in 2007, one of few landmarks in Eastside San José. (Photograph by Mary Andrade, courtesy of *La Oferta* newspaper.)

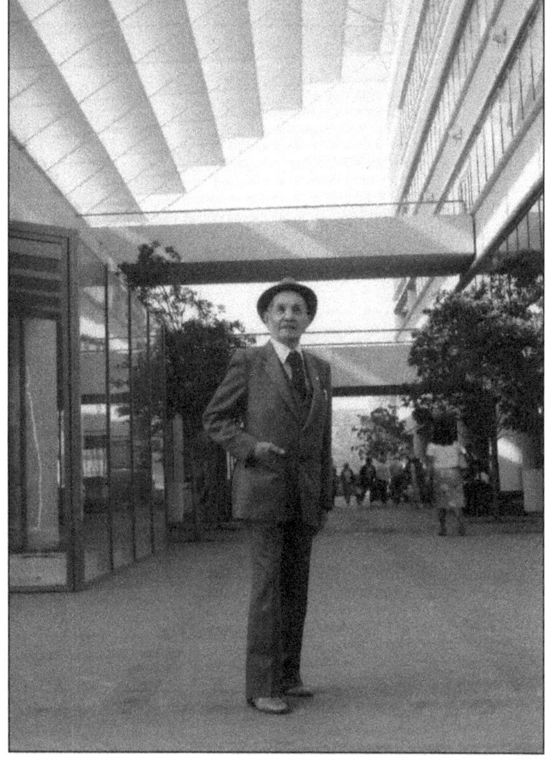

Born in Mexico during the Mexican Revolution, Joe Gaxiola was a cousin to Mexican president Francisco Madero. Gaxiola was the president of the Community Service Organization (CSO) in San José. In that capacity, he helped Mexicans and Mexican Americans become active in their community. (Photograph by Mary Andrade, courtesy of *La Oferta* newspaper.)

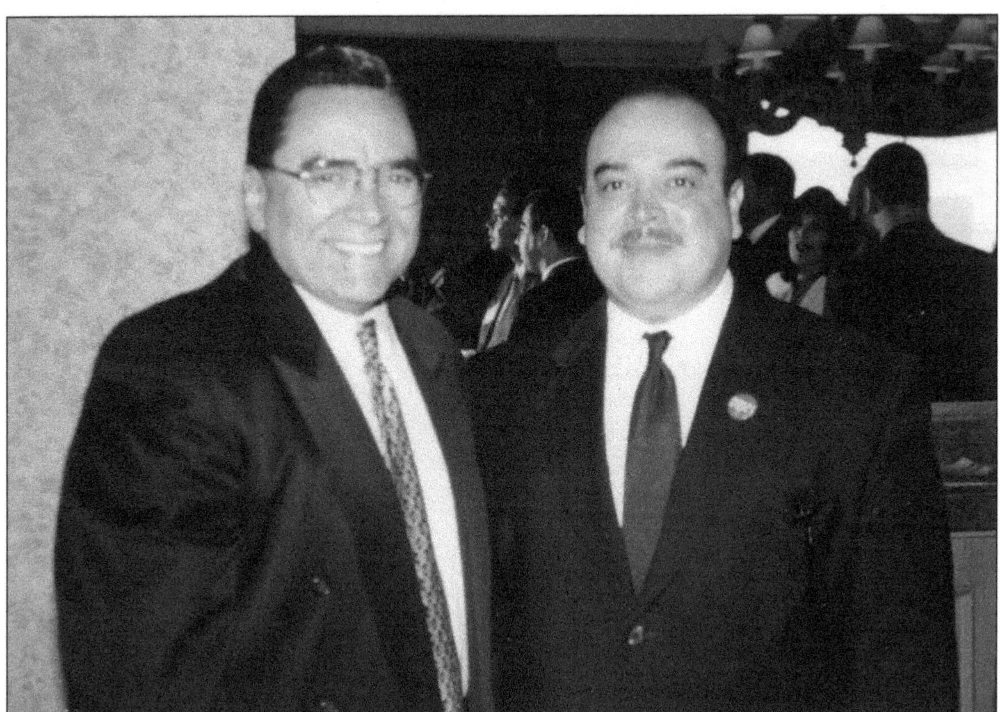

As the first Mexican American mayor of San José since 1850, Ron Gonzales (left) poses for a photograph with California lieutenant governor Cruz Bustamante in 1998. Ron served as mayor for two terms from 1998 to 2006. Dedicated to improving schools, he initiated programs to attract teachers to San José by providing a teacher-homebuyer program and programs to provide role models for youth. (Courtesy of Victor Garza.)

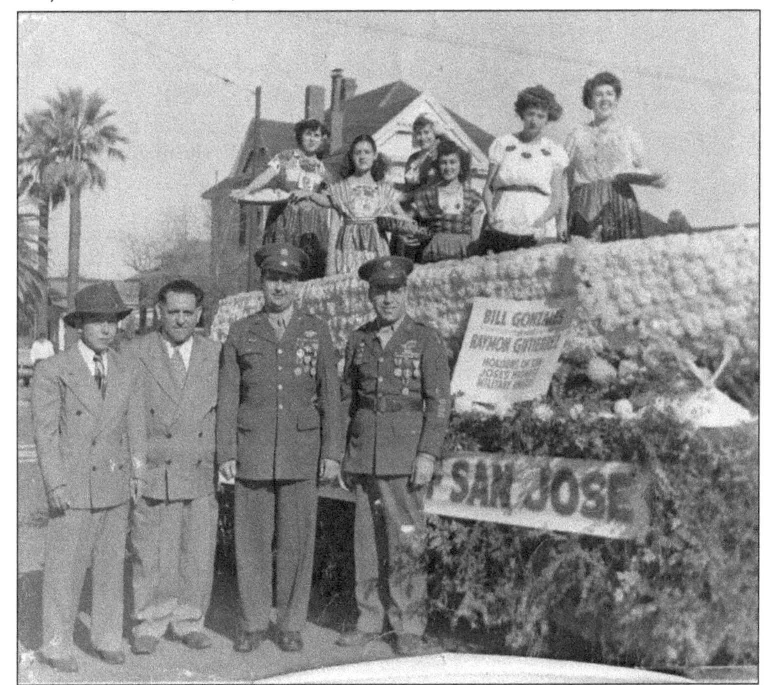

Bill Gonzales (far right) and Raymon Gutierrez (second from right) are honored at the Cinco de Mayo festivities as holders of San José's highest military awards in the 1950s. Bill served valiantly in the U.S. Air Corps in World War II. He was a prisoner of war in the Pacific. Impressively, he earned 14 medals for his military service. (Courtesy of the Bill Gonzales family.)

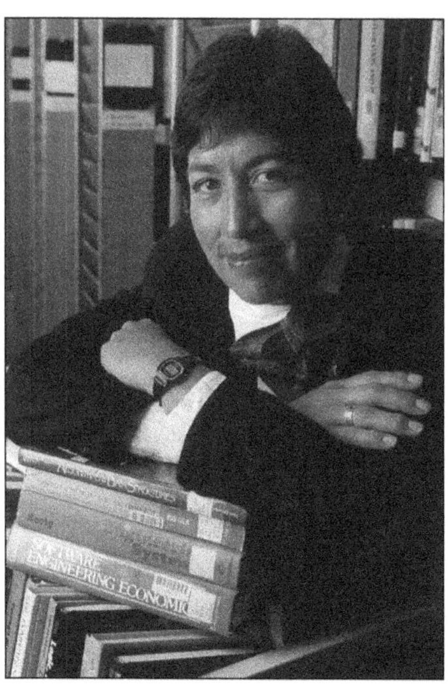

Maria Magaña grew up in Visalia, California. She earned her college degrees from the University of California, Los Angeles and Berkeley in computer science. By 1991, she was a senior engineering department manager at IBM in San José. She is one of few female Mexican scientists and engineers. (Courtesy of George Castro.)

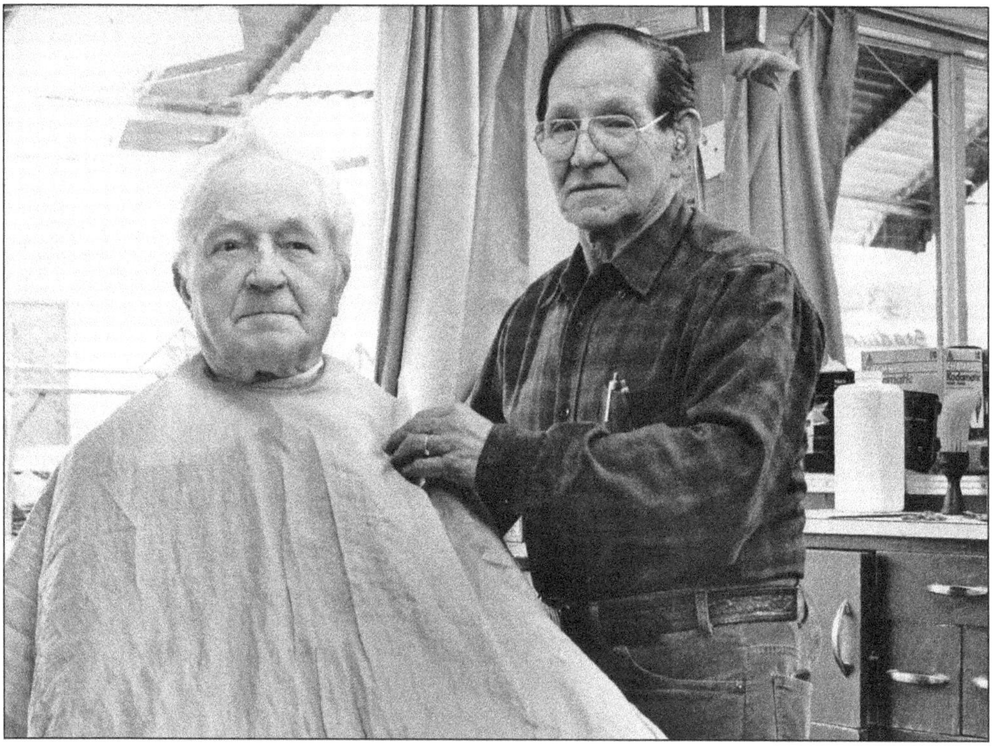

John Torres Sr. was known not only for his mastery as a barber but also for his sage advice. He often kept his Eastside San José shop open until well past midnight on Saturdays so that canning and packing workers coming from the end of a week's work could have their hair cut. He was president of the CSO in San José in the early 1960s. (Photograph by Mary Andrade, courtesy of *La Oferta* newspaper.)

Born to blind parents, Jim Plunkett (seated) attended James Lick High School in Eastside San José. He attended Stanford University and was the quarterback for the football team, winning the Heisman Trophy in 1970. He played professional football for the San Francisco 49ers and Oakland Raiders. In 1981, as the quarterback, he led the Raiders to victory in Super Bowl XV and received the Most Valuable Player Award, making him the first Mexican American to earn the award. This image includes Plunkett along with Victor and Leticia Garza. (Courtesy of Victor Garza.)

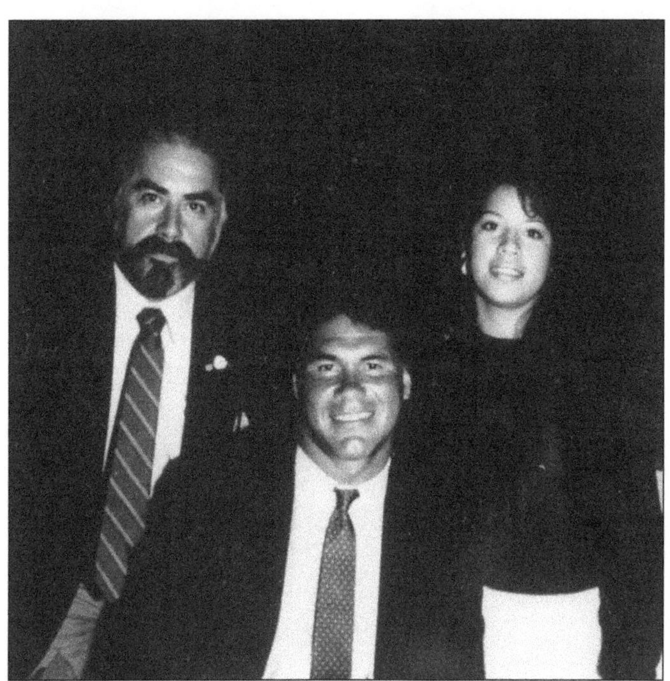

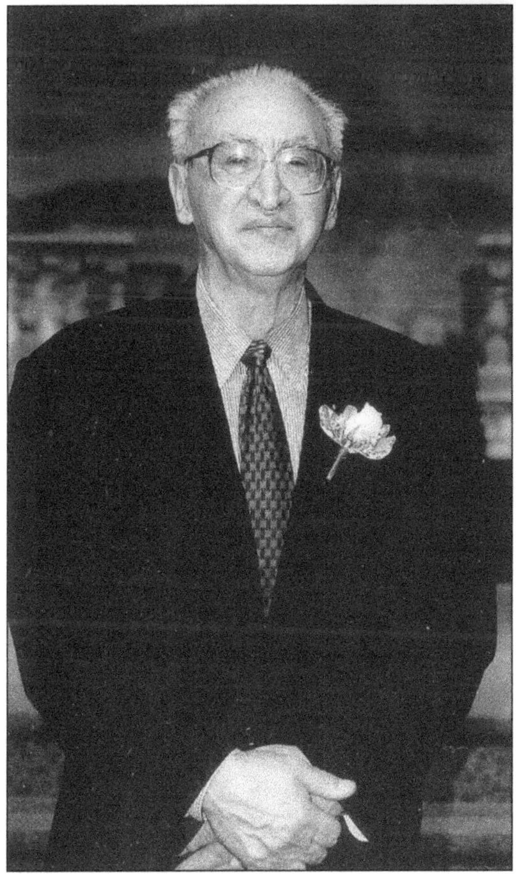

In the 1950s, J. Hector Moreno Sr. was the first Mexican American to graduate from Santa Clara University Law School. He was one of the first Spanish-speaking attorneys in San José and Santa Clara County. He was a member of San José's G.I. Forum chapter and a founder of Mexican American Political Association (MAPA). As president of the CSO chapter in San José, he worked to register Mexican American voters. (Courtesy of the J. Hector Moreno family.)

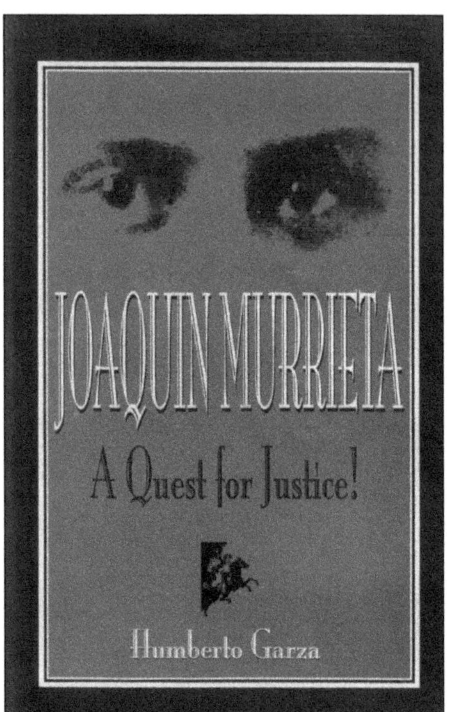

Educator, community organizer, and author Humberto Garza wrote *Joaquin Murrieta: a Quest for Justice*, a revealing account of Joaquin Murrieta, a Mexican gold prospector in the California Gold Rush who was accused of stealing a mule and was pursued statewide by California law enforcement authorities. Many Mexicans viewed him as a victim of racism and discrimination. In addition to this book, Humberto has produced several other books on Mexicans and Mexican Americans. (Courtesy of Humberto Garza.)

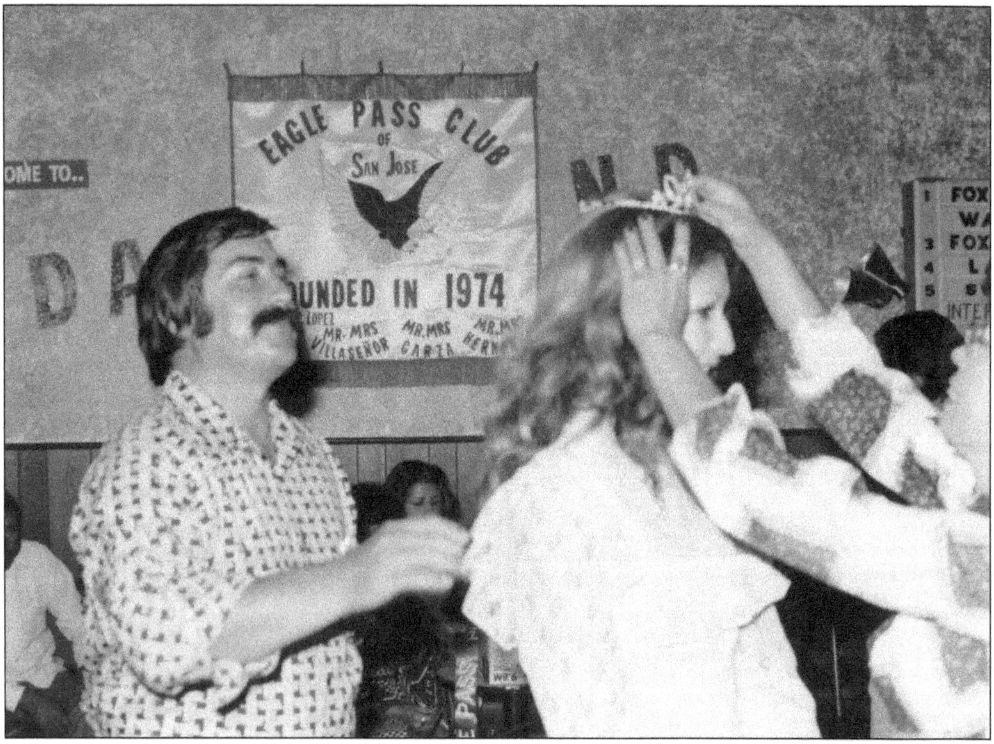

One of the founders of the Eagle Pass (Texas) Club of San José in 1974, Victor Garza looks on at the crowning of the Eagle Pass princess. Mexicans in San José take pride in their hometowns and continue their loyalty by establishing clubs and organizations. (Courtesy of Victor Garza.)

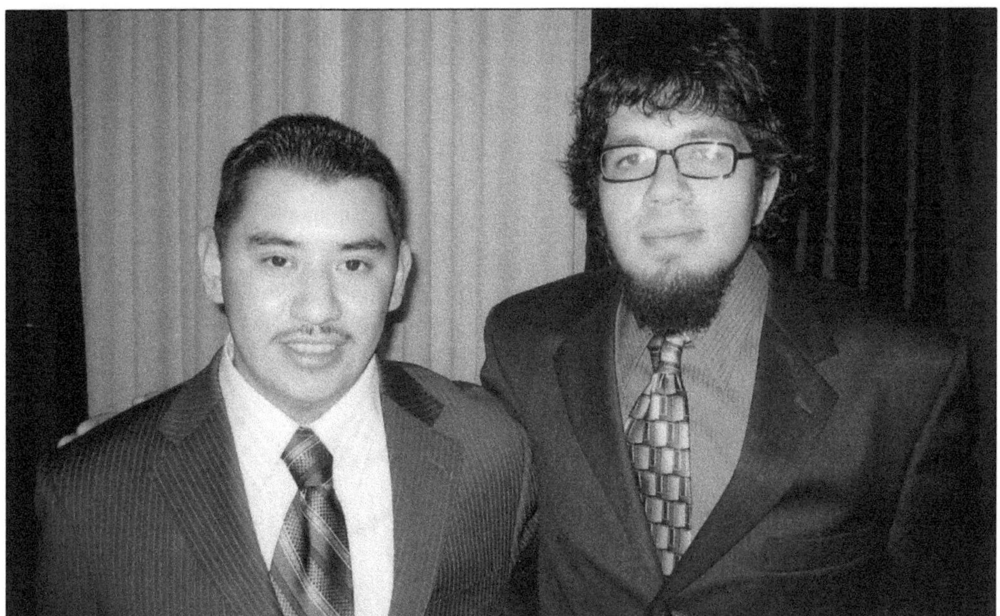

In 1974, John Parraz, Vicente Calderon, Richard Reyes, John Aleman, and Mariano Flores founded the Latino Peace Officers Association (LPOA), now a national organization. They created an association dedicated to seeking change in the law enforcement and policy administration process in the community. The LPOA provides programs for youth and seniors. In this photograph, Robert Corpus (left) and Emmanuel Mendoza, students of the Enlace Program of Evergreen Valley College, receive LPOA scholarships at the annual scholarship banquet. (Courtesy of Richard Regua.)

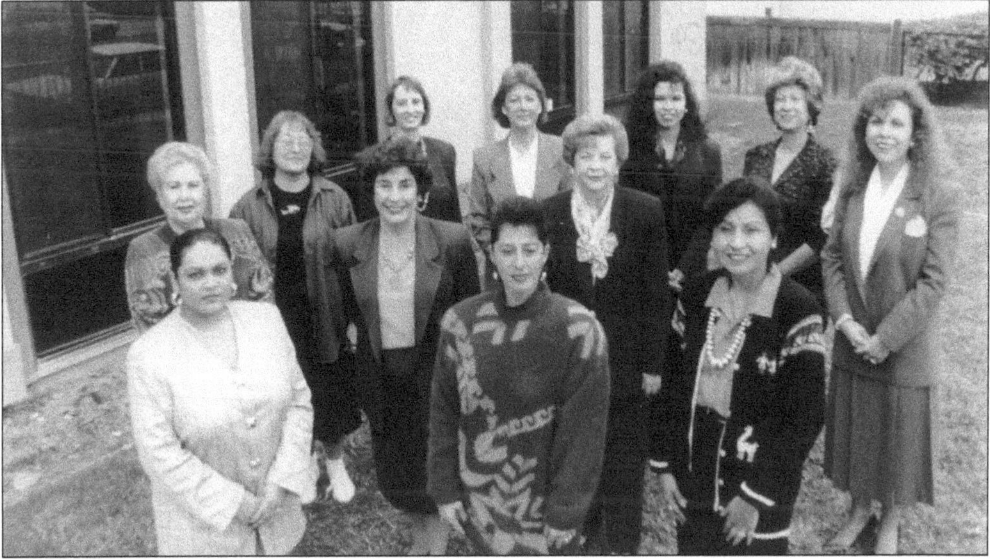

The Hispanic Women's Council of Northern California, founded in 1991, worked to improve the status of Hispanic women through education, career, and leadership development activities in Northern California. From left to right are (first row) Olga Enciso Smith, Luz Alba Agudelo, and unidentified; (second row, center) Carmen Johnson and unidentified; (third row) Lucy Rodriguez, Yolanda Reynolds, Ivonne Montes de Oca, Elisa Goti, Gloria Flores, Mary Andrade, and Sandra Escobar. (Courtesy of *La Oferta* newspaper.)

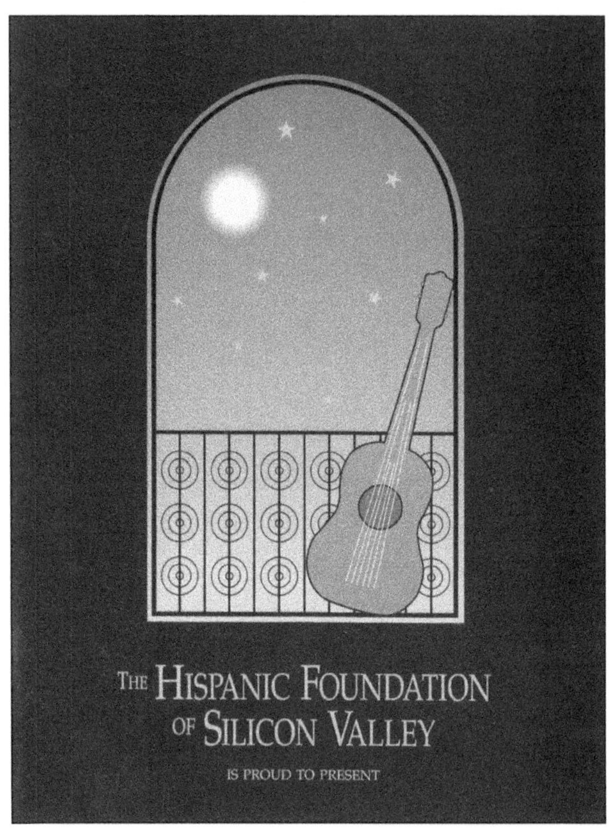

The Hispanic Foundation of Silicon Valley grew out of the Hispanic Charity Ball (HCB). The HCB was first inaugurated in 1990. It helped to raise awareness about issues affecting the Hispanic community and to promote volunteerism, celebrate philanthropic leaders, and provide cash grants to support nonprofit organizations serving the Hispanic community. This image is the cover of the program for the 11th Annual Hispanic Charity Ball. (Courtesy of Vickie Romero.)

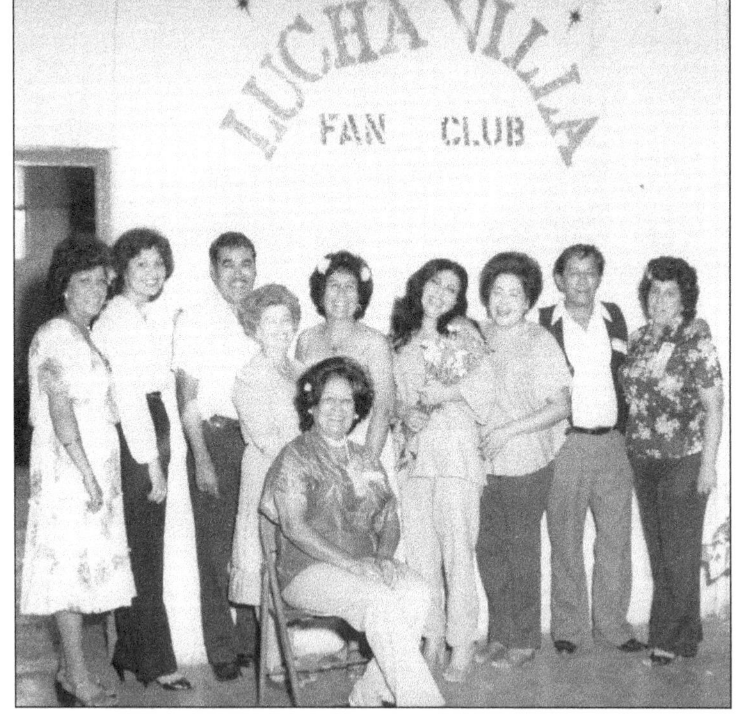

In the late 1960s, Richard Diaz established a fan club for Mexican actress and singer Lucha Villa. Annually, the volunteers of the fan club cooked and donated food and soft drinks for the Mexican performers playing at the Santa Clara County fairgrounds on the Cinco de Mayo and September 16 holidays. (Photograph by Richard Diaz, courtesy of El Fotografo del Estrellas.)

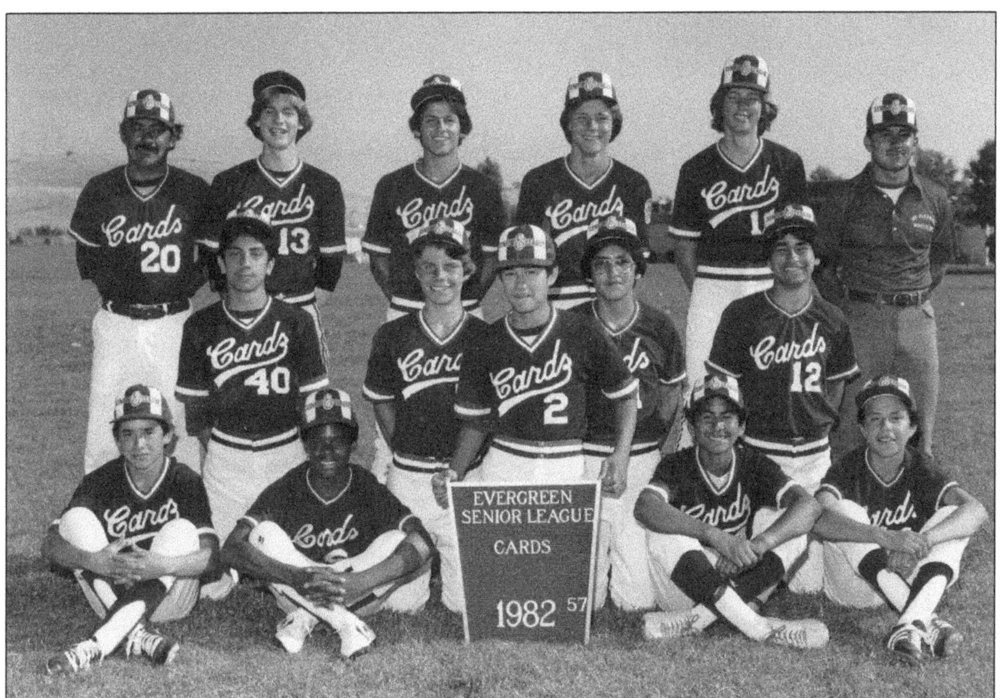

Ken Carrasco (second row, second from right) and the Cards baseball team gather for a photograph in 1982. In addition to being a member of the Evergreen Senior League, Ken attended and graduated from Silver Creek High School. (Courtesy of Connie Carrasco.)

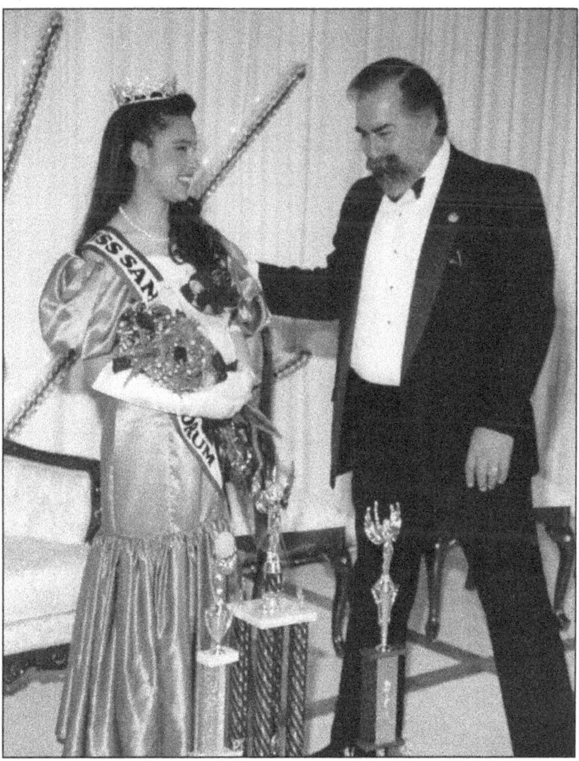
Each year, the G.I. Forum chapter of San José offered quality programs, including a scholarship foundation, the Vida Nueva alcohol recovery program, and the Flores Mexicana, a queen pageant. In 1990, Monica Gomez was selected as Miss San José, the chapter queen. Monica, a graduate of Notre Dame High School, later competed and won Miss California State G.I. Forum and Miss National G.I. Forum. (Courtesy of Victor Garza.)

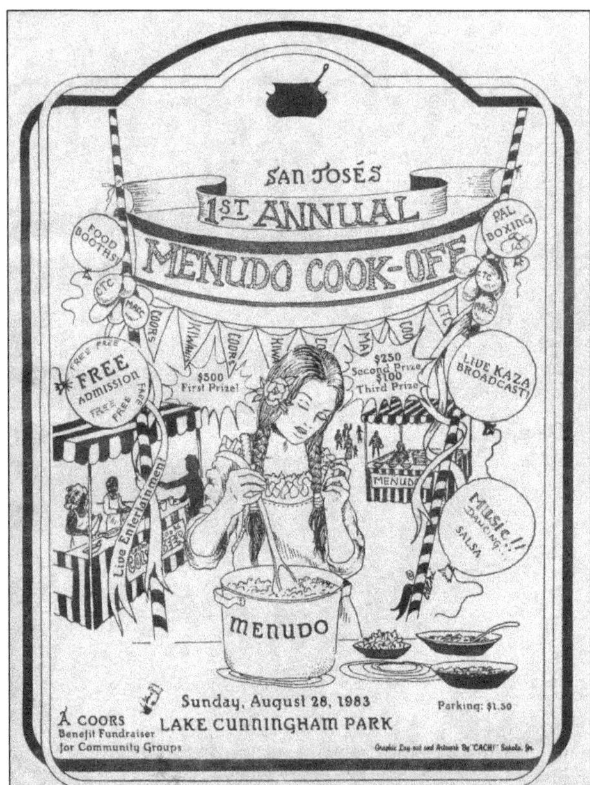

With funding from donors, the Menudo Cook-Off committee established the 1st Annual Menudo Cook-Off in 1983 at Lake Cunningham Park. Admission was free with prizes awarded for the best *menudo*, a tripe and hominy stew. The Menudo Cook-Off provided live entertainment, food booths, dancing, and other family-centered activities. (Graphics by Cachi Sabala Jr., courtesy of Victor Garza.)

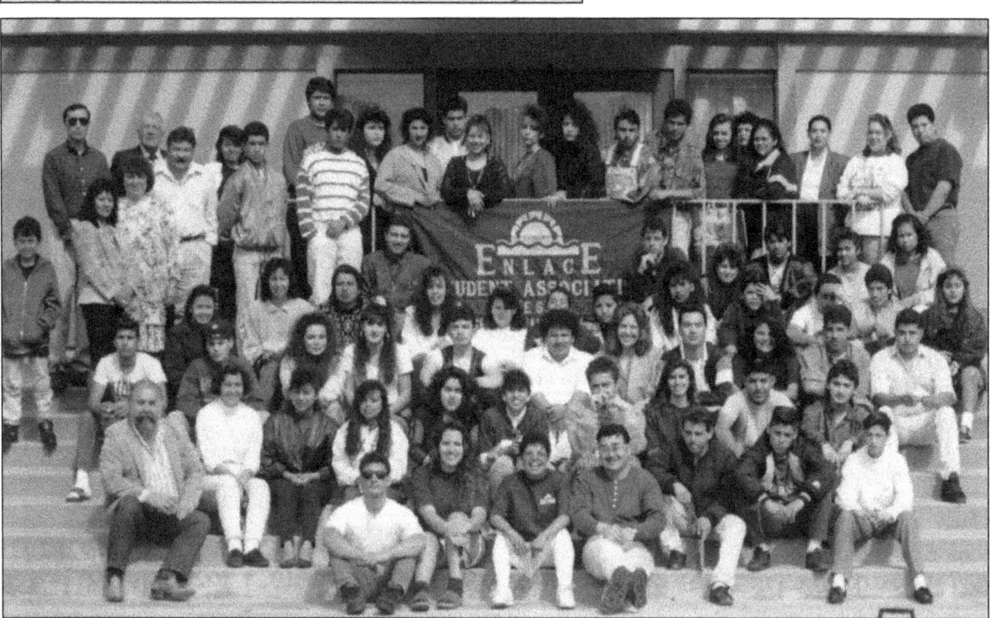

This late-1980s group photograph displays the membership of the Enlace Student Association of Evergreen Valley College. The Enlace program, with the mission of increasing the graduation and transfer rates of Latina/o students, was started by Evergreen Valley College instructors Dr. Mauro Chavez, Angelo Atondo, and Richard Regua and community members Dr. George Castro and Victor Garza. (Courtesy of the Enlace Student Association, Evergreen Valley College.)

Seven

Religion and Family

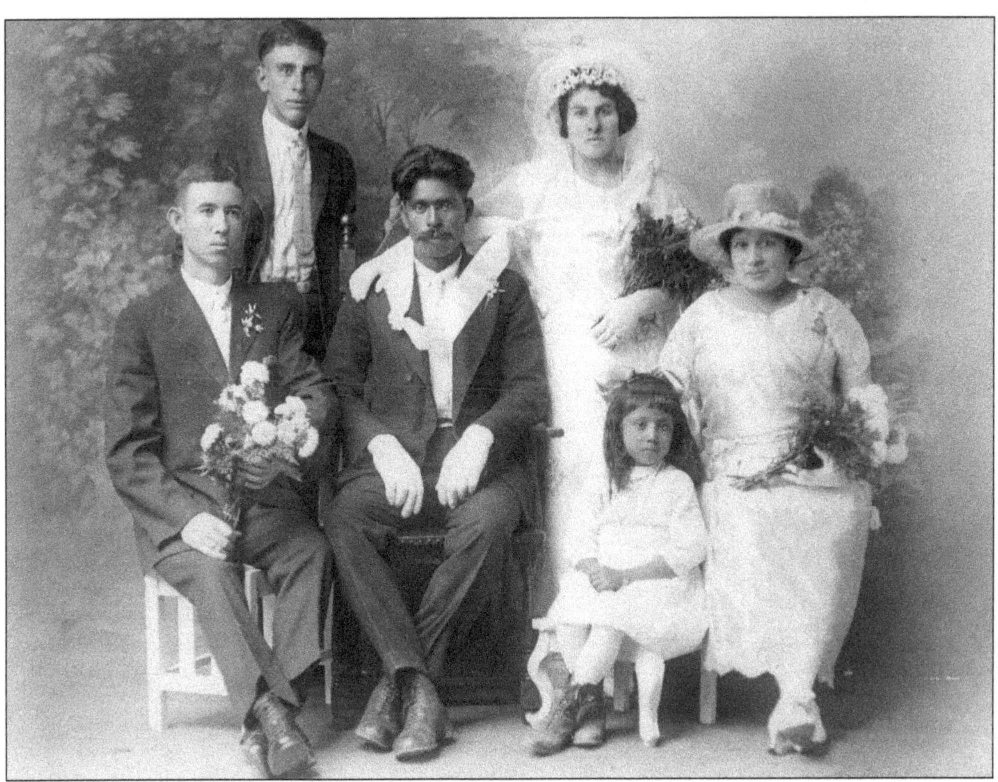

On October 5, 1923, Pedro Lara (seated, center) married Guadalupe Rodriguez (arm over groom) in Bakersfield, California. Pedro, born in Mexico in 1884, migrated to the United States during the Mexican Revolution. He was a veteran of World War I. Shortly after their wedding, the bridal couple moved to Tenth and Santa Ana Streets in San José and started a family. Pedro worked as a street-paver, and his wife, Guadalupe, became a homemaker. (Courtesy of the Lara Luna family.)

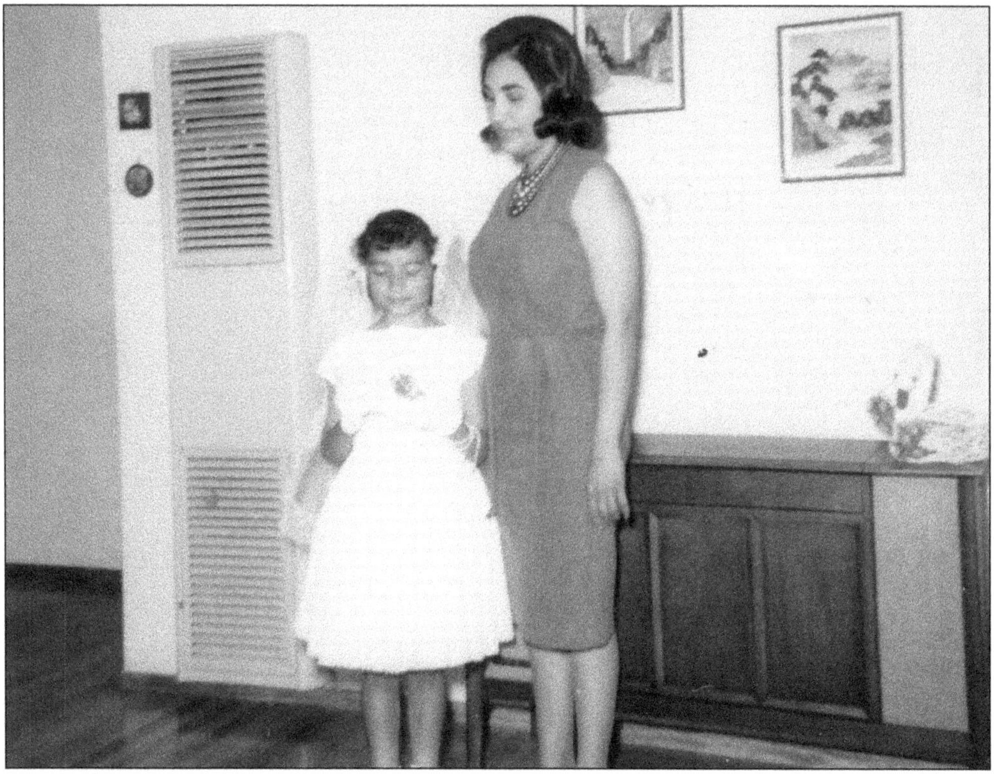

Elaine Ortiz poses in 1963 with her mother, Jennie Ortiz, at their home on McKee and White Roads for her first communion at St. John Vianney Church. (Courtesy of Elaine Ortiz-Kristich.)

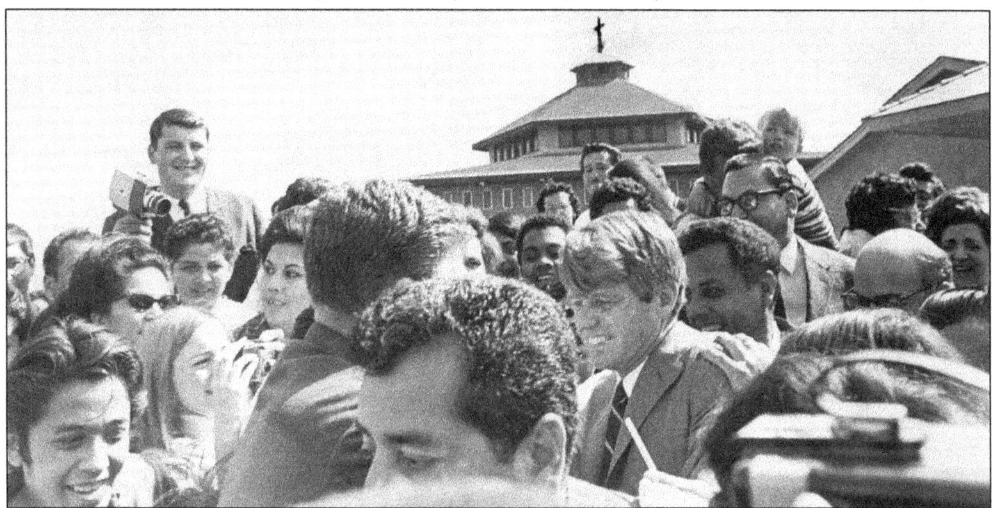

U.S. senator Robert F. Kennedy (center, smiling) visited Our Lady of Guadalupe Church in March 1968. That same month, Kennedy traveled to Delano to break bread with San José's homegrown leader Cesar Chavez, marking the end of Chavez's 25-day fast against the unfair labor practices of grape growers. Kennedy was assassinated the same year on June 6 in Los Angeles after earning the nomination as the California Democratic presidential candidate. (*San José Mercury News* photographer, courtesy of Mercury News Archives, *San José Mercury News*, © 2009. All rights reserved.)

Church attendees T. Pagan (left) and Caridad Caballero (right) with Caridad's grandson, George Herrera, pose for a quick photograph after a Pentecostal church service in 1952. The church was located in downtown San José on Race Street. A majority of Mexicans identify themselves as Catholic; however, a significant number of Mexicans follow other denominations. (Courtesy of Eppie Regua.)

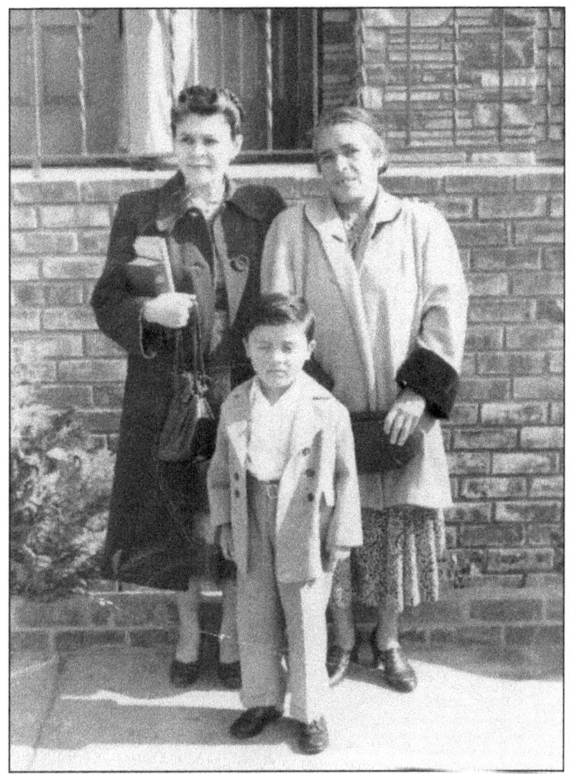

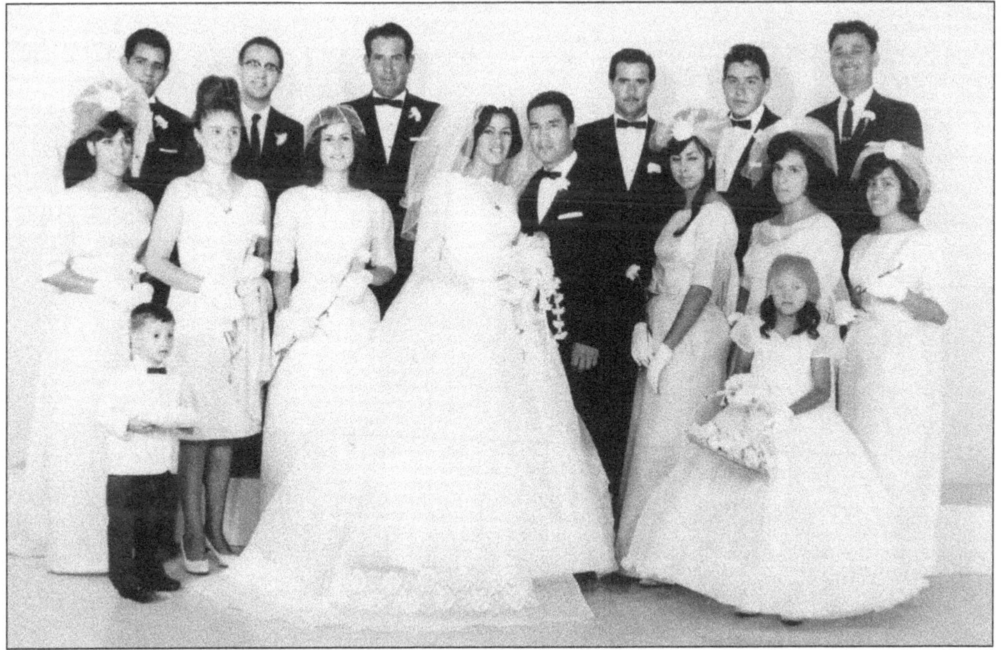

Maria Isabel Ortiz and Richard Gutierrez married in July 1967. The wedding was at Holy Family Church, located near the old St. Joseph's school off of West San Carlos Street. The area has since been redeveloped. Holy Family Church was rebuilt in a new location on the west side of San José. (Courtesy of Carmen Ortiz Mendez.)

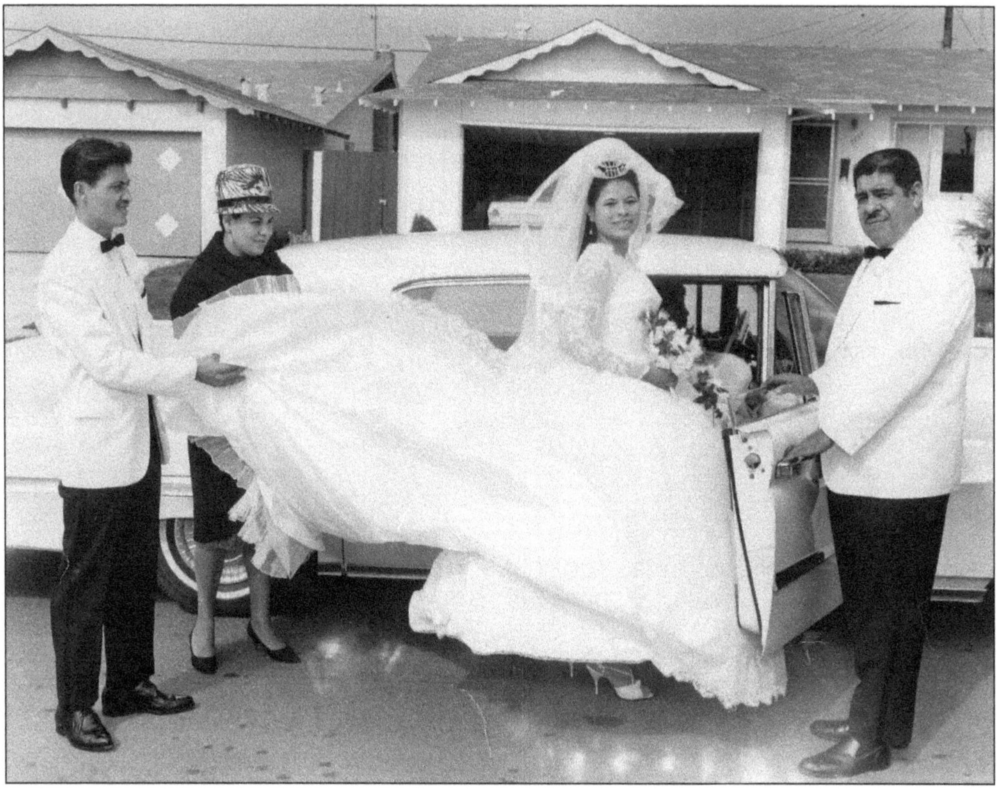

In the 1960s, Ernest Lara (far left) married Gloria ? in San José. Holding the car door open for the bride is Silvestre Ignacio. Ernest's sister, Katie, is helping the bride with her dress. (Photograph by Richard Diaz, courtesy of the Lara Luna family.)

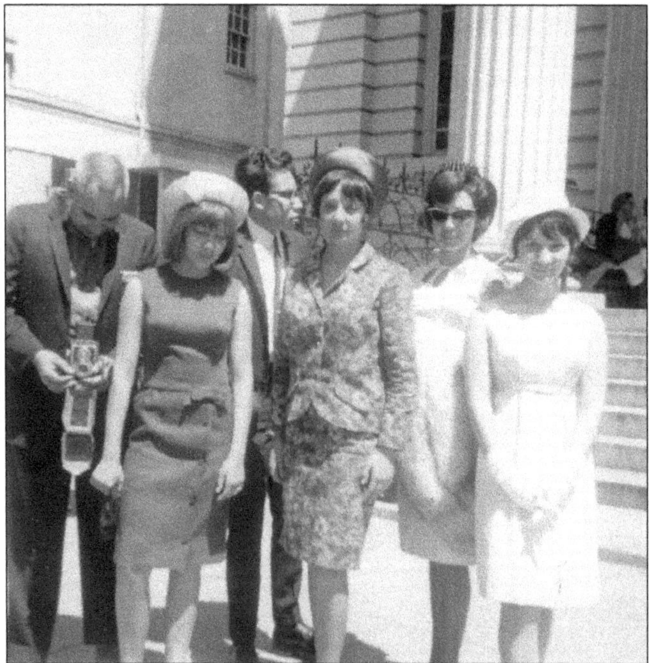

The Villagran family comes out of St. Joseph's Cathedral in 1964 after attending a friend's wedding. Gilberto takes a photograph of his wife, Graciela, who is photographing the family. From left to right are Gilberto, Laura, Gil, Jasmine, Nicole, and Nora. (Photograph by Graciela Villagran, courtesy of Gil Villagran.)

In 1964, a bride and groom get into their car as they leave St. Joseph's Cathedral on Market Street. Across the street is the Liberty Theater, which showed Mexican films in Spanish. In the 1960s, it was one of few San José theaters that featured films in Spanish. (Courtesy of Gil Villagran.)

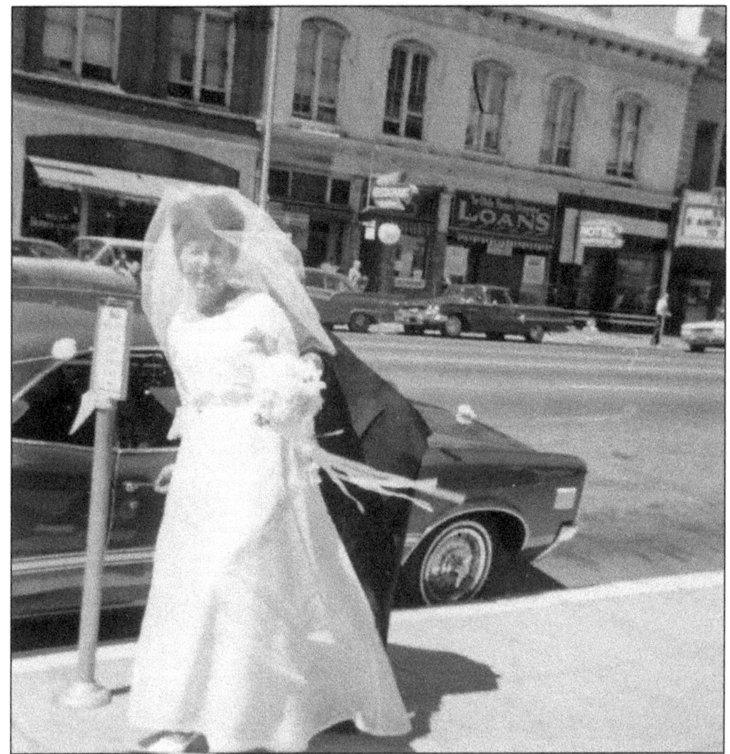

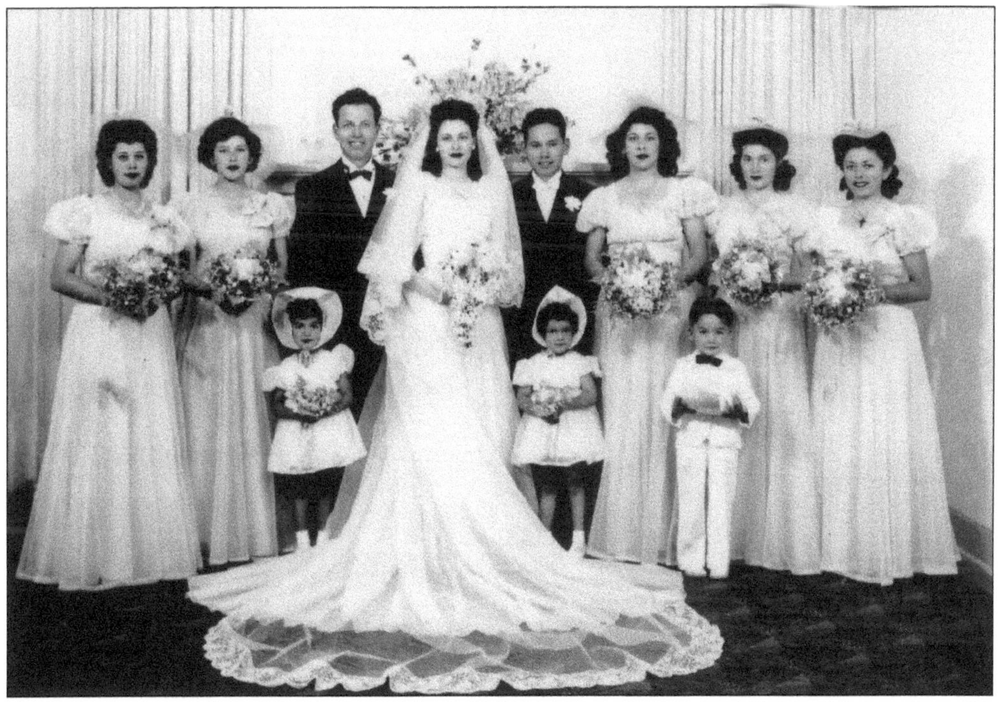

At St. Patrick's Catholic Church on July 7, 1943, Andrew Gaiton and Angie Medrano tie the knot. Angie was the former queen of San José's 127th Mexican Independence Day celebration in 1937. (Courtesy of Art Peredia.)

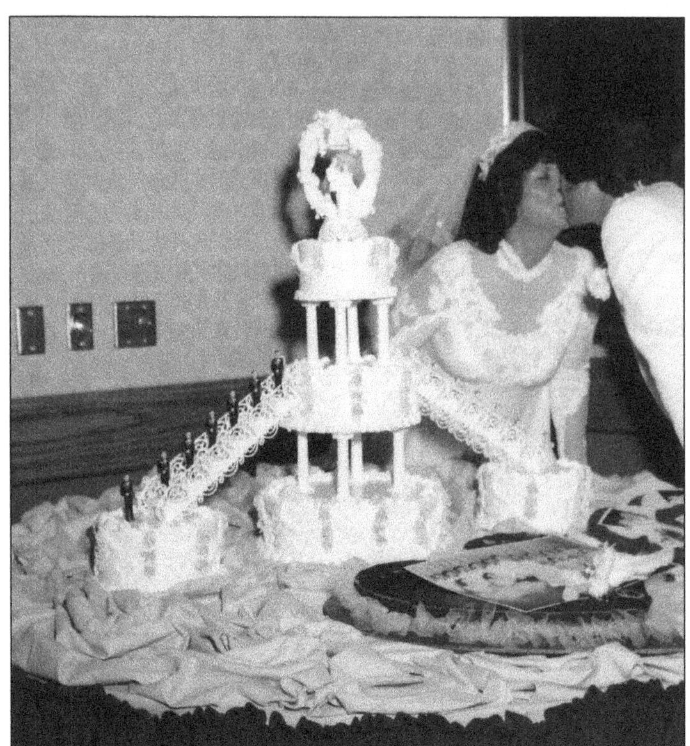

Korean War veteran Moses Carrasco and his wife, Connie, celebrate 25 years of marriage in 1984. Moses and Connie were married on Valentine's Day in 1959. Their anniversary was one of the first and largest Mexican celebrations at the newly opened Red Lion Inn. All original bridal party members came from throughout California to celebrate the Carrascos' anniversary in San José. (Courtesy of Connie Carrasco.)

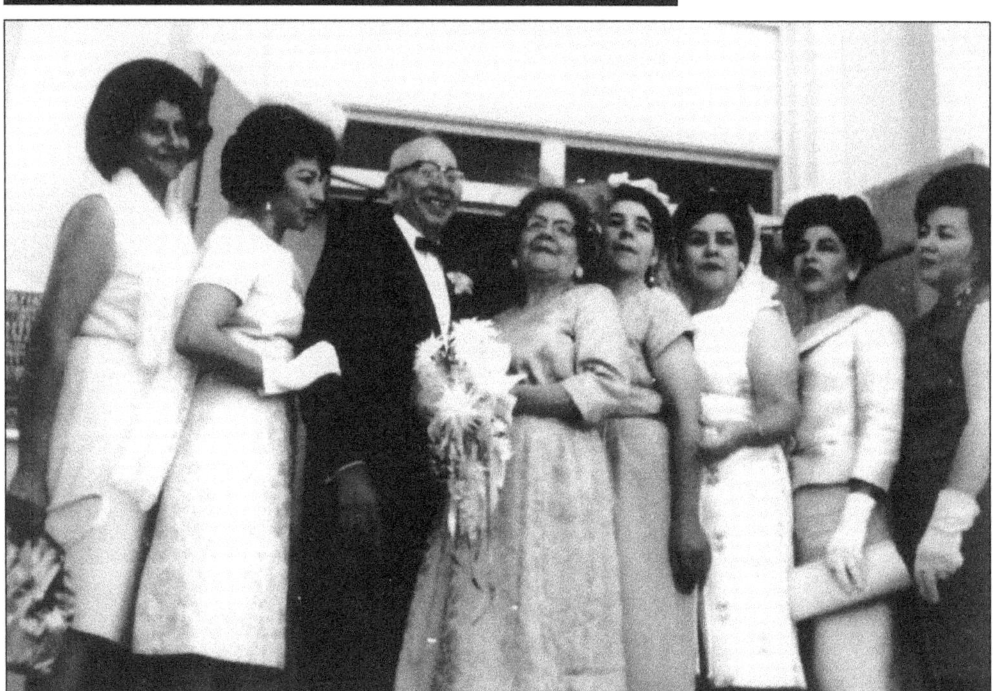

Celebrating 50 years of marriage, Jesus and Rafaela Medrano renew their vows at Holy Family Catholic Church in July 1966. Standing outside of the church from left to right are Eva Medrano, Esther Medrano, Jesus Medrano, Rafaela Medrano, Beatrice Peredia, Angie Medrano, Erlinda Medrano, and Amelia Medrano. (Courtesy of Art Peredia.)

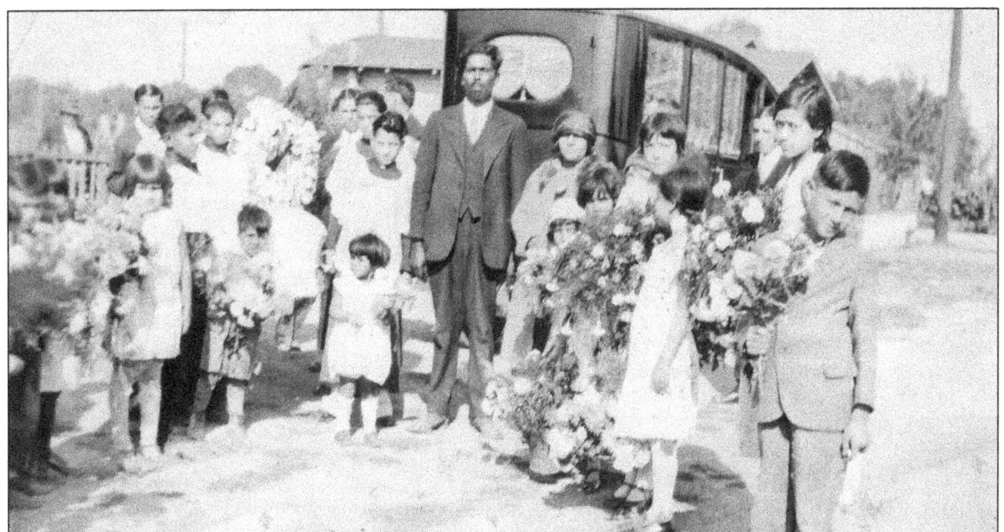

In this 1931 image, Pedro Lara (center) and his family, the boy's choir, and guests pose for a sorrowful photograph as they accompany the casket of little Rocindo Lara in a funeral car for a burial at a local cemetery. Seven-year-old Rocindo Lara was struck by a car and killed while walking with his father, Pedro, in front of the San José Civic Auditorium. Rocindo was the firstborn son of the family. (Courtesy of the Lara Luna family.)

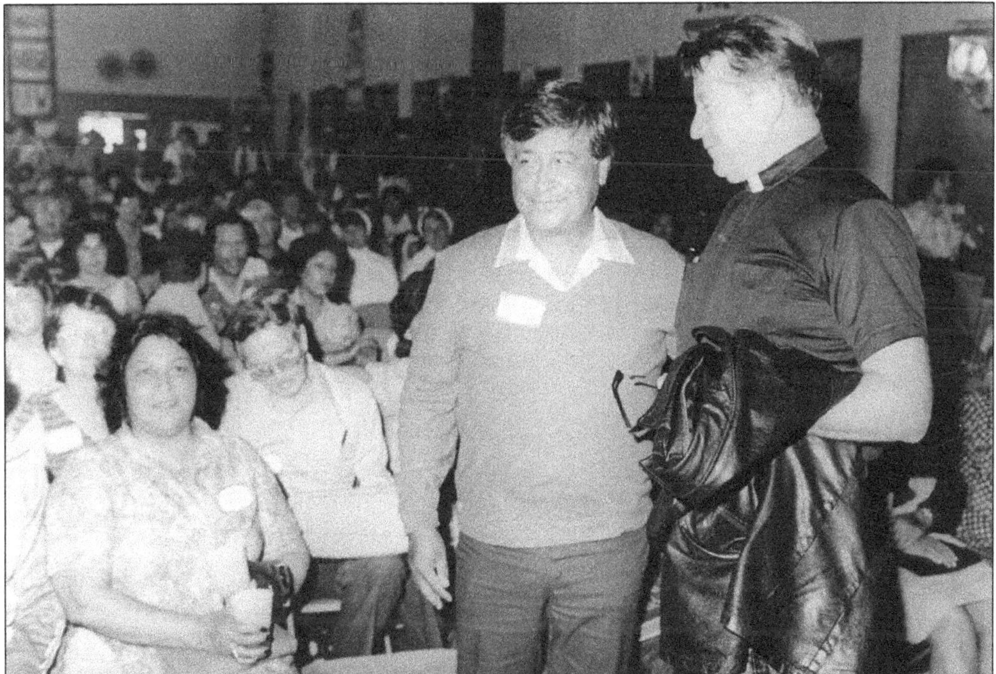

Cesar Chavez speaks with Fr. Donald McDonnell at the 20-year anniversary of the United Farm Workers union in 1982. Helen, Cesar's wife, is seated on the left. Father McDonnell is credited for mentoring Cesar Chavez and introducing him to renowned community organizer Fred Ross. Father McDonnell was one of the first missionaries to help establish Our Lady of Guadalupe church in East San José. (Courtesy of the Chicano Collection, Cultural Heritage Center, Dr. Martin Luther King Jr. Library, San José State University.)

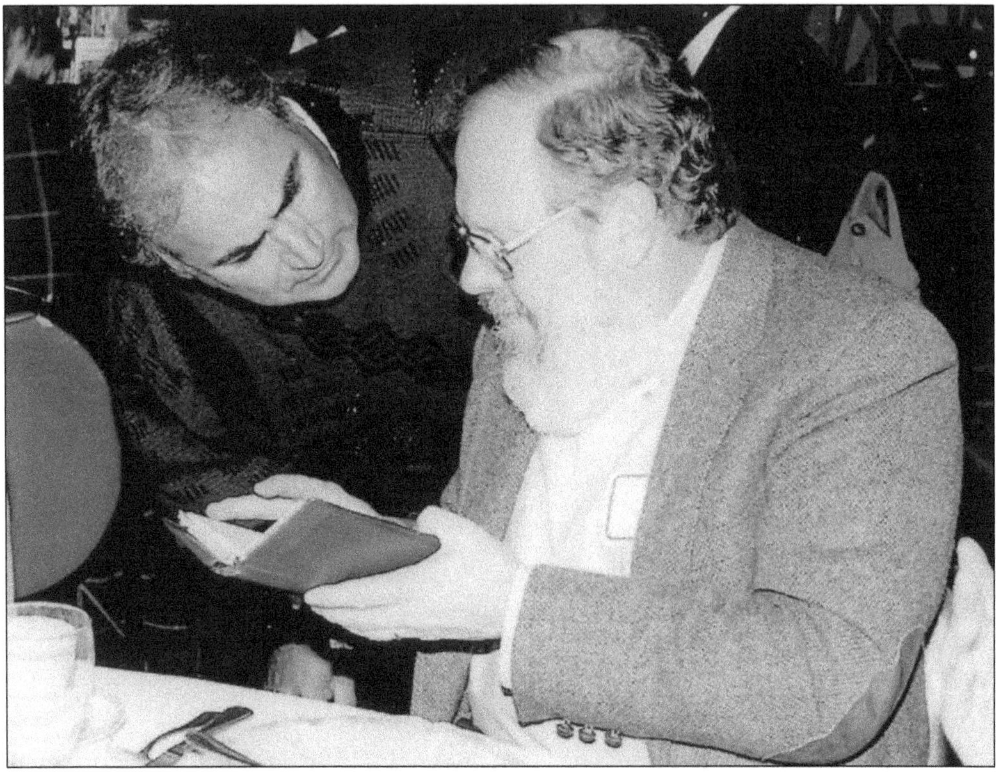

Fr. Mateo Sheedy (seated) began serving the fellowship at Sacred Heart Church shortly before the church suffered devastating damage from the 1989 Loma Prieta earthquake. Sheedy was instrumental in raising funds to complete the church's restoration. Since the early 1960s, Deacon Sal Alvarez (standing) has been a community activist and a steadfast fighter for social justice. Alvarez is the director of the Institute of Non-Violence. (Courtesy of People Acting in Community Together.)

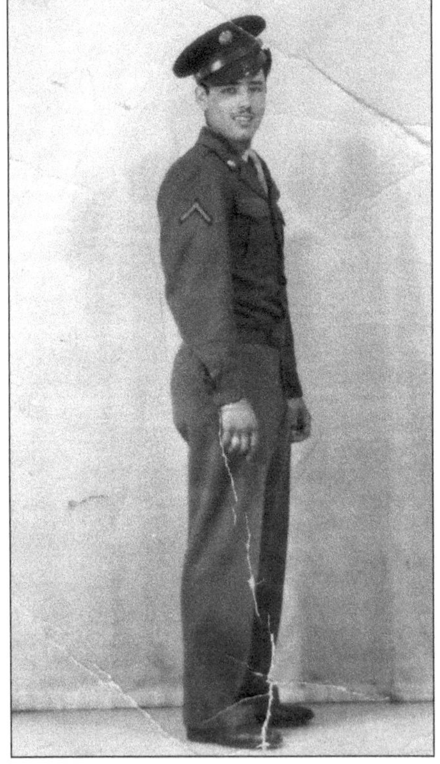

PFC Delfino Caballero poses in his army uniform for a photograph at Hollywood Studios in San José in 1945 after serving in Europe during World War II. His family moved to San José from Jerome, Arizona. He attended Lincoln High School. He was one of over 350,000 Mexican Americans who served their country during World War II. Like Delfino and his brothers, Alvino Jr., Eduardo, and Refugio, Mexican Americans have served patriotically in all branches of the military. (Courtesy of Eppie Regua.)

Ysidor Sanchez served in the U.S. Army in World War II. Born in Sonora, Mexico, he migrated with his family to San José. In 1942, he was drafted into the army. He was sent to France eight days after D-Day in June 1944. To this day, Ygnacio honors the memory of the brave soldiers who served with him and sacrificed their lives for their country. (Courtesy of the Lara Luna family.)

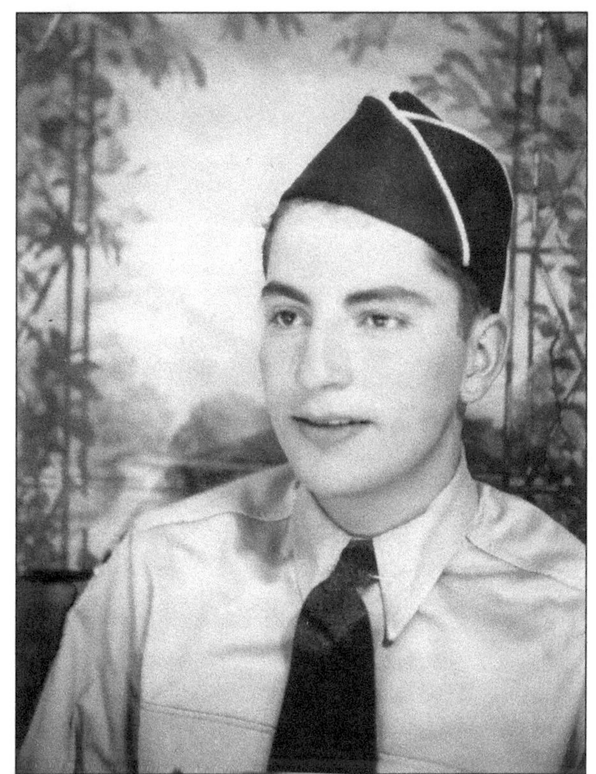

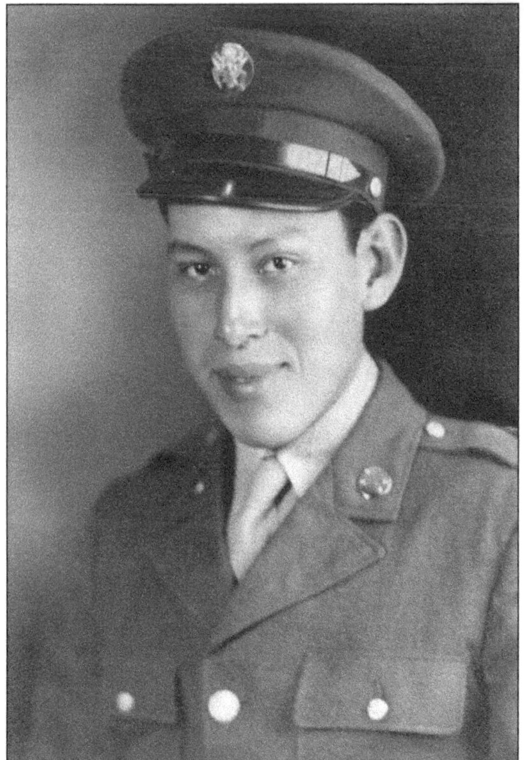

Tomás Cortez was a field worker in his youth. He recalls the years of poverty and financial struggles that he and his family endured in California. The struggles of working in the fields prepared him to withstand the struggles of war. He served in the U.S. Army in World War II. Learning that the war was over, he rejoiced at church and gave thanks to God. (Courtesy of Darrell Cortez.)

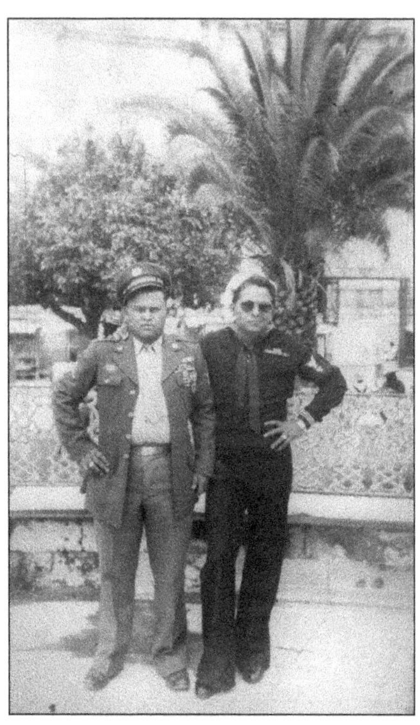

Brothers Daniel (left) and Frank Martinez served respectively in the U.S. Army and U.S. Navy in World War II. Frank served in the navy on the U.S. Destroyer *Walker*. They were raised in Jerome, Arizona. After the brothers returned safely home from the war, the family moved to San José. Daniel became a San José Police Department officer, and Frank became a machinist. (Courtesy of the Ralph Chavira family.)

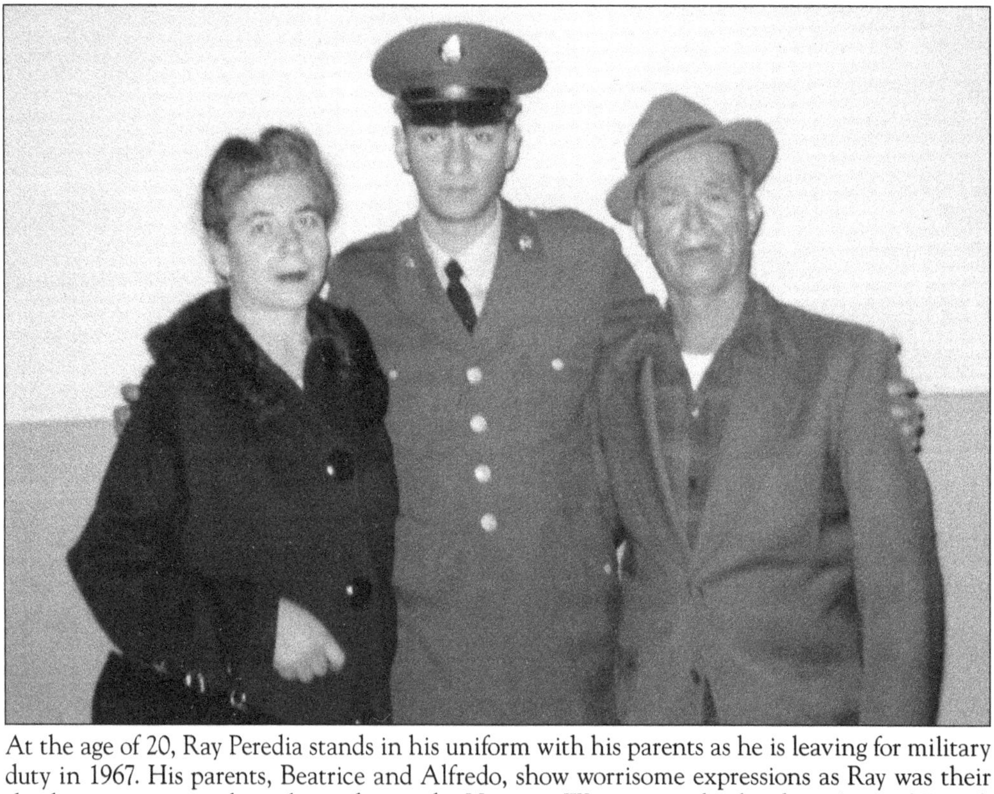

At the age of 20, Ray Peredia stands in his uniform with his parents as he is leaving for military duty in 1967. His parents, Beatrice and Alfredo, show worrisome expressions as Ray was their third son to serve in the military during the Vietnam War, joining his brothers Art and David. All three brothers were San José High School graduates. (Courtesy of Art Peredia.)

Mary Montez (left) and her sister Jennie pose in a tree on Fourteenth and Julian Streets in front of their home in 1947. In their early teens in this photograph, they attended San José High School. (Courtesy of Elaine Ortiz-Kristich.)

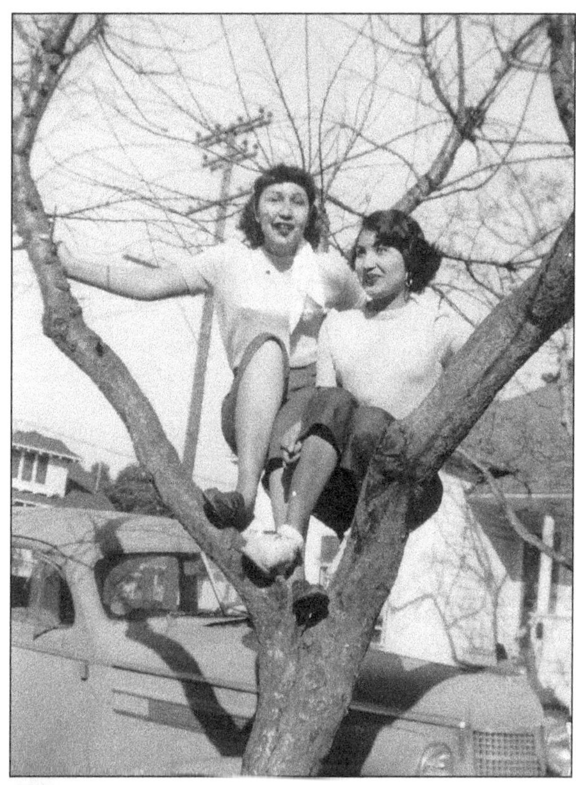

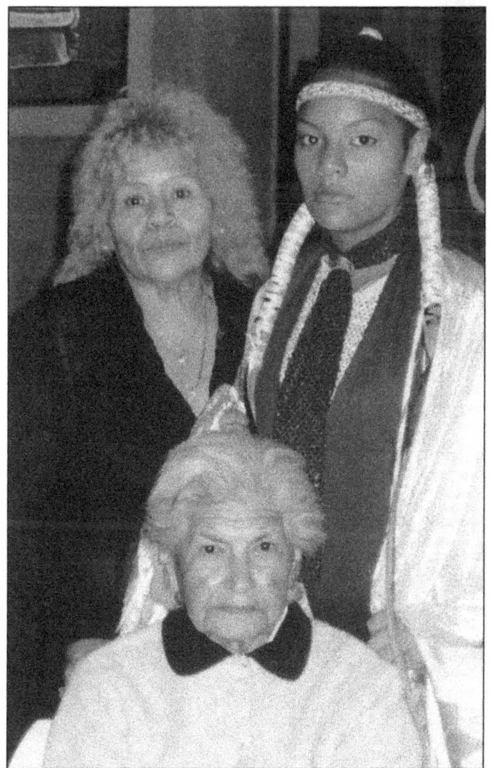

Pictured are three generations of women of Muwkema Ohlone and Mexican heritage. Shown are Margaret Martinez (seated), her niece Julia Lopez (left), and her great-niece Julie Dominguez (right), wearing a traditional Native American dress. Julie is a Fancydance performer. (Courtesy of Geraldine "Gerri" Garcia.)

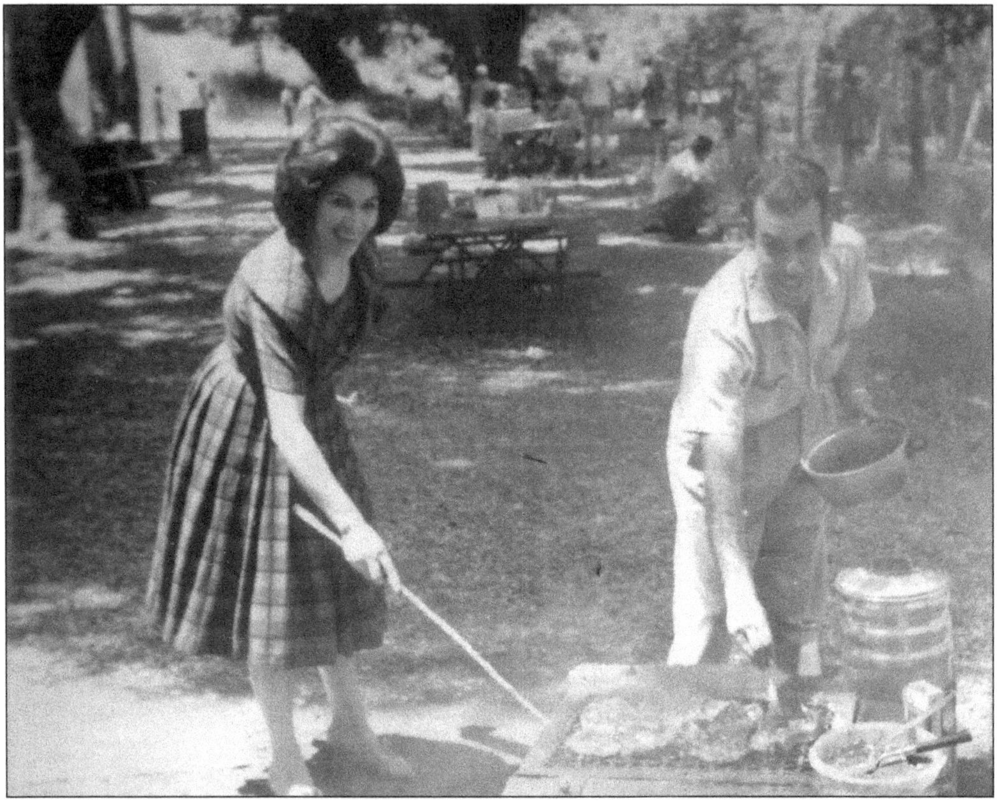

Bertha Lopez and her husband, Jesus, enjoy barbecuing for their family at Alum Rock Park in the foothills of East San José. Bertha and Jesus are busy turning and basting chicken on the barbecue pit. Consistent with the fashion of 1958, the Lopezes are dressed very well for a barbecue at the park. With her carefully styled hair, Bertha is wearing high-heeled shoes and a dress. (Courtesy of History San José.)

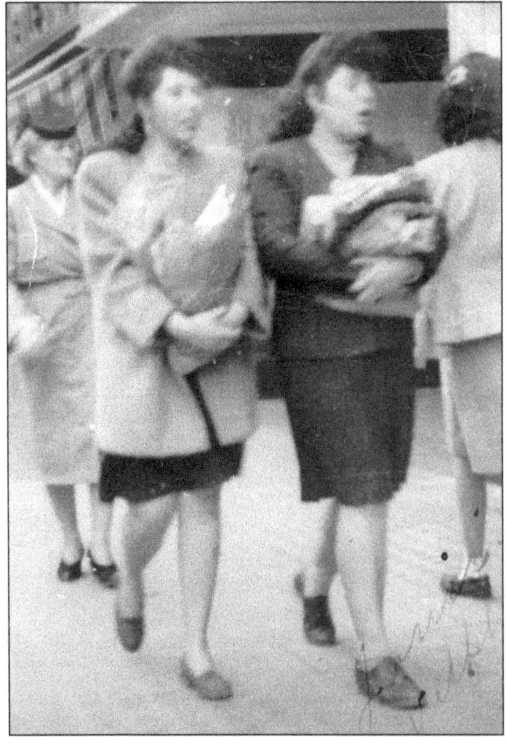

Louisa Montez (left) shops with friend Delfina Hernandez in downtown San José in 1946. They are walking by the popular Crest movie theater on First Street. (Courtesy of Elaine Ortiz-Kristich.)

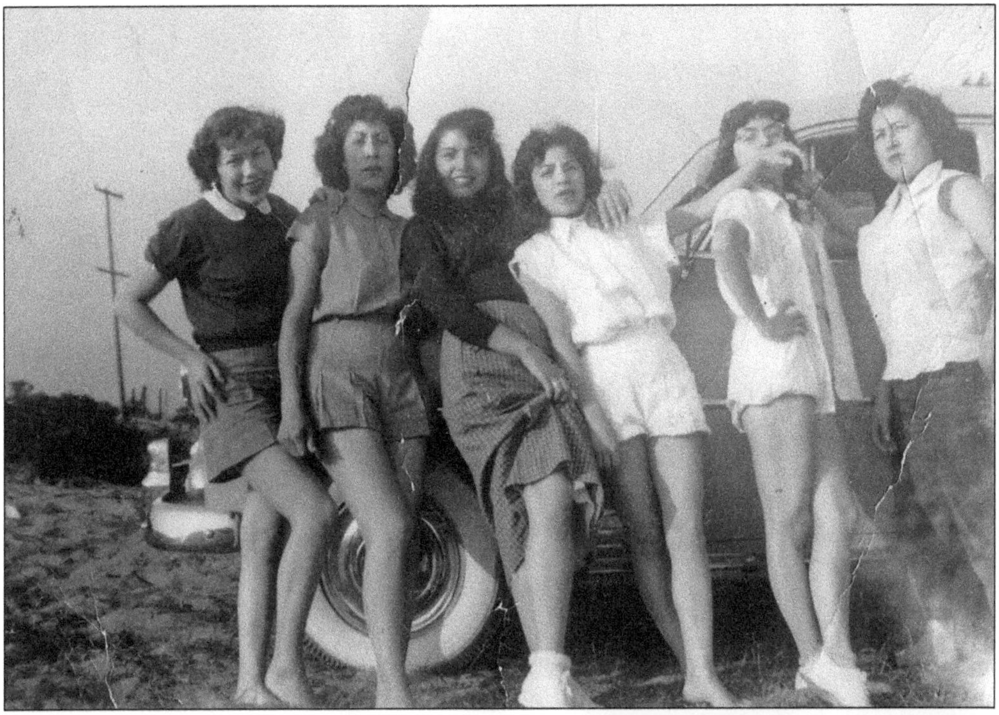

Six female cousins and friends from San José and nearby San Juan Bautista relax in 1949 during one of their few days off from working in the fields. From left to right are Lorenza Pedregon, Eulalia Pedregon, Esther Gonzales, Casimeda Reyes, Ida Reyes, and Estella Lopez. The Pedregons and Reyeses were first cousins, and the other two ladies were close friends, or *comadres*. (Courtesy of Rita de la Cerda.)

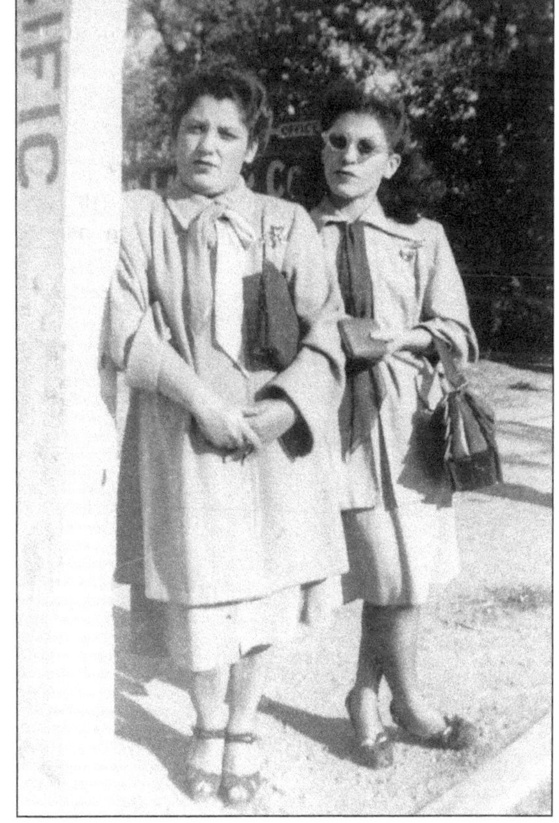

In 1952, Martha Perez (left) and Angie Herrera wait for a bus by the Southern Pacific Railroad tracks on Twenty-eighth and Santa Clara Streets. They are headed for a day of shopping in downtown San José. Downtown San José offered numerous shops, restaurants, and theaters for the women to enjoy on a sunny day. (Courtesy of George Perez.)

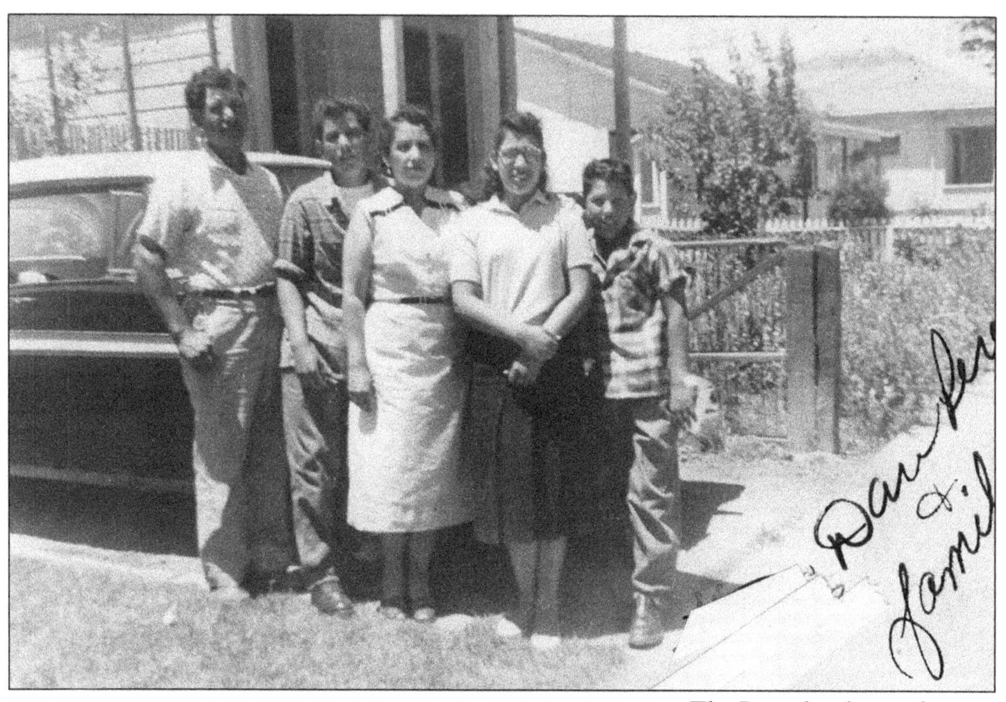

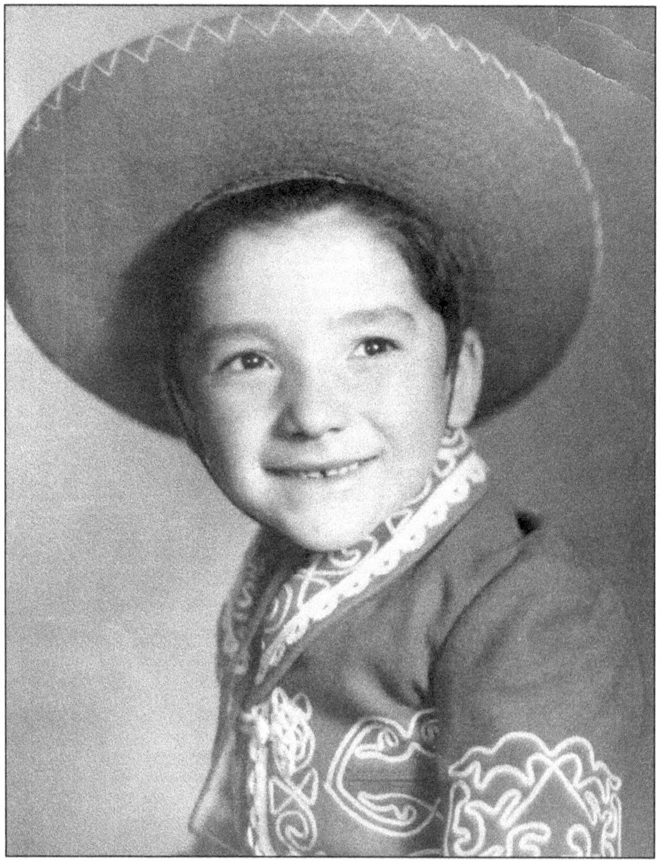

The Perez family stands in front of their home on Spring Street in north San José in 1956. The family purchased the home for $3,200. Later, due to the expansion of the San José Airport, residents in the nearby vicinity were forced to relocate. From left to right are Daniel Sr., Daniel Jr., Martha, Jennie, and George. (Courtesy of George Perez.)

At the age of four, Fernando Zazueta poses in a *charro* outfit, which was purchased by his beloved uncle, Tomas Barba. A child of a migrant farm worker family, Zazueta recalls living in a tent with a makeshift kerosene stove for cooking. His chores included sprinkling water on the dirt floor to keep the dust from rising in the tent. (Courtesy of Fernando Zazueta.)

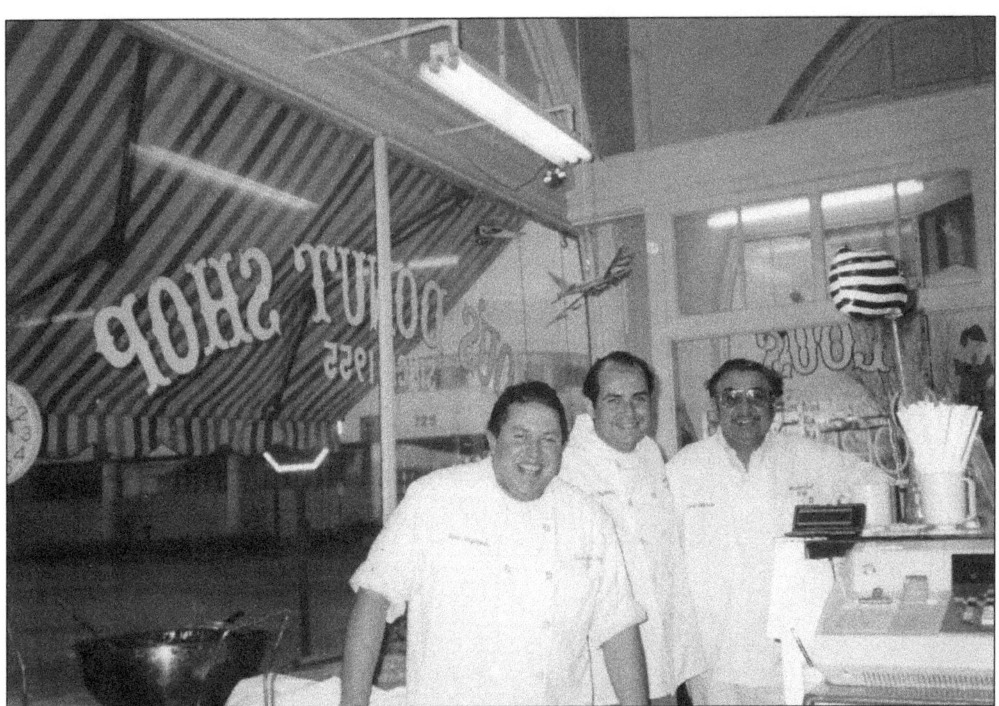

The Chavira brothers Rick (left) and Chuck (center), with the help of their parents, Ralph (right) and Connie, purchased Lou's Donut in 1981 from its original owner, Lou Ades. The shop was located on Santa Clara Street across the street from San José Hospital. Mexicans in San José recall patronizing the shop after mass on Sundays. In 1996, the donut shop moved to Auzerais and Delmas Avenues and established a history museum honoring military veterans. (Courtesy of the Ralph Chavira family.)

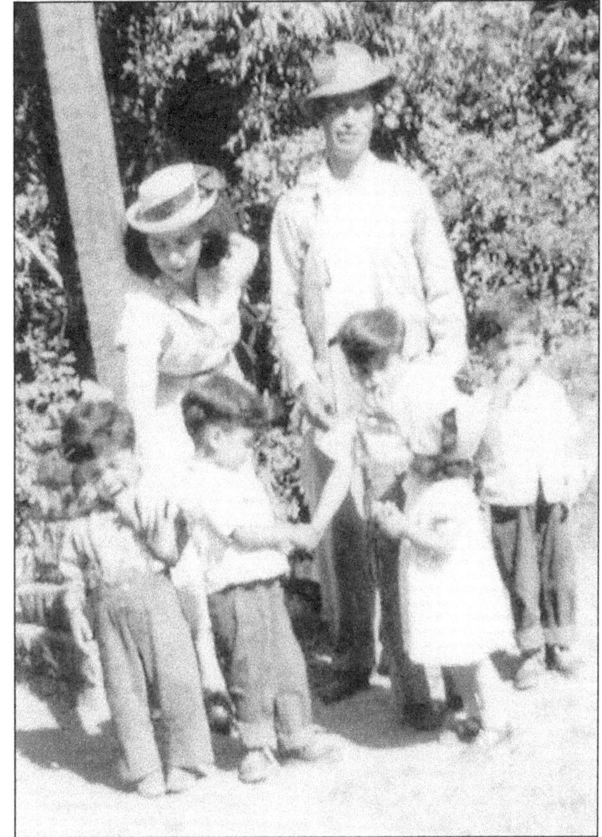

Alfredo and Beatrice Peredia take their children to Alum Rock Park in 1950. Beatrice has her hands full with five young children. From left to right, the children are Sam, David, Ray, Lidia, and Art. (Courtesy of Art Peredia.)

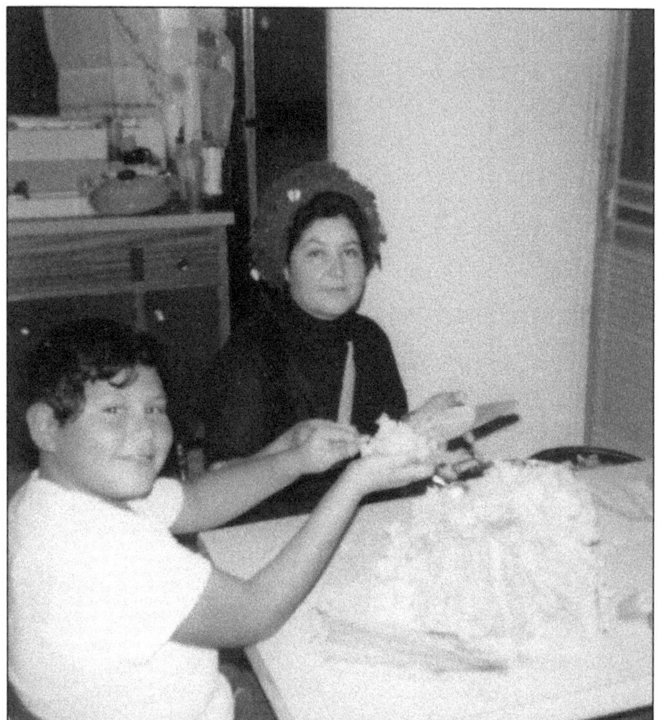

Lupe Payne Gonzalez spreads *masa*, a cornmeal for tamales, onto corn husks, called *ojas*, at her kitchen table on White Road during Christmas 1970. Joseph, her son, helps with the spreading of the *masa*, which is in a mound in the center of the table. (Courtesy of Alfred Gonzalez II).

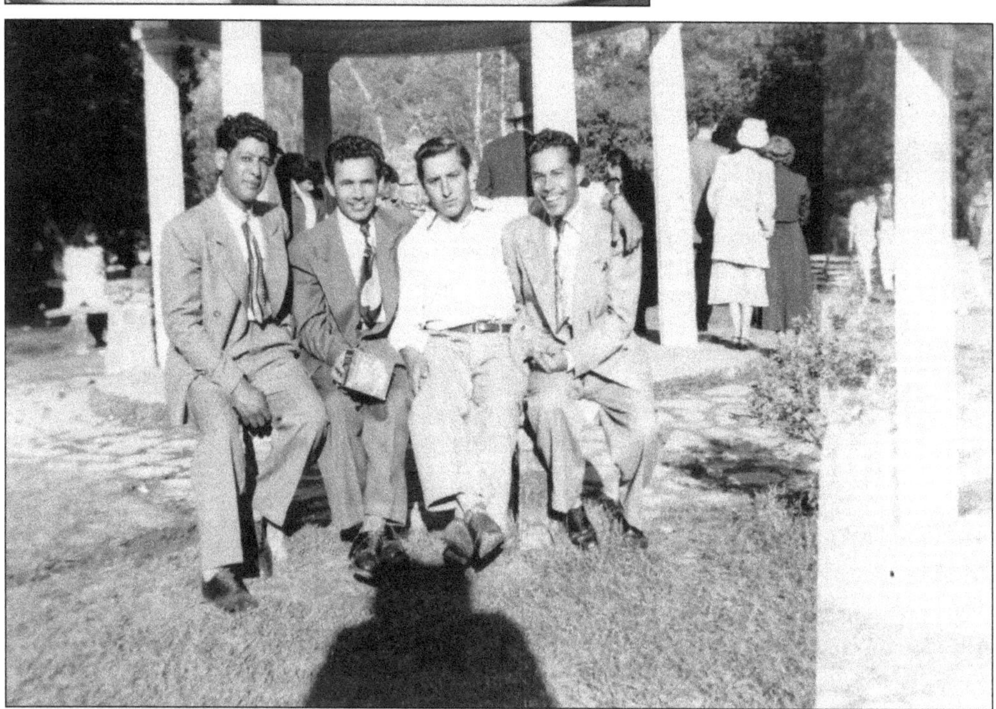

Daniel Perez (far left) sits on a bench with his two brothers-in-law and friend Hector Herrera (second from left), Rudy Rey, Richard Herrera (far right), at the water fountain in Alum Rock Park in 1952. The men gathered in the park with their families after attending mass at St. Joseph's Cathedral. (Courtesy of George Perez.)

Eight

Arts and Entertainment

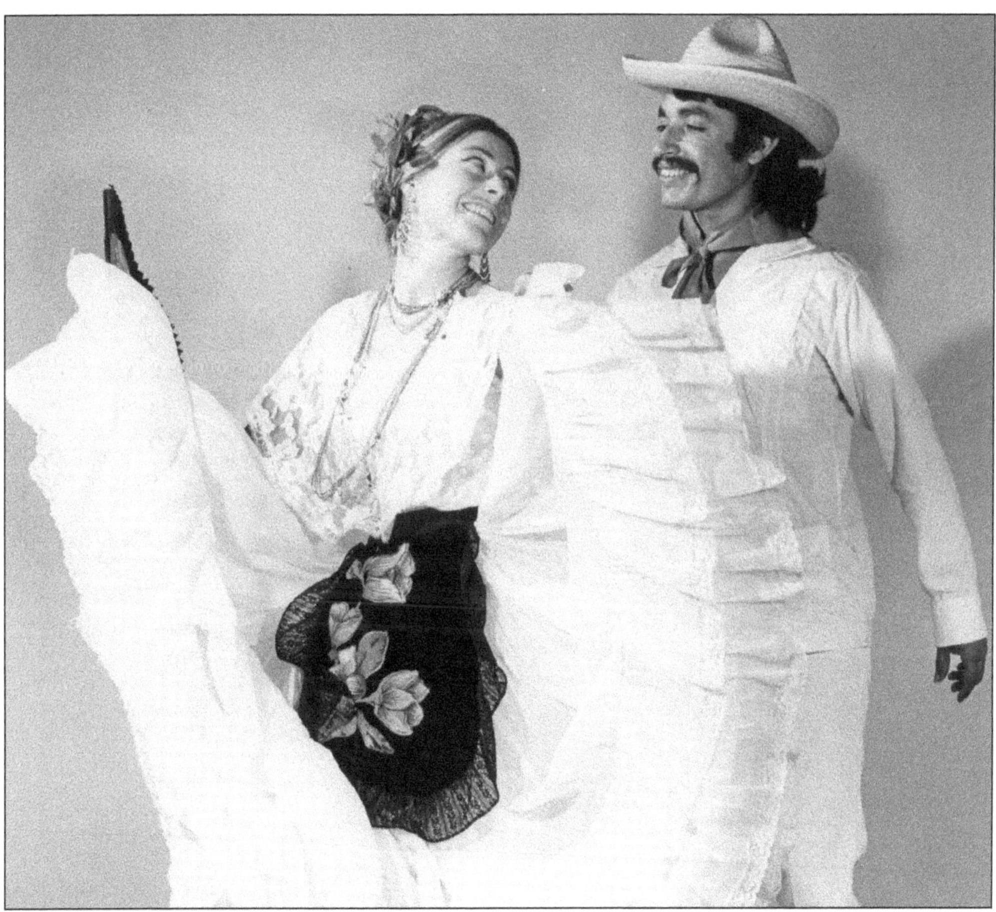

Los Lupeños de San José was cofounded by Dr. Susan Cashion and Ramón Morones (both shown above) in 1969 with support from Daniel Galán, the Consul General de México in San José, and Guadalupe Suarez, a local civic leader in Mexican affairs. Showing appreciation for Guadalupe Suarez's immense support, the folklórico dance company named itself after her, "Los Lupeños." In 1969, Los Lupeños had one of its first performances at San José City College's men's gym. Quickly, they established a dedicated following of fans and outgrew the men's gym at San José City College and moved to its theater until finding a larger facility. Los Lupeños is highly regarded in San José, the San Francisco Bay Area, and Mexico. In 2004, the company celebrated its 35th anniversary. (Courtesy of Susan Cashion.)

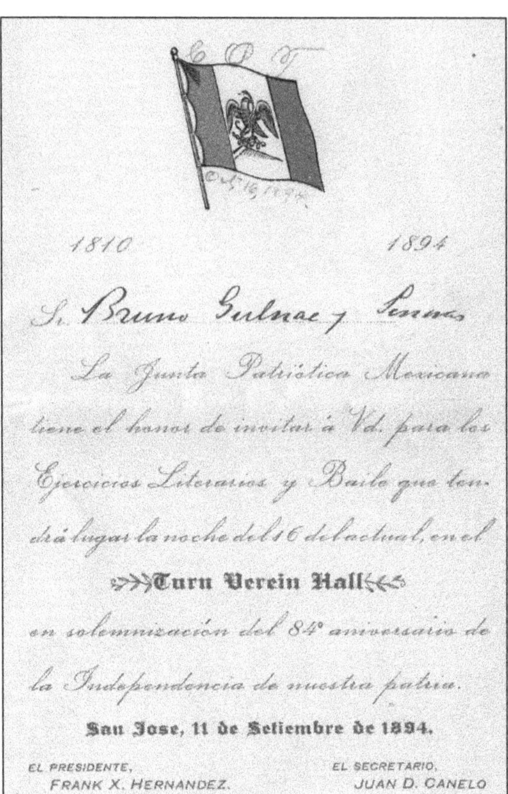

1810 1894

Sr. Bruno Gulnac y Pennas

La Junta Patriótica Mexicana tiene el honor de invitar á Vd. para los Ejercicios Literarios y Baile que tendrá lugar la noche del 16 del actual, en el

Turn Verein Hall

en solemnización del 84° aniversario de la Independencia de nuestra patria.

San Jose, 11 de Setiembre de 1894.

EL PRESIDENTE,
FRANK X. HERNANDEZ.

EL SECRETARIO,
JUAN D. CANELO

When the French occupied Sonora, Mexico, during 1864 and 1865, many Sonoran communities in Northern California organized *Juntas Patrioticas*, "patriotic committees," to provide aid and support for the people in Mexico. This 1894 invitation to the 84th anniversary celebration of Mexican Independence demonstrates that celebrations of Mexican Independence and Cinco de Mayo were observed in 19th-century San José. (Courtesy of History San José.)

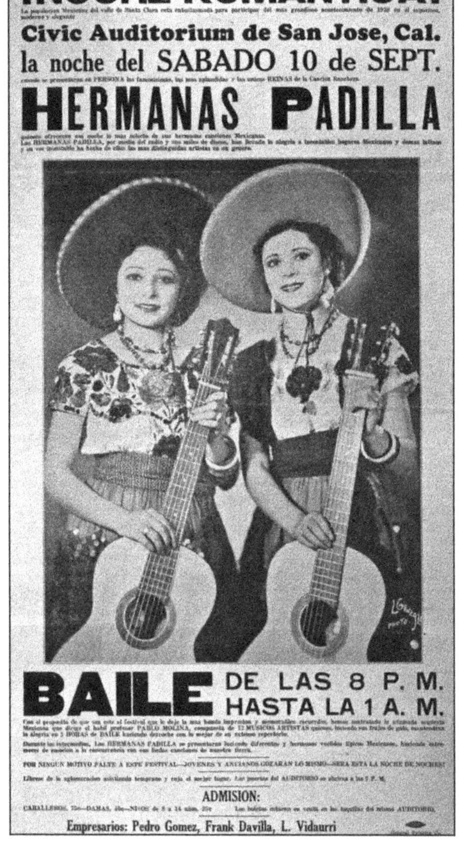

In this 1935 dance poster, the featured performers are the Padilla sisters. The poster advertises a romantic night of dance to be held at the Civic Auditorium in San José on Saturday, September 10 from 8:00 p.m. until 1:00 a.m. (Courtesy of History San José.)

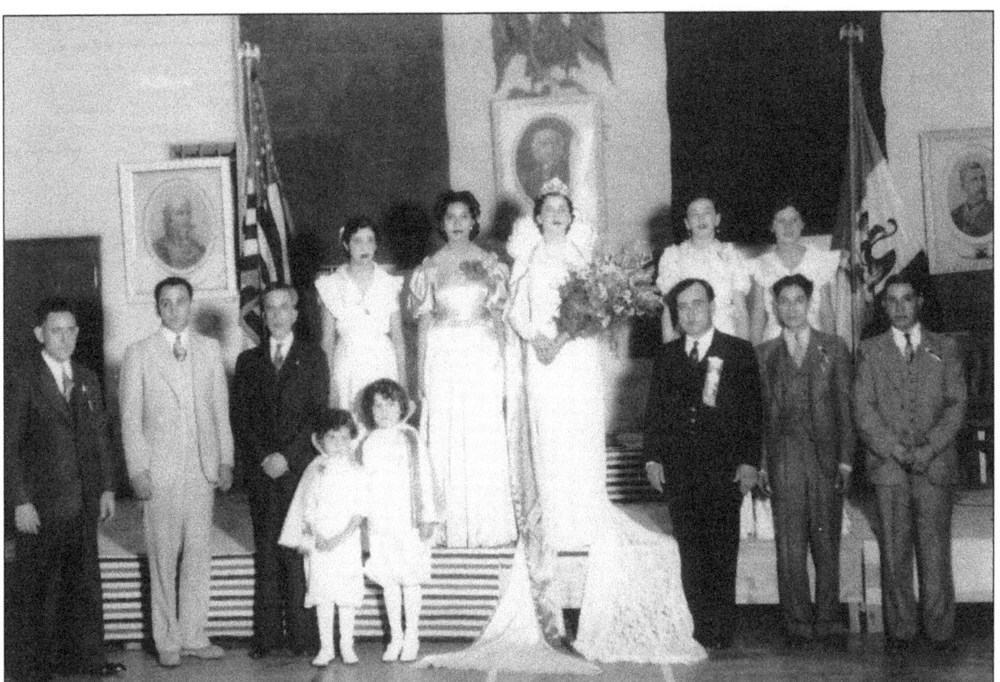

In 1937, Angie Medrano was crowned queen of the 127th anniversary of Mexico's independence from Spain on September 16. An article in the *San José News* on September 15, 1937, includes her name and photograph and the agenda of San José's two-day festivities, sponsored by the Sociedad Mexicana de Beneficencia Mutua. (Courtesy of Art Peredia.)

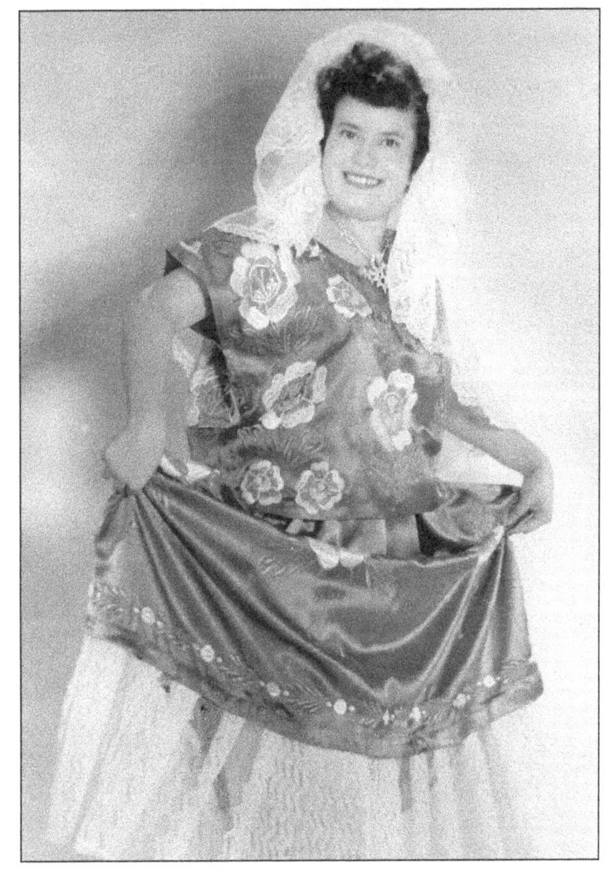

Connie (Martinez) Chavira performed at the San José Civic Auditorium in 1952. She sang and danced for the Cinco de Mayo and September 16 festivities annually. Her mother emphasized the importance for Connie to retain her Spanish culture through dance and song. (Photograph by Reyes Studio, courtesy of the Ralph Chavira family.)

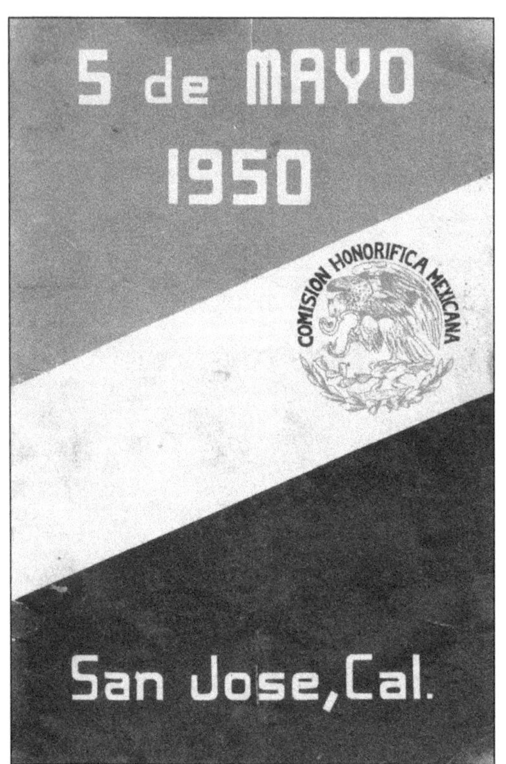

The 1950 program at left for the Cinco de Mayo events in downtown San José was distributed to participants and attendees. The steering committee that oversaw the festivities was the Comission Honorifica Mexicana. Below is radio announcer Jesus Valenzuela participating in the parade with two women in a car and his son on the car hood, wearing a child's mariachi outfit. (Both courtesy of the Jesus Valenzuela family.)

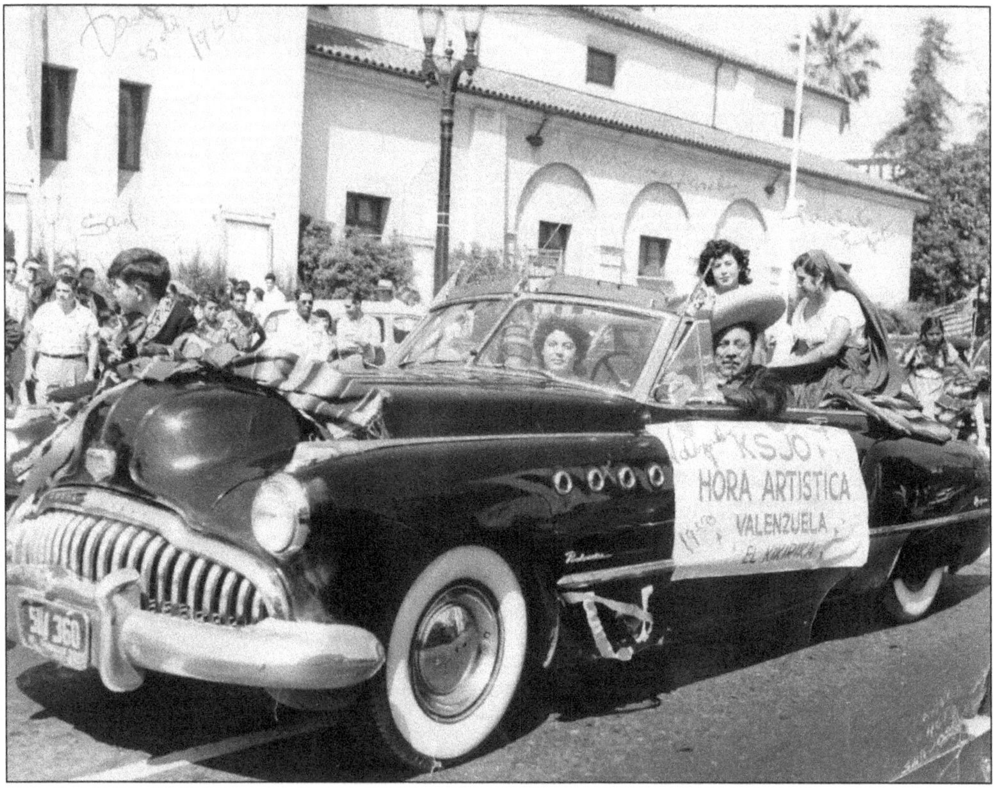

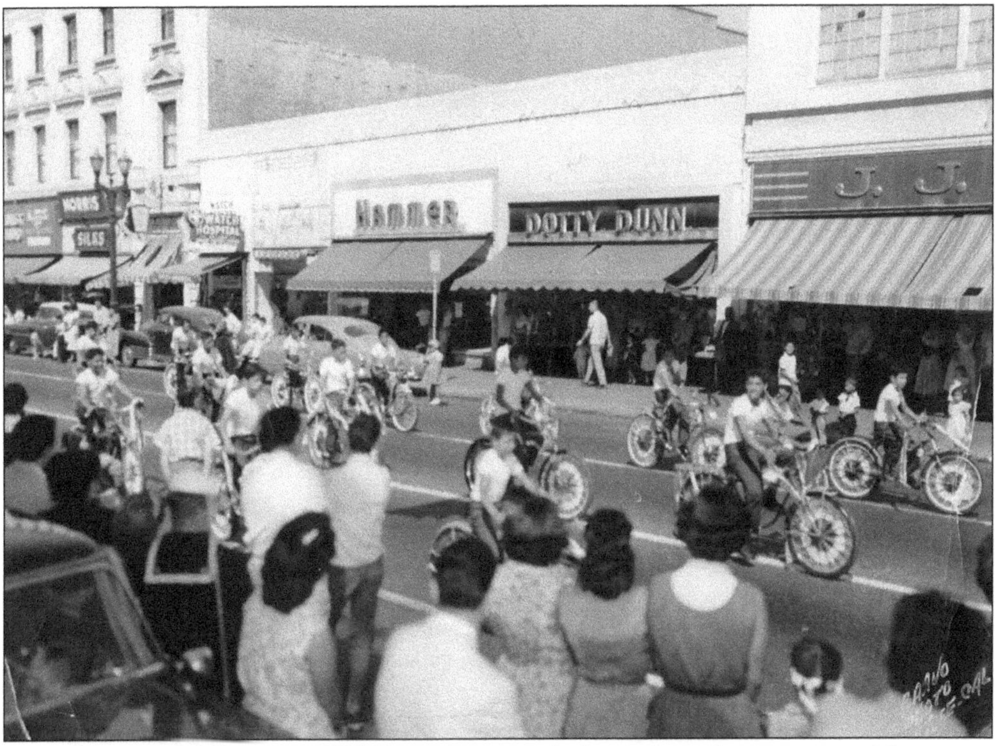

Spanish-language radio station KSJO's employees worked actively in the community. The station employees encouraged the formation of a boy's bike club in 1954. During the Cinco de Mayo parade, the boys formed a figure eight on their bikes in front of the San José Civic Auditorium. (Courtesy of the Jesus Valenzuela family.)

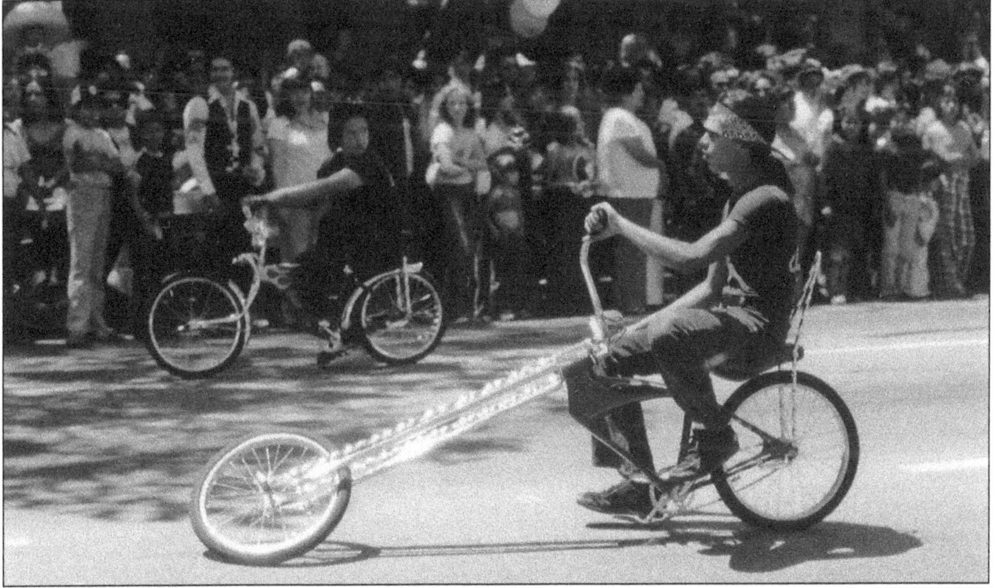

Customized cars and bikes have been of interest to generations of Mexicans and Mexican Americans in San José. In this 1980s image, two Cinco de Mayo parade participants ride their low-rider bikes in a procession. (Photograph by and courtesy of Paul Ortiz.)

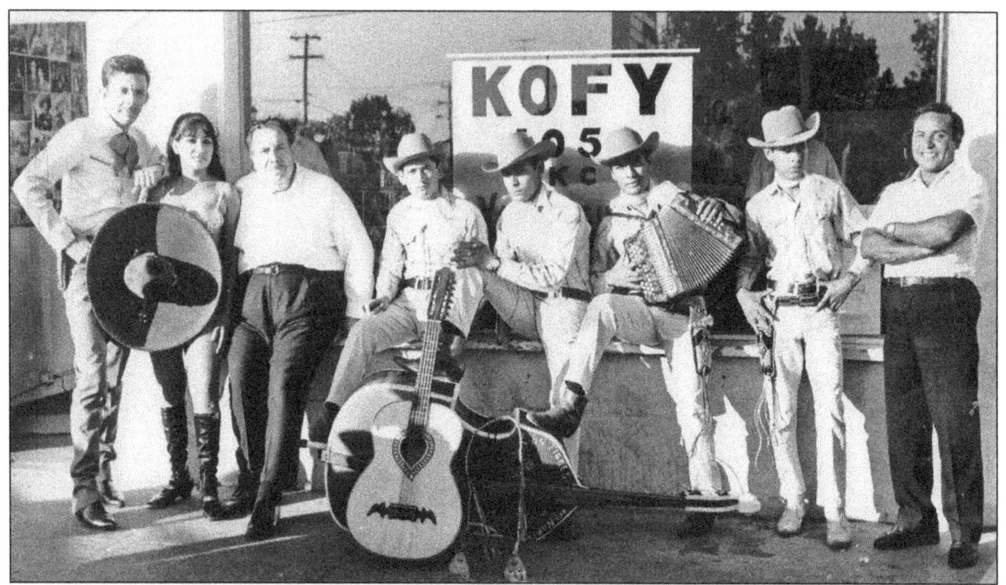

In the late 1960s, members of the musical group Los Tigres del Norte stand in front of KOFY radio station. San José–based Los Tigres del Norte earned multiple Grammy and Latin Grammy awards for their Norteño music, which combines corridos, ballads, cumbias, and rancheras. (Courtesy of the Jesus Valenzuela family.)

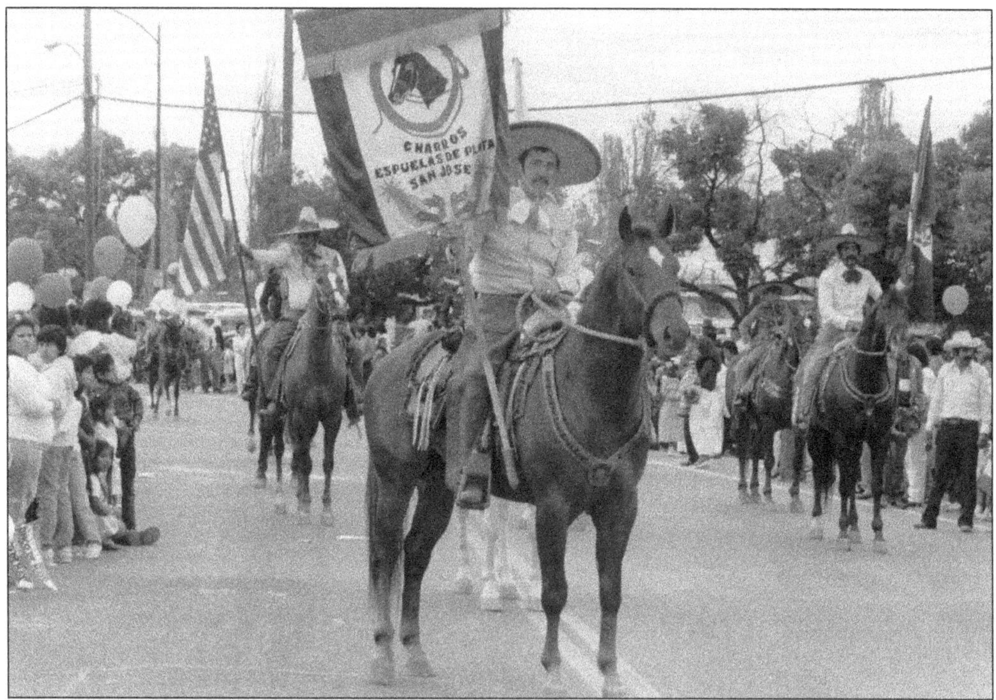

In Mexico, a *charro* is a term referring to a skilled horseman or cowboy. The traditional Mexican charro is known for colorful clothing and participating in *charreadas*, a type of rodeo. This cultural tradition continues in San José. This image includes the Charros Espuelas de Plata San José at the Cinco de Mayo parade in the 1980s at the Santa Clara County Fairgrounds. (Photograph by Mary Andrade, courtesy of *La Oferta* newspaper.)

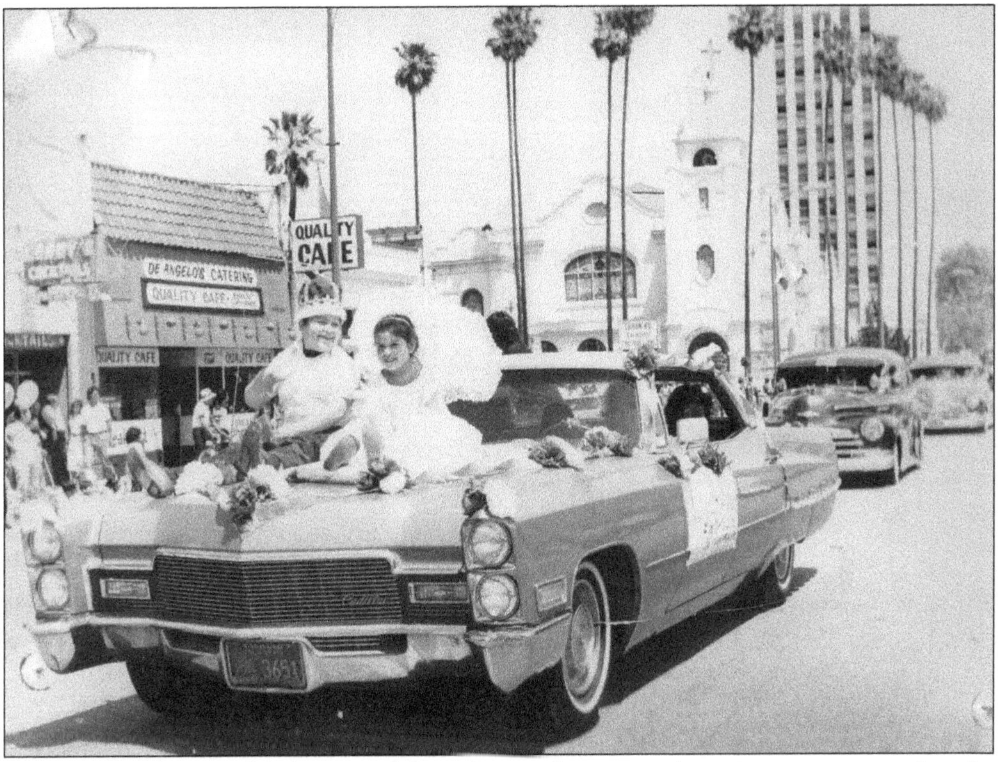

The Lucha Villa Fan Club, honoring Mexico's most famous ranchera singer, participated in the annual September 16 and Cinco de Mayo parades. Grandchildren of photographer Richard Diaz join the parade as the king and queen of the Lucha Villa Fan Club in the 1970s. In this image, the parade, which includes classic lowrider cars, is traveling on Santa Clara Street. (Photograph by Richard Diaz, courtesy of El Fotografo del Estrellas.)

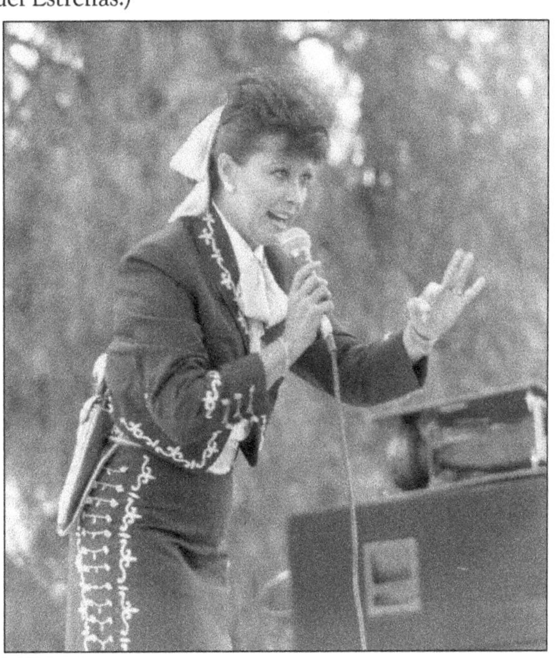

Mexican singer and actress Roz(s)enda Bernal performs at the Santa Clara County Fairgrounds for Cinco de Mayo in the 1980s. She is well known in Mexico as a ranchera singer. She has also acted in more than 200 Mexican films. She acted alongside Vicente Fernandez in the film *La Ley del Monte* in 1976. (Photograph by Mary Andrade, courtesy of *La Oferta* newspaper.)

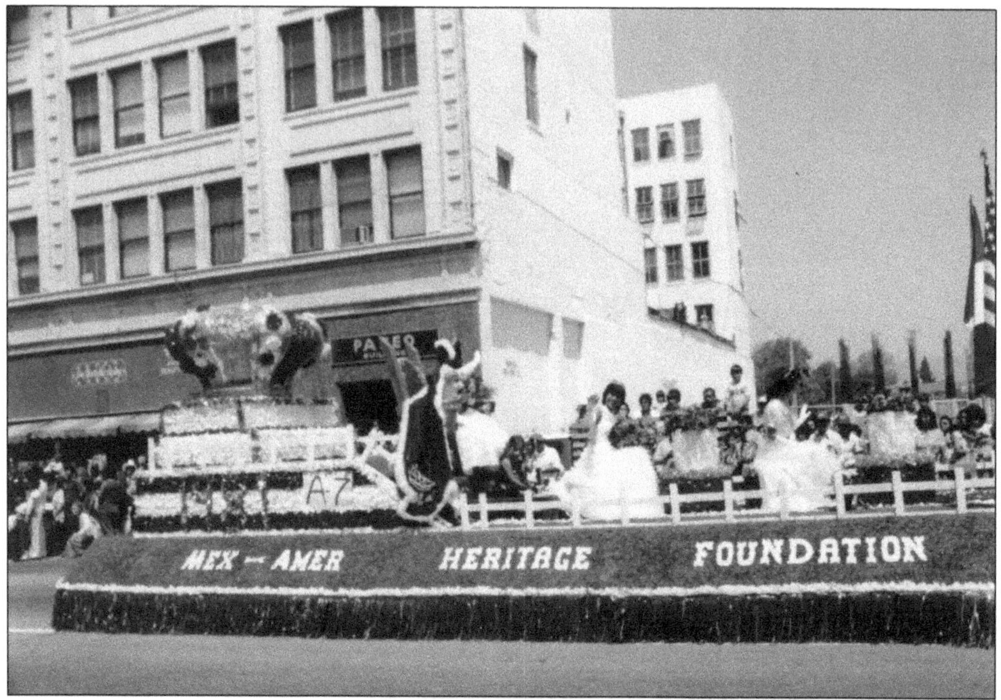

In a Cinco de Mayo parade in 1970, beauty queens wave to the crowd in downtown San José on the Mexican American Heritage Foundation float. (Courtesy of Connie Carrasco.)

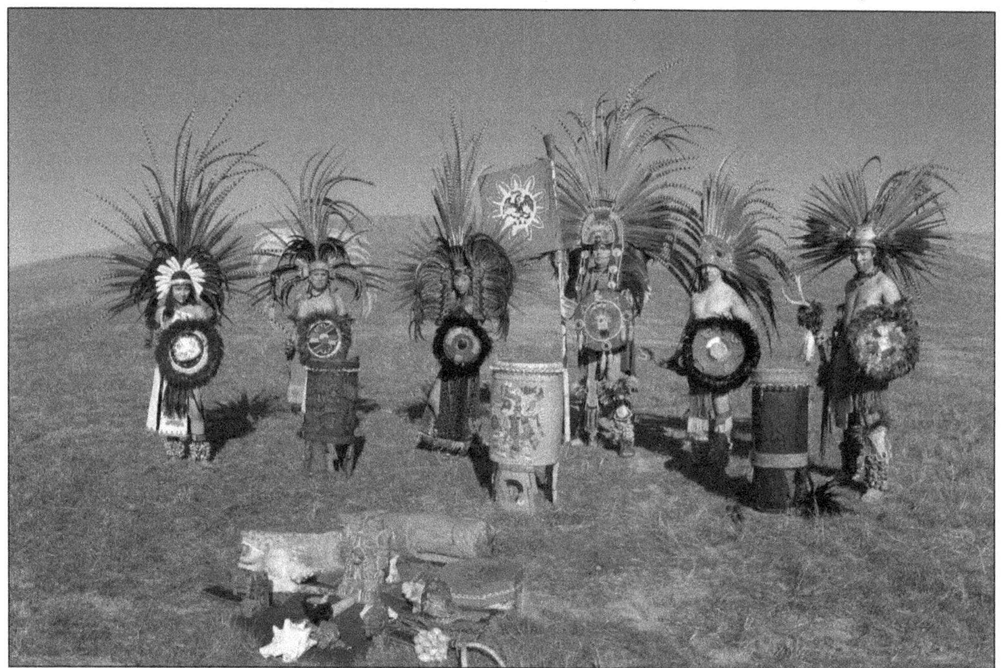

Calpulli Tonalequeh is a San José–based Mexica/Azteca *danzante* group. The *danzantes* have been performing ceremonies and dances for many years throughout the Bay Area and beyond. They are under the leadership of Adam "Mitlalpilli" Gonzalez. (Photograph by Robert Emery Smith, courtesy of Calpulli Tonalequeh.)

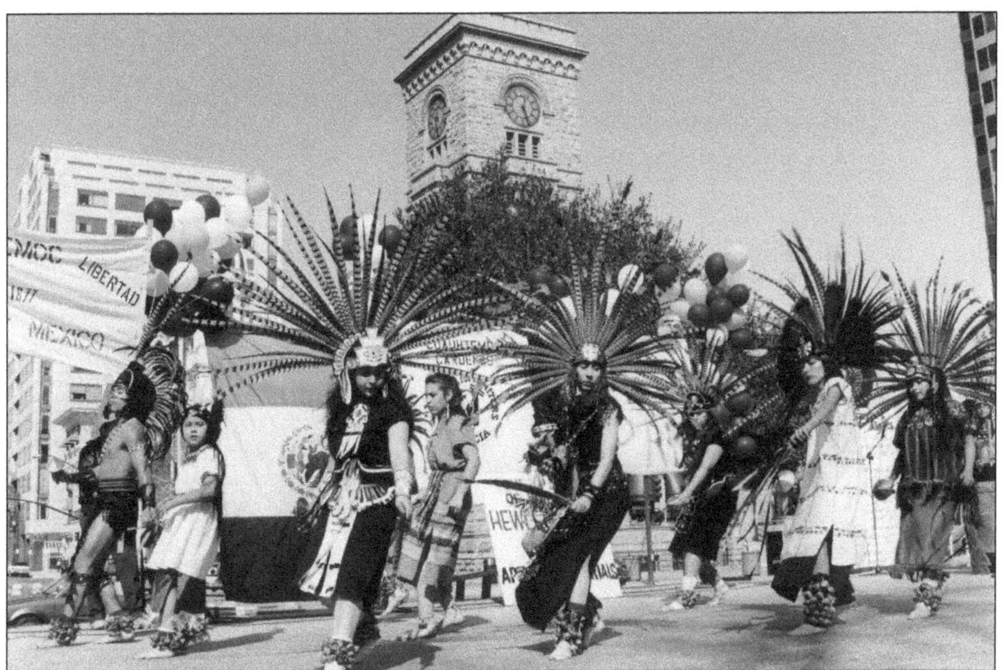

Aztec dancers perform in downtown San José for Cinco de Mayo. They are dancing on Market Street at Cesar Chavez Park. The dancers vary in ages, instilling cultural pride into the youth. (Photograph by Mary Andrade, courtesy of *La Oferta* newspaper.)

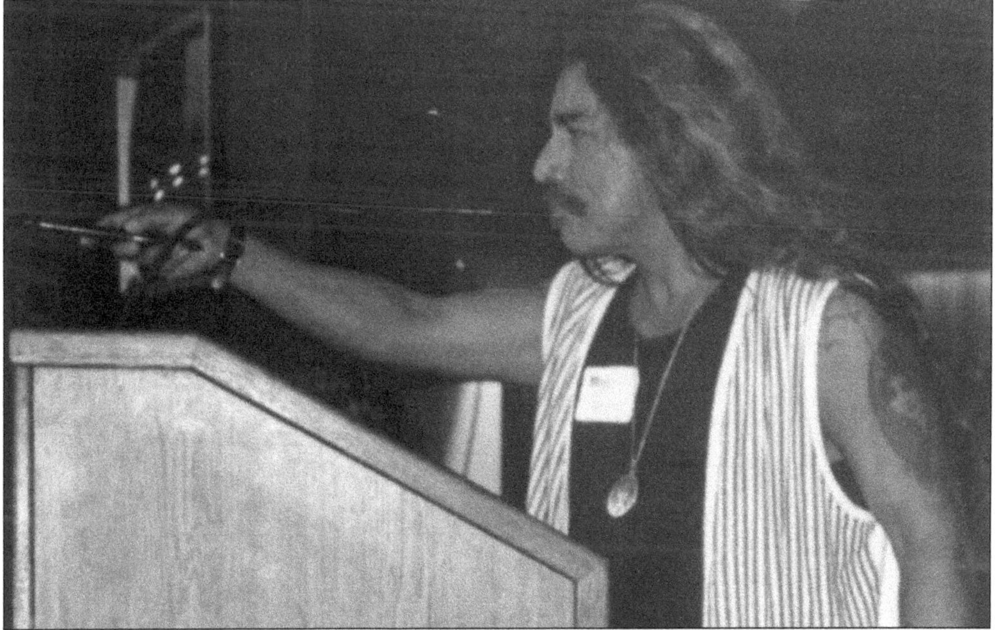

Roberto Duran was born and raised in Eastside San José. He attended San José City College and received a Bachelor of Arts degree in social work from San José State University. He is the author of *A Friend of Sorrow*, *Triple Crown*, *Reality Ribs*, and *Dark Spark*. He has created compact discs featuring original poetry and lyrics: *86ed again*; *Poetry Pie*; and *Darkspark*. (Courtesy of Roberto Duran.)

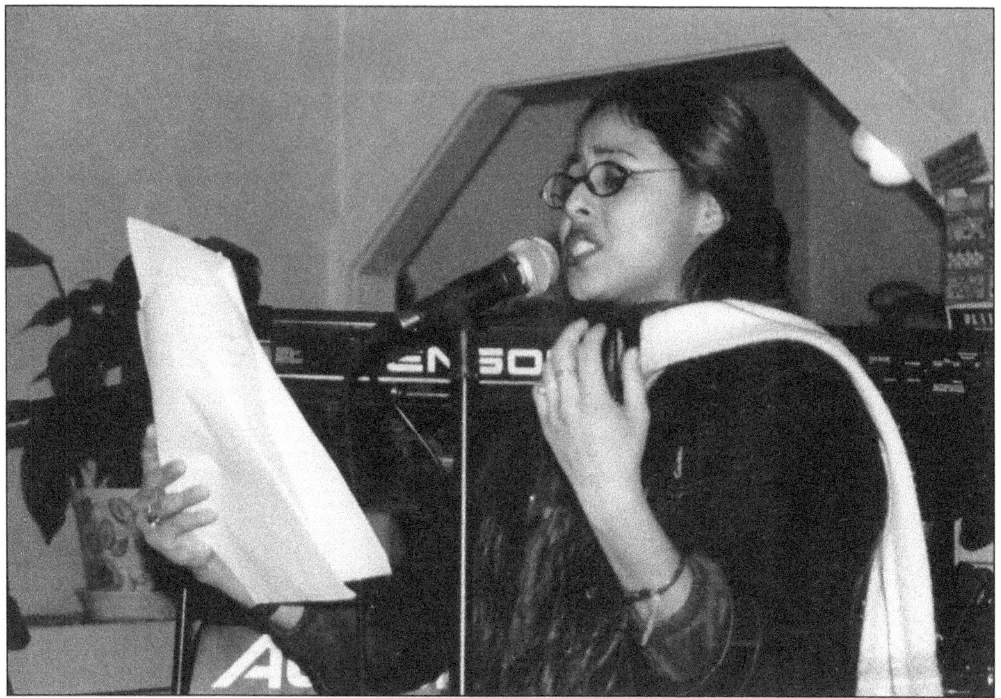

Adriana Garcia Cabrera is a poet and community activist currently attending San José State University, completing a Master of Arts in Mexican American studies. She received a Bachelor of Science degree from San José State University in public relations in 2003. (Courtesy of Adriana Garcia Cabrera.)

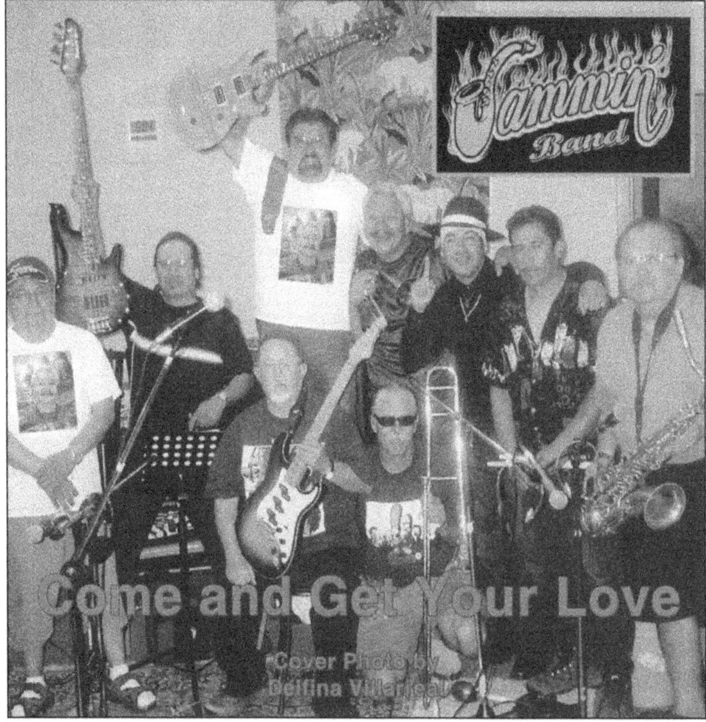

The Jammin' Band is a San José–based band. The band plays in San José and the San Francisco Bay Area. Their music is a variety of Mexican, Chicano rock and roll, and oldies. The group is led by Jerry Melendrez. (Courtesy of the Jammin' Band.)

Charley Trujillo founded Chusma House Publications in 1990. A Vietnam War veteran, Trujillo received a Bachelor of Arts degree in Chicano studies from the University of California at Berkeley and a Master of Arts degree from San José State University. He is the author of *Soldados: Chicanos in Viet Nam*. He also produced a documentary based on his book *Soldados*. He is currently completing a documentary on Tiburcio Vasquez. (Courtesy of Chusma House Publications.)

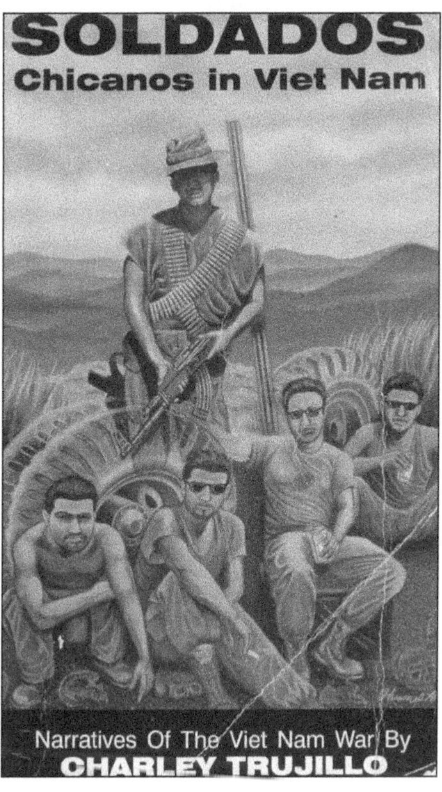

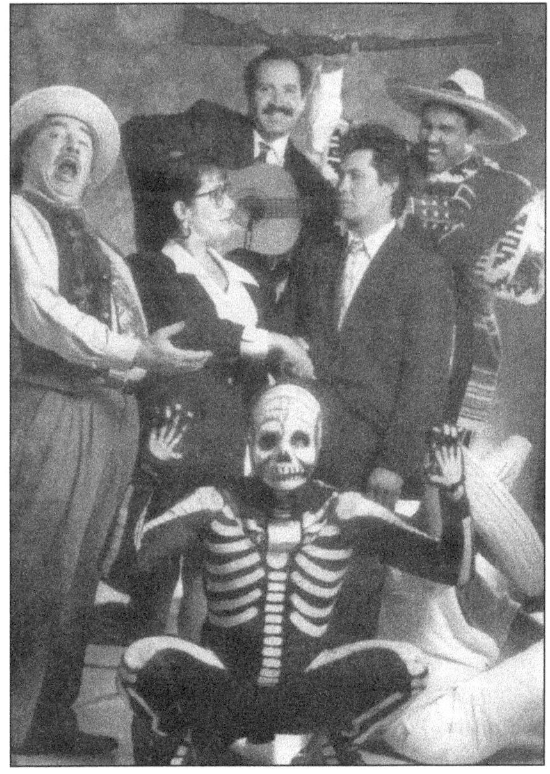

Teatro Familia Aztlan is a San José–based Mexican American theater troupe that has performed for many years. They were cofounded by Adrian Vargas. They hold acting classes and have performances at the Mexican Heritage Plaza and other locations. (Courtesy of Adrian Vargas.)

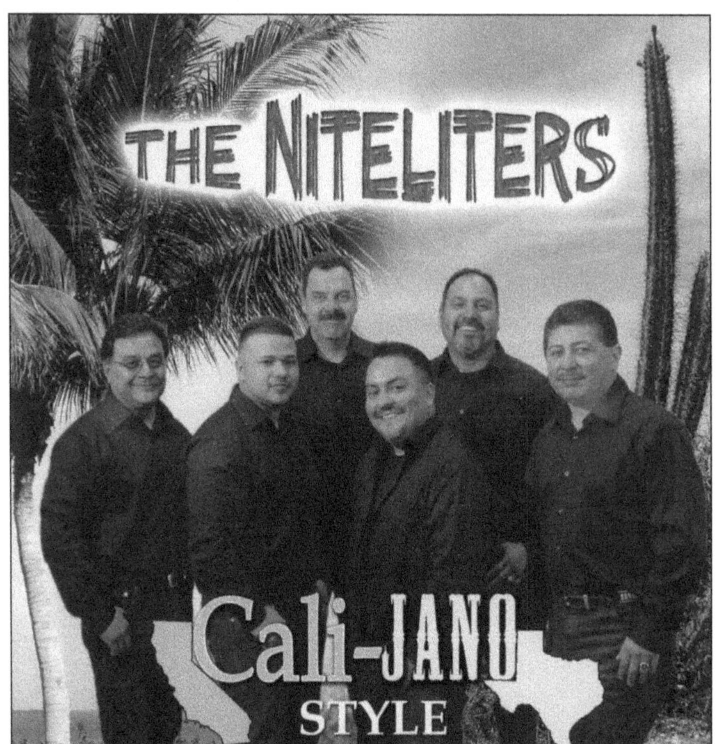

The Niteliters is a Latino band based in San José. The group traces its origins to the 1970s when it was founded by the Espinoza family of Hollister, California. Over the years, the group evolved through various genres of Latino music and has developed into one of Northern California's favorite bands, playing a wide range of music from Tejano, salsa, cumbias, funk, and rhythm and blues. (Courtesy of Jesus Covarrubias.)

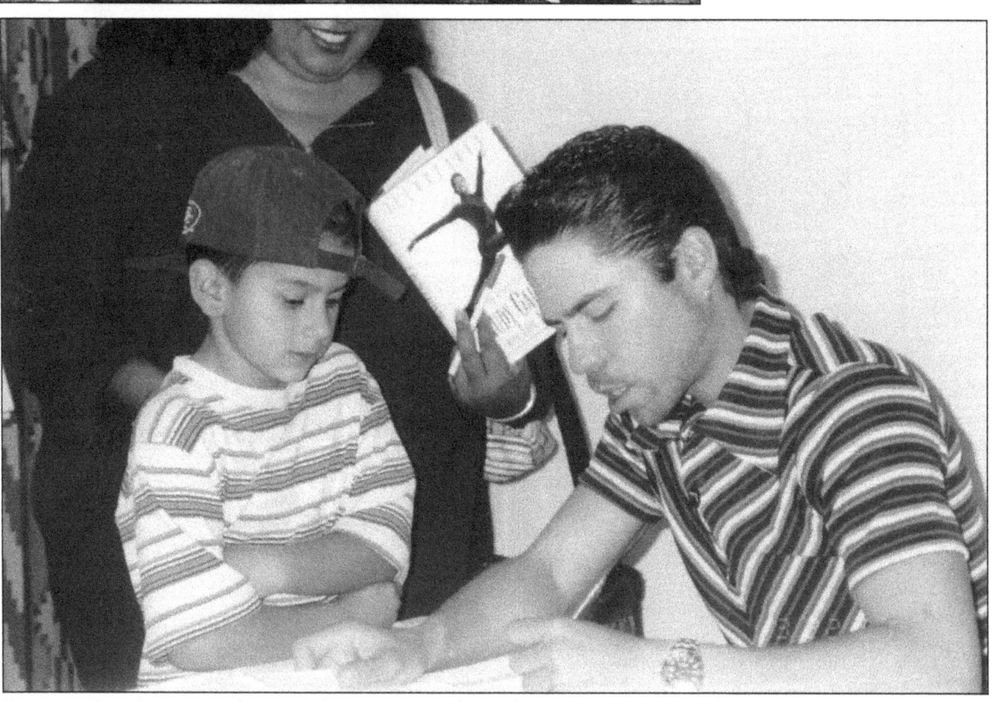

Born in San José, ice-skating champion Rudy Galindo signs his autobiography, *Icebreaker*, for a young fan. In 1996, Galindo won the men's title at the U.S. Figure Skating Championships at the San José Arena, becoming the oldest male to win this title in almost 50 years. (Photograph by Mary Andrade, courtesy of *La Oferta* newspaper.)

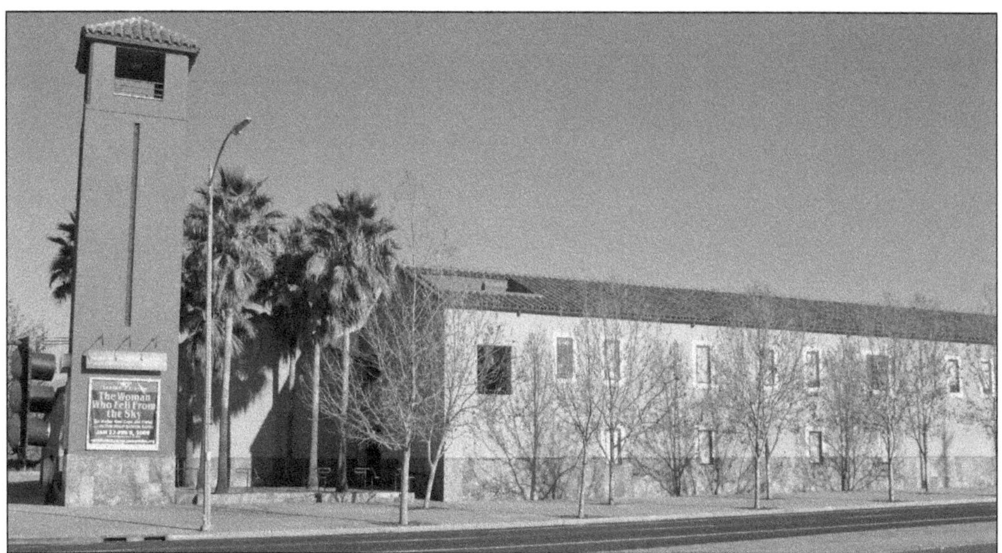

The Mexican Heritage Plaza is a unique community and cultural arts facility located at the corner of Alum Rock Avenue and King Road in the Mayfair district of Eastside San José. The site was formerly a Safeway grocery store that was the location of one of the first boycotts of grapes grown in Delano, California. The plaza features a theater, pavilion, art gallery, classrooms, and an outdoor square and gardens built in the architectural style of a traditional Mexican plaza. (Photograph by and courtesy of Ernie de la Torre.)

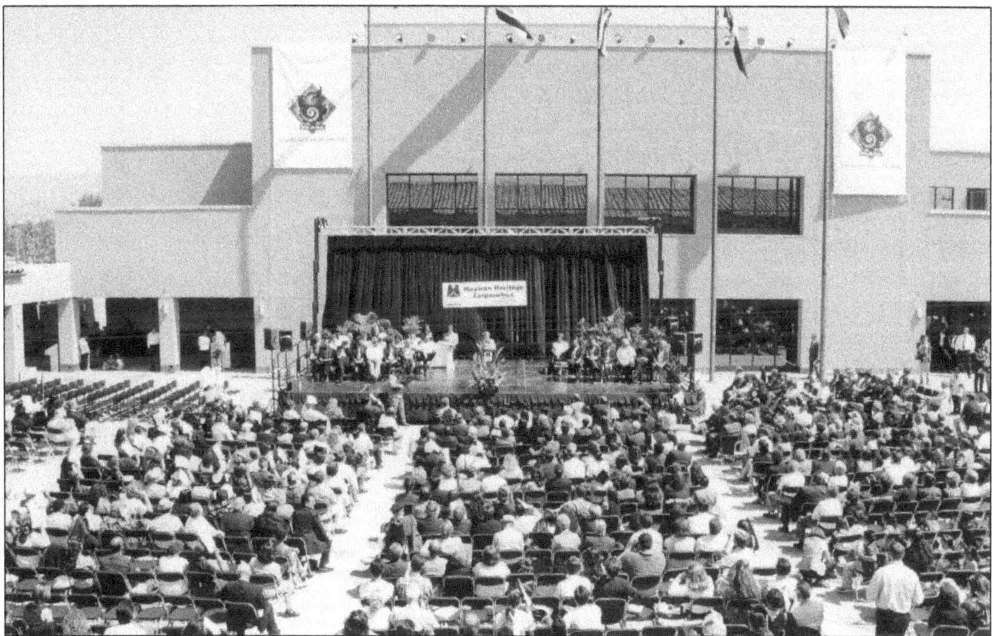

On Thursday, September 9, 1999, the official dedication of the Mexican Heritage Plaza took place, and an extraordinary fund-raiser gala followed to honor those who played a significant role in the development of this cultural masterpiece. Members seated on the stage include Blanca Alvarado, Manny Diaz, Susan Hammer, Fernando Zazueta, Arturo Rodriguez, Adrian Vargas, Victor Arrañaga, José Villarreal, Ron Gonzales, Dan Perez, and other notable individuals. (Photograph by Mary Andrade, courtesy of *La Oferta* newspaper.)

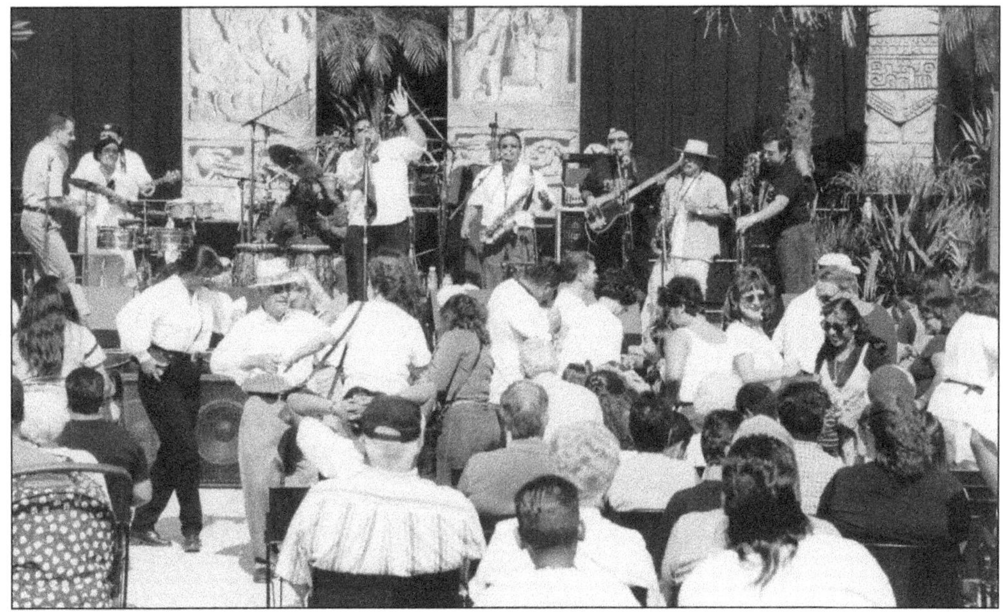

The sound of music filled the streets of Eastside San José, people danced, and an array of activities took place, highlighting the opening of the Mexican Heritage Plaza. In this image, grand opening revelers dance to the sounds of local band Mystique. (Photograph by Mary Andrade, courtesy of *La Oferta* newspaper.)

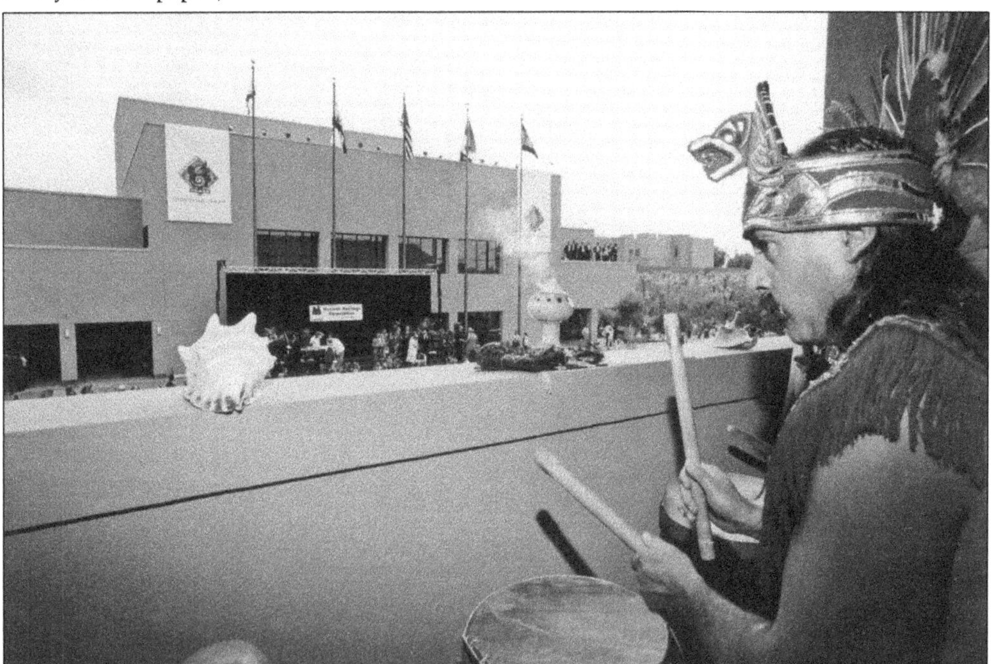

Combining the indigenous and the contemporary, the plaza is a place where the community can meet, exchange ideas, and reflect upon and appreciate the arts, culture, and heritage of the Mexican community. The plaza represents an important milestone in the community's efforts to preserve and promote the rich cultural diversity and history of Mexicans in San José. (Photography by Mary Andrade, courtesy of *La Oferta* newspaper.)

BIBLIOGRAPHY

Beebe, Rose Marie, and Robert M. Senkewicz, eds. *Lands of Promise and Despair: Chronicles of Early California, 1535–1846*. Berkeley, CA: Heyday Books, 2001.

Bouvier, Virginia M. *Women and the Conquest of California, 1542–1840: Codes of Silence*. Tucson, AZ: University of Arizona Press, 2001.

Bulmore, Laurence, and Milton Lanyon. *Cinnabar Hills: The Quicksilver Days of New Almadén*. Los Gatos, CA: Village Printers, 1967.

Fox, Frances. *Luis Maria Peralta and His Adobe*. San José, CA: Smith-McKay Printing, 1975.

Garcia, Alma M., Francisco Jimenez, and Richard Garcia. *Ethnic Community Builders: Mexican Americans in Search of Justice and Power: The Struggle for Citizenship Rights in San José, California*. Lanham, MD: AltaMira Press, 2007.

Loomis, Patricia. *Signposts*. San José, CA: San José Historical Museum Association, 1982.

Margolin, Malcolm. *The Ohlone Way: Indian life in the San Francisco-Monterey Bay Area*. Berkeley, CA: Heyday Press, 1978.

McKay, Leonard. *Clyde Arbuckle's History of San José*. San José, CA: Memorabilia of San José, 1986.

Munoz, Carlos. *Youth, Identity, Power: The Chicano Movement*. New York: Verso, 1989.

Payne, Stephen M. *Santa Clara County: Harvest of Change*. Northridge, CA: Windsor Publications, 1987.

Pitt, Leonard. *The Decline of the Californios: A Social History of the Spanish-Speaking Californians, 1846–1890*. Berkeley, CA: University of California Press, 1966.

Pitti, Stephen. *The Devil in Silicon Valley: Northern California, Race, and Mexican Americans*. Princeton, NJ: Princeton University Press, 2003.

Olmstead, Alan, and Paul Rhode. *Creating Abundance: Biological Innovation and American Agricultural Development*. Cambridge: Cambridge University Press, 2008.

Robinson, W. W. *Land in California: The Story of Mission Lands, Ranchos, Squatters, Mining Claims, Railroad Grants, Land Scrip, Homesteads*. Berkeley, CA: University of California Press, 1948.

San José Studies Special Issue By and About Chicanas and Chicanos. San José, CA: San José State University, 1993.

Soto, Anthony. "New Almadén Quicksilver Mines." *Southwest Labor Studies Conference*. San José: Chicano Library Resource Center, San José State University, 1984; pp. 1–46.

Teixeira, Lauren S. *The Costanoan Ohlone Indian of the San Francisco and Monterey Bay Area*. Menlo Park, CA: Ballena Press, 1977.

Valencia, Francisco. *New Almadén and the Mexican*. Master's thesis. San José, CA: San José State University, 1977.

Zavella, Patricia. *Women's Work and Chicano Families: Cannery Workers of the Santa Clara Valley*. Ithaca, NY: Cornell University Press, 1987.

www.ingramcontent.com/pod-product-compliance
Lightning Source LLC
LaVergne TN
LVHW060625110826
845147LV00015B/942

* 9 7 8 0 7 3 8 5 6 9 3 0 7 *